Hunting Preserves
for
Sport or Profit

by

EDWARD L. KOZICKY

CAESAR KLEBERG WILDLIFE RESEARCH INSTITUTE

TEXAS A&I UNIVERSITY
KINGSVILLE, TX 78363

1987

International Standard Book Number 0-912229-16-0

Library of Congress Catalog Card Number 86-073206

Available from:
    Caesar Kleberg Wildlife Research Institute
    Campus Box 218
    Texas A&I University
    Kingsville, TX 78363

Printed by Grunwald Printing Co., 1418 Morgan, Corpus Christi, TX 78404.

CONTENTS

INTRODUCTION

Prior to my retirement from the Winchester Group, Olin Corporation, in January 1983, I realized that a new book on hunting preserves was a necessity, but time to research new material and write was not available. New preserve management techniques and types of preserves needed to be recognized for the good of the concept; the old Nilo book (1966) was both out-of-date and out-of-print. So, with the encouragement of friends as well as for peace of mind in retirement, I embarked on a very enjoyable 3-year effort.

Whereas the Nilo book was based on 1 management system, this book is based on my 26 years of experience at Nilo plus visitations to many hunting preserves and innumerable conversations and correspondence with preserve operators, gamebird breeders, university scientists, and wildlife biologists throughout the United States. Since some phases of hunting preserve management are still being developed, there will be criticism. All one can do is to frankly express his ideas and deductions as tempered by experience and the findings of others. To the best of my ability, each chapter is treated as an entity with reference to other chapters and literature that contains supplemental information. However, it should be noted that the magazine, *Modern Game Breeding,* ceased publication more than a decade ago, and publications by the Sportsmen's Service Bureau are no longer available.

The book is not written as a scientific treatise but rather as a how-to reference book for sportsmen, preserve operators, and state wildlife personnel. Hopefully, it will provide them with guidelines on how hunting preserves, commercial and non-commercial, can help provide quality hunting for landless sportsmen and alleviate hunting pressure on both landowners and dwindling supplies of wildlife.

Any mention of commercial products within the book does not imply endorsement by CKWRI or me.

Finally, the book project gave me the opportunity to make a contribution to a lifetime vocation as well as avocation — sport hunting. And, if I have been successful in recording the current state-of-the-art and providing a blueprint of action for the enjoyment of tomorrow's outdoorsmen, the whole effort will have been worthwhile.

Edward L. Kozicky

ACKNOWLEDGEMENTS

In writing a book of this scope it is impossible to properly acknowledge all the individuals and groups that helped with information, encouragement, and hospitality. My first expression of appreciation goes to my wife, Carolyn. She is the one who kept the home fires burning without complaint during my long absences.

The cooperation and friendship I received from hunting preserve owners and operators (Appendix A) I visited was overwhelming. Their home was my home, and I was treated like family.

Without the encouragement of Dr. George V. Burger, Manager, Max McGraw Wildlife Foundation, Dundee, Illinois, the project would have never been initiated; but equally important, he devoted many hours editing each chapter. John B. Madson, my co-worker at Winchester (Olin Corp.) for 22 years, helped with suggestions and editing and convinced his wife, Dycie, to design and do the artwork for the chapter headings with the exception of chapters 1, 12, 21, and 22.

A meeting with Dr. Charles A. DeYoung through the courtesy of Dr. James G. Teer, Welder Wildlife Foundation, Sinton, Texas, brought me to the Caesar Kleberg Wildlife Research Institute (CKWRI), Texas A&I University, Kingsville, Texas, where Dr. Sam L. Beasom, the Director, provided me an office and complete freedom to write. Through the patience and persistence of Dr. Alan R. Tipton of CKWRI, I learned to operate a word processor which eliminated the drudgery of writing. Drs. Sam L. Beasom and Fred S. Guthery of CKWRI helped immensely with the final editing and the chore of proofreading galleys.

My stay in Texas was most pleasant, thanks to the hospitality of Dr. and Mrs. James G. Teer, Mr. and Mrs. Val W. Lehmann, Dr. and Mrs. Sam L. Beasom, Dr. Ralph L. Bingham, and Mr. and Mrs. William B. Mason, plus the staff at CKWRI.

Other people to whom I am indebted are the guest authors of various chapters. They gave freely of their time and knowledge without compensation. Then there are others who helped: John Mullin, Editor, *Wildlife Harvest*, Goose Lake, Iowa; Steve Johnson, Red Bank Ale & Quail Gamebird Club, Red Bluff, California; Dr. J. Richard Cain, Poultry Science Department, Texas A&M University; Dr. Herb Jordan, Pennsylvania State University; Terry Musser, Illinois Department of Conservation; and Jack Downs, Nilo, Brighton, Illinois.

I owe a debt of gratitude to financial contributors for the publication of the book: The Max McGraw Wildlife Foundation, Dundee, Illinois; The Caesar Kleberg Wildlife Research Institute, Texas A&I University, Kingsville; The Winchester Group (Olin Corp.), E. Alton, Illinois; and Mr. Eugene F. Williams, Jr., St. Louis, Missouri. In addition, both the National Rifle Association of America, Washington, D.C., and the National Shooting Sports Foundation, Riverside, Connecticut, contributed by prepublication orders for the book.

Personnel within Winchester (Olin Corporation) were most gracious with their time, patience, and professional skill. With the approval of Mr. G. W. Bersett, Vice-president and General Manager of North American Ammunition, W. Orrill, Facilities Engineer, supervised the preparation of the engineer drawings and Paul DeRanek, Photographer, supplied the Winchester photos and the development and enlargement of others. Winchester also granted me permission to use photos, cartoons, artwork, and/or text from the book, *Shooting Preserve Management — The Nilo System.*

Carol Altman and Anna Salinas, Learning Resources Center, Texas A&I University, were most helpful with the final editing of the engineer's drawings.

Sincere appreciation is also due Grunwald Printing Co., Corpus Christi, Texas, for their special efforts in designing and printing this book.

APPENDIX A

Hunting Preserve and Game Farm Cooperators

Max McGraw Wildlife Foundation
Dr. George Burger, Ole Oldenburg,
Clark Ganshirt, and Bob Montgomery
Dundee, IL

Nilo
Winchester Group (Olin Corp.)
Leo George and Jack Downs
Brighton, IL

Richmond Hunting Club
Mike Daniels and "Chuck" Wunderlich
Richmond, IL

Arrowhead Hunting and Conservation Club
John and Gloria Mullin
Goose Lake, IA

Hunters Creek Club
Preston Mann
Metamora, MI

Longleaf Plantation
Robert Clanton
Purvis, MS

Hillendale Game Farm
Tom Crawford
Tyrone, PA

Flying MK Ranch
Bill McKee
Honey Grove, TX

Running High Hunting Club
Mike Pitman
Bowie, TX

Bull Valley Hunt Club
Orrin and George Wold
Woodstock, IL

Hopewell Views Game Farm & Hunting Preserve
Rick Wombles
Rockport, IL

Whistling Wings
Leo and Bill Whalen
Hanover, IL

Oakview Hunting Club and Kennels
Ron De Bruin
Prairie City, IA

Wild Wings of Oneka
Jeff Hughes
Hugo, MN

Elkhorn Lake Shooting Park
Charles Baehr
Bucyrus, OH

Duck Creek Game Farm
Jack Campbell
Spur, TX

Hawkeye Hunting Club
Jerry Waters
Center, TX

Morris Quail Farm
Edward Morris
Goulds, FL

Bonnette Hunting Preserve
Bill Bonnette
Lake Park, FL

Riverview Plantation
Cader Cox
Camilla, GA

Quailridge
Edwin Norman
Norman Park, GA

Tom's Quail Farm
Tom Brown
Gulfport, MS

FOREWORD

Dedicated to

JOHN MERRILL OLIN
A Man, A Cause, An Industry

Every worthwhile effort in our society has been sparked by visionary men and women who were not satisfied with status quo and sought a better answer or way. Such a person was John M. Olin — inventor, industrialist, philanthropist, sportsman, conservationist, champion of private enterprise, and the man to whom this book is dedicated.

His contributions to sport hunting were manifold and of great historical interest. In every sense he was a steward of sport hunting within the Sporting Arms and Ammunition Manufacturers' Industry (SAAMI) throughout his life, yet he never sought recognition or credit for his efforts. He was at the helm of important SAAMI committees and helped to guide the management of our wildlife resources out of the political and into the biological arena — the basis of modern game management.

The story of John Olin as a sportsman and conservationist should be recorded, but within the limitations of this book one can hardly do more than list his major accomplishments as they related to the hunting preserve industry.

He grew up with the old Western Cartridge Company at East Alton, Illinois. His apprenticeship afield was served at the turn of the century when the nearby Mississippi and Illinois rivers teemed with wildfowl, and the rough little family farms of eastern Missouri and southwestern Illinois were bobwhite country supreme. Olin was a lifelong sportsman who embodied the deepest meaning of the term, investing his hunting and fishing with pride, honor, and tradition.

Olin joined his father at Western Cartridge in 1913 as a chemical engineer, and shortly after World War I applied progressive-burning, smokeless powder to paper shotshells for the first time

— resulting in the famous Super-X load. During the 1920s, John Olin became First Vice-president and member of the Board of Directors at Western Cartridge Company. Here he forged his convictions into policy.

One of his most important involvements during that period was as Chairman of the SAAMI Committee on Restoration and Protection of Game. It was this committee, under Olin leadership, that directed Aldo Leopold's classic, "Game Survey of the North Central States." According to the late Senator Harry B. Hawes, author of the Duck Stamp Act, it was this "that brought Aldo Leopold into active work in the field of game management...."

Begun on July 1, 1928, Leopold's monumental study was the first of its kind. Its purpose was to appraise the chance for the practice of game management as a means of game restoration in the north central region.

In his preface, Leopold noted, "The survey was financed by the sporting arms and ammunition industry. The motive hardly requires explanation. Success in game restoration means continuance of the industry; failure in game restoration means its shrinkage and ultimate liquidation."

Begun at a time when American game supplies were at an all-time low ebb, the game survey was a comprehensive, objective, and professional analysis of the game resources of a large region. Many of the findings were used in developing "An American Game Policy," adopted by the American Game Conference in 1930. It was one of the first and greatest blueprints for game management and marked the dawn of scientific game management. Leopold was encouraged to write his classic book, *Game Management*, which is

John M. Olin at Nilo.

still the bible of the game management profession.

When John Olin was chairman of that historic SAAMI committee, one of the most pressing problems was a growing rift between 2 key conservation groups.

The Game Conservation Society was found in New York in 1912, just 1 year after the legalizing of the hunting preserve concept in that state. The main interest of the Society was the propagation of game, and the group sponsored the original Game Conservation Institute at Clinton, New Jersey, to train game breeders.

The American Game Association had begun in New York in 1911 as the American Game Protection and Propagation Association. It was backed by SAAMI and directed its principal efforts to awakening the public to the need for wildlife restoration; however, the group's early interest in game propagation had vanished, and it had begun opposing the sale of pen-reared gamebirds for table use.

John Olin appreciated the purposes of each and endorsed their programs. He knew that enhancement of the nation's wildlife resource depended on habitat restoration, efficient protection, and game propagation. Outlawing the sale of pen-reared gamebirds for table use could greatly restrict their commercial use — hampering the young hunting preserve industry and other private management efforts. As chairman of the SAAMI committee, Olin channeled financial and moral support to both the Game Conservation Society and the American Game Association — and it's not surprising that he was successful in persuading the Association to withdraw its opposition to the sale of pen-reared gamebirds.

The Game Conservation Society, with support from SAAMI, continued to operate the "Clinton Game School" until 1935. During the 4 years the school was in operation, it trained 145 men, of whom two-thirds were professionally engaged in game breeding and game management. These were among the first technically trained employees of state game and fish departments. The Game Conservation Society was incorporated into More Game Birds In America — which eventually became Ducks Unlimited. Another branch of the Society would become the current North American Gamebird Association.

The American Game Association became the American Wildlife Institute — which in turn became the Wildlife Management Institute of today.

Although most of these original groups are nearly forgotten, they were of great importance as citizen efforts in early game management. Some of these early programs were milestones in wildlife conservation, shaping actions and policy for generations. For example, John Olin's SAAMI committee also initiated fellowships for game management research at 4 state universities — the real beginning of the cooperative wildlife research programs between state universities, the U.S. Biological Survey (now the U.S. Fish and Wildlife Service), and state wildlife agencies.

In 1931, when the Game Survey was published, John Olin and the Western Cartridge Company bought the foundering Winchester Repeating Arms Company. It was a bold move at a time when the economy was plunging to new depths — and it committed John Olin more fully to game restoration than ever before.

Some efforts in game restoration had been made by the Western Cartridge Company as early as 1910, but the real beginning came during the 1930s when Nash Buckingham was hired as an advisor for projects involving bobwhite quail. John Olin was becoming increasingly interested in quail management — an interest that had been fueled by Herbert Stoddard, the great Georgia quail biologist. (In later years, at his plantation near Albany, Georgia, Olin would break the traditional "1-quail-per-acre" barrier. With his characteristic attention to detail, and by putting large landholdings under intensive management with the help of Herbert Stoddard, he would achieve an average of more than 2 bobwhite quail per acre.)

Beginning in 1933, the gun industry had been subjected to a 10% federal excise tax — a levy that evoked no cheers from the gunmakers or anyone else. After all, this was in the depths of the depression when the excise tax on a $30 shotgun would buy 24 pounds of pork chops! The little matter of a gun excise tax tacked on to the retail cost could (and probably did) turn away customers.

The original excise tax on firearms was channeled directly into the general fund. None of it was spent for wildlife purposes; however, in 1937, the Pittman-Robertson Federal Aid in Wildlife Restoration Act was passed, providing that the federal excise tax on sporting arms and ammunition be earmarked for ''wildlife restoration.'' It was a principle heartily endorsed by the sporting arms and ammunition industry, a way to implement the findings of Aldo Leopold's game survey. As a member of SAAMI's executive committee, John Olin lent his full support to the new program.

In 1935, Olin formed the Western-Winchester Game Restoration Department, based at East Alton. This began as a small game farm mainly concerned with habitat improvement and quail stocking. Working with landowner cooperators and leased land, game managers stocked wild-trapped and pen-reared birds in the spring and fall. The Western-Winchester Game Restoration Plan was developed, combining new techniques of gamebird rearing with habitat development. When the first soil conservation district in Illinois was set up in the mid-1930s, Western-Winchester (the name would be reversed in later years) was designated by the trustees of the district as wild-life management consultants.

The old W-W Game Restoration Department was disbanded in 1946, transferring certain functions and personnel to the newly organized Wildlife Management Institute (WMI) in Washington, D.C. In fact, some of the first projects of WMI were applications of the Western-Winchester Game Restoration Plan on a national basis.

During World War II, all excise taxes were increased, and the tax on sporting arms and ammunition was hiked from 10 to 11%. Excise taxes were rescinded after the war, but the sporting arms and ammunition industry specifically requested that the full 11% tax on their products be retained. Such voluntary taxation was unique, an eloquent testimony to the fact that the gunmakers believed professional game management was worth investing in.

The years after World War II brought vast changes to the American hunting scene. Almost overnight, great new pressures were beginning to weigh on America's gamelands and wildlife. The Depression and World War II were past; there was more discretionary money, and a flood of consumer goods on which to spend it. Road systems were being expanded and there was a rising tide of new cars filled with hunters enjoying their release from economic and military restrictions. A new era in outdoor recreation had arrived, and with it came a highly efficient new agriculture. Nothing would ever be the same again.

All the developments in game restoration, game management, and conservation before World War II were groundwork for those postwar years. The impact on our gamelands was greatly buffered by existing conservation programs and the small corps of trained game managers who held the line and bought time while new programs gained strength. The Pittman-Robertson Act was providing more money each year — and just as important, it was money reserved for solid game management and not political boondoggles. New ground was being broken by such professionals as Aldo Leopold, Seth Gordon, Ira Gabrielson, and others, and the first contingent of game managers to be trained in their new art-science. If the foundation of modern game management had not been laid during the late 1920s and 1930s by men such as John Olin, effective game management on a national scale might never have been developed in time. Today's outdoorsmen owe a great deal to those conservation pioneers — men who may have done more to perpetuate American hunting than anyone before or since.

In 1952, John Olin formed the Winchester Conservation Department. The official charge went beyond the old Western-Winchester Game Restoration Plan. The main charge would be to promote professional game management in all its aspects — and particularly the hunting preserve concept.

By nature, John Olin was visionary, always concerned with the future. He became increasingly aware that a soft spot of the sporting arms and ammunition business was in densely settled regions where access to hunting was becoming more difficult. There might be game enough in such areas — but there was also a growing number of ''No Hunting'' signs. There were 2 general solutions: to acquire more public hunting lands with private money, and to develop hunting on private lands with private money. In spite of expanding land acquisition programs, it was obvious that the first method could never keep pace with growing demand. Public effort must be augmented with private enterprise — and its most effective form was felt to be the Commercial Hunting Preserve where the public could hunt released gamebirds for a fee. As commercial ventures swallowed up more and more gamelands, it grew plain that only private enterprise could save some of these lands for hunting. Olin became a member of the Fin & Feather Hunting Preserve (now the McGraw Wildlife Foundation), Dundee, Illinois, and the Rolling Rock Hunting Preserve, Ligonier, Pennsylvania. He must have liked what he experienced on these hunting preserves because he swung into action.

Through the leadership of John Olin, SAAMI hired a field staff of 3 men: Charley Dickey, Joe Davidson, and Kenneth Dodd. When Dodd resigned, he was replaced by Dr. George Burger. These dedicated men worked in various regions of the country and were instrumental in the passage of necessary state legislation and in assisting hunting preserve operators with management and promotional problems.

By design, the efforts on the SAAMI field were reduced over the years until only 1 man was left. Charley Dickey made the promotion of hunting preserves a labor of love, and did much through writing and consulting to develop the concept on a regional and national basis; however, in 1964, his talents were redirected to the National Shooting Sports Foundation.

John Olin also knew that the preserve concept could succeed only if it maintained a high degree of "quality hunting in natural surroundings" where the average hunter could enjoy good dog work and sporty gunning. With this in mind, he founded Nilo Farms (now called Nilo) near East Alton in 1952 and made it the main assignment of the new Winchester Conservation Department. Nilo Farms would promote the hunting preserve concept, serve as a demonstration area for potential preserve operators, and conduct experiments to improve preserve management techniques.

At the same time, Olin established Nilo

Kennels. He believed devoutly in the retriever breeds and the necessity of good dogs in reducing losses of game in both upland and wetland hunting. The black Labradors of Nilo would become famous in the national field trial campaigns, especially King Buck. Trained by the Manager of Nilo Kennels, T. W. "Cotton" Pershall, King Buck won national championships in 1952 and 1953 and, to this day, is the only retriever to complete 63 consecutive series in the National Championship Stake. King Buck was featured on the 1959-60 Federal Migratory Waterfowl Stamp — the only dog ever to appear on the annual stamp.

There is little doubt that Nilo Farms was a key factor in the rise of the hunting preserve concept — and it surely had great influence in establishing standards. For over 3 decades, Nilo has been the hallmark of hunting preserve quality, promoting its concept of "quality hunting in natural surroundings" through publications, workshops with game managers and extension specialists, field days with students, and on-the-job training programs for hunting preserve managers. It is not surprising that the North American Gamebird Association recognized the contributions of John Olin by presenting him their first annual award.

John Olin was in a special position to defend and promote hunting preserves and modern game management. He not only headed one of the great sporting goods industries of the world, but also the giant corporation that bears his family name. He was in a unique position to influence sportsmen, other members of the sporting arms and ammunition industry, and governments and business leaders on a national level. This was apparent when he wrote his peers in the business world on behalf of a fund-raising campaign for The Wildlife Society — and obtained funds from sources that probably never before contributed to wildlife conservation.

John Olin was not prone to make a decision in haste nor was he reluctant to seek information on a problem from knowledgeable people, regardless of their station in life. He had a genius for absorbing and evaluating details on any subject of personal interest. Within the field of wildlife management and sport hunting, everything that captured his fancy benefitted by his attention — hunting preserves, Labrador retrievers, springer spaniels, Atlantic salmon, bobwhite quail, sporting firearms and ammunition, and even fishing reels.

It has been said that the Age of Giants has passed. Politics, business, labor, art, science, and religion are staffed by men and women who vary in competence but have 1 thing in common: they are rarely larger than life-size. This is as true of game management as any other profession. Most of game management's giants, including John M. Olin (1893-1982), are gone, having blazed the trail for the competent, life-sized professionals now in charge of our wildlife resources and the future of sport hunting.

Chapter 1

WHY HUNTING PRESERVES?

John B. Madson
Godfrey, IL

Sooner or later, when hunters get together, a certain question comes up. If they're new to the game, it's asked right away. And, even if they're old-timers, they may have lost some of their contacts out there on the land and the question is just as urgent:

Where can a guy find good hunting these days?

A public hunting area is 1 answer. Especially if you don't mind red tape and drawings, and lots of company, or all 3. Or you can knock on doors until you find a farmer who's willing to share his good game cover. As a third choice — and often the best — there may be commercial hunting preserves.

When that comes up, someone usually says that hunting preserves are just too expensive, and that he can't afford it. He wants some good free hunting. Wants some good hunting that doesn't cost anything.

Who doesn't? Well, I've been looking for that sort of thing for nearly 50 years, and haven't

found much good hunting that was "free." If it was any good, it always ended up costing something in time, effort, and usually money. The better the hunting was, the more I had to pay of something, and most of my hunting today costs more than it used to. Not because I needed any fancy trimmings, because I don't. But consider my annual Iowa pheasant hunts, for example.

For years I have gone back to Iowa to hunt in some of the best pheasant range in the world. I hook up with old friends like Glen Yates and his son Steve, and we have at it — combing the weedpatches and cornfields for what Steve calls "those rockin', rollin' roosters." There are red-letter days filled with cackling ringnecks and the smell of burnt powder. But there are other days, too — the grinding, grueling days when the few roosters we do see are all flushed far out of range, and we may never once cheek a gun. Either way, it's getting downright expensive.

It's not quite 400 miles to central Iowa from my home in southwestern Illinois. I can count on

1

getting about 23 miles per gallon in my 4-cylinder car. This adds up to about $40 in gasoline. I stay with relatives in Iowa, so there's no lodging cost.

My non-resident Iowa hunting license costs $47.50. Add to that a $3 wildlife habitat stamp. For a 3-day hunt I can count on dropping at least $40 in local restaurants. If I end up spending less than $125 and 16 hours of driving time, I'm lucky — and I usually make 2 of those trips every fall.

So why not hunt near home? Because I live south of the main pheasant range and there are no birds. The last time I hunted pheasants on a farm in northern Illinois I drove 4 hours, and shot 1 bird, drove 4 hours home and spent about $15 on meals. So much for ''free'' pheasant hunting.

I'm not griping. Even when the shooting is poor, there's rich companionship with dogs and old friends, and exercise to clear away cobwebs. I'd probably go back if it cost twice as much. There is, however, another way.

I didn't get back to Iowa for pheasants last fall. My work kept me tied up until late November, when we headed up to Chicago area for Thanksgiving. My son-in-law, John Venere, who isn't the most loquacious guy in the world, had told me on the phone, ''Bring field clothes and your old pump gun. Be ready to walk.'' I wasn't sure where I'd be walking, or why, much less what I might be shooting at.

Of course, the women were glad to be rid of us. Nothing's quite as worthless as men hanging around the house on Thanksgiving Day, getting in the way and interfering with kitchen gossip and general efficiency. And so, on a silver-and-gold Thanksgiving morning, before the frost had left the swales and shaded cornrows, we were ''out amongst 'em'' at a commercial hunting preserve up near the Wisconsin line.

At this point, let me present some bona fides.

I've hunted ring-necked pheasants since 1938, growing up in central Iowa when and where pheasants were plentiful. There was never a problem finding a place to hunt. We would hunt after school and on weekends, never far from home. In that wonderful fall when I owned my first good shotgun, I was 15 years old and bagged exactly that many rooster pheasants. Four years later, just before I entered the army, I sometimes sacked that many in a week. That was no big

deal; however, for in the late 1930s it wasn't unusual for a hunter in northern Iowa to bag 75 ringnecks between Iowa's traditional November 11 opening and New Year's Day. None wasted — not in those times, near the end of the Great Depression.

After the war, majoring in game management in college, we G.I.-Bill students not only hunted pheasants for our groceries but as an actual part of our coursework! Still later, with the Iowa State Conservation Commission, we were expected to spend part of the pheasant season afield, gun in hand. After that I was with Winchester-Western's Conservation Department at East Alton, Illinois, for nearly 22 years. A good part of that time was spent at Nilo Farms, W-W's famous experimental and demonstration hunting preserve, where I saw at least 5,000 pheasants bagged by hunters — and possibly another 1,000 or more flush out of range or otherwise escape.

So, at one time or another, in front of the gun and otherwise, I've seen ring-necked pheasants in a wide spread of conditions. And although no one *really* knows what a pheasant is going to do from one moment to the next (least of all, the pheasant), I think I have a fair handle on what constitutes quality pheasant hunting.

Anyway, there we were on a crisp Thanksgiving morning, combing pheasants out of the field borders, thickets, and feed patches of a commercial hunting preserve. They were beautiful birds — brassy, clattering, long-tailed roosters that were doing about everything a pheasant can do to make things tough for the shooters, which is considerable.

Being an old pro and a dead shot (but far too modest to ever mention such things), I held back while John and his friend Gene did the shooting — making helpful comments whenever they missed. They did not seem to appreciate this, which was most ungrateful. But then a fine, brassy rooster flushed on my side where they couldn't safely shoot. Time for the master to show the kids how. Smoothly and easily, I brought up the old model 12. *Boom. Boom. Boom.* As the pheasant scaled off over the horizon, every feather still in place, there was a good deal of rude and disrespectful laughter. The trouble with kids today is that they don't recognize real skill and experience when they see it. Too much television, I guess.

But, during the next few hours, we all redeemed ourselves, and when the morning stretched well into the afternoon, we called it quits and left for home. We had shot 4 birds apiece, seen some good dogwork, honed our appetites, and had a ball. A red-letter day.

Later on, John and Gene asked me what I really thought of the day's action and how the pheasants had compared with pheasants anywhere. I thought the quality of the birds had been excellent; although they had been pen-reared and released not long before we hunted, they were touchy, strong-flying, and beautifully plumaged. The cover was typical of good pheasant range, and the preserve was safety conscious and professional. All in all, a class operation.

Come to think of it, I've yet to see a pen-reared hunting preserve pheasant do anything a "wild" bird doesn't do. All strong, healthy ring-necked pheasants are essentially wild. It goes with the breed, pen-reared or not. High quality pheasant hunting is possible on a commercial hunting preserve, and may be as affordable as any other kind. And, as preserve operators learn more about the proper management of bobwhite quail, mallard ducks, and chukar and gray partridges, the same is true of those gamebirds.

Quality, of course, means many things to many people — particularly as it applies to hunting. It may or may not mean tough hunting and/or a lot of shooting, and the hunting preserve operator must be able to judge what the individual hunter has in mind, and how to tailor the hunting to that person. A good hunting preserve has something for everyone, and can offer hunting to the rank beginner, the physically handicapped, or to the old-timers who can no longer handle rough cover and tough going.

One concern among hunters is that hunting on preserves may be too easy. If you really want it tough, a good preserve can offer something stronger. If you don't believe that, find a quality hunting preserve and brag to the operator, "Buddy, there's no hunting around here that's too tough for *me!*" and see what he does.

Chances are he won't say much. But his eyes may sort of light up, and he'll go into a huddle with your guide. Remember, you asked for it.

It is quite possible, in fact, for the skillful preserve operator to furnish hunting that is just too tough and demanding for his average client. The hunting preserve operator must be able to read his clients, be a shrewd practical psychologist, and be able to offer something for everyone. But, first of all, he must know what quality hunting really is, and be a professional hunter in every sense of the word. The best preserve operators fill that bill.

Which isn't to say that there is isn't a bad side to the commercial hunting preserve concept. As there is in any form of private enterprise, there have been fly-by-night hunting preserves that degrade the word "hunting" — shoddy, fast-buck operations that are doomed to failure but do great damage to the preserve industry before they fold up. Such places can leave bad tastes in hunters' mouths for years, and one of the salient problems in the hunting preserve industry today is that few state game agencies choose to take the responsibility of policing such operations or even shutting them down if necessary. As long as their hunting preserves are licensed and keep proper records, most state agencies seem indifferent to the general quality of operation.

Aside from the out-of-pocket cost of gunning on a hunting preserve, many sportsmen have a basic objection to paying for what they feel is their God-given right to hunt free. Anything else, they feel, smacks of "The European System." But, as I noted in the beginning, I doubt if there's very much "free" hunting anymore. Not if it's any good, that is. Good hunting these days is going to cost in terms of time, money, effort or all 3. No hunter has a right to expect good sport without paying something in those terms.

A hunting preserve lacks the uncertainty of "wild" hunting. The basis of the hunting preserve concept is certainty. In "wild" hunting there are no guarantees; you head out into the boondocks and hope for the best. On a good hunting preserve the hunter is assured of at least a sporting opportunity to shoot game, but is *not* guaranteed birds for his efforts. He pays on the basis of either sporting opportunities to shoot at birds or on the number of birds released. If he misses — well, he pays anyway.

It comes down to this: A topnotch hunting preserve is run with skill and imagination by people who know what hunting, *real* hunting, is all about. And although they may not be offering "wild" hunting in its exact sense, you will have great difficulty in telling the difference. It all depends on high quality birds, fine cover, and good guides and dogs. The best preserves will offer all that — and maybe good biscuits, too.

In addition, the hunting preserve has some special advantages not found in ordinary hunting. For one thing, hunting preserve seasons are far longer (up to 6 months or more) than the regular hunting season, and there are no bag limits. Furthermore, there's no better place for a beginner to learn proper shotgun handling in and out of the field, and preserves are ideal for inexperienced shooters. Trap and skeet is an excellent start, and will take the new shooter a long way, but actual wing shooting can be learned in only one way — and you'll find that way on a hunting preserve.

The same things that apply to young shooters apply to young bird dogs or retrievers. Canvas dummies and pheasant wings are useful training devices, but there is no substitute for the tantalizing scent, sound, and action of a real pheasant or mallard. There are hunting preserves that will allow you to use your own dog — either a finished dog or a young one — and there are some preserves that will even board and train your dog for you.

Bird for bird, there's no doubt that a hunting preserve can offer at least as much for the money as a wild shoot — and often more. There's no question that the hunting preserve can save the sportsman a great deal of time — and in this day and age, time is money. I've a hunch that many businessmen have hung up their guns not because of hunting's cost in dollars, but because of time. A good hunting preserve is the answer to that, and many feature half-day hunts for businessmen.

And there's another thing: on a hunting preserve you aren't just tolerated, you are welcomed. You are a hunter among hunters in a hunting environment, and that's worth a lot to many of us.

There's been some concern that hunting preserves will replace "free hunting" in some areas. Indeed, there are places where this has happened, and will continue to happen — but such "free" hunting was not eliminated by hunting preserves, only succeeded by them. Free hunting was really eliminated by rising populations and soaring land costs. Even under such conditions, some of the public will still want to go hunting, and they can with an expenditure of time, effort and/or money. Through personal effort, time and some money, they can operate a Do-it-yourself or a Co-op Hunting Preserve. Or, if they don't choose to do that, they can always hire someone else's time and effort at a Commercial Hunting Preserve. Hunters in areas of high population and land-use pressures are the first to face a growing truism. Through almost all of human existence, huntable land and huntable wildlife have preceded the hunter. They *caused* the hunter. But, in the future, this must be reversed; it is the hunter who must cause huntable wildlife and land.

There's no reason to believe that hunting preserves will crowd out all American hunting. Preserves can replace such hunting only where it has already ceased to exist; otherwise, there's no need. But, to the extent that "free" hunting is lost, and that people still long for a day afield with dog and gun, even in areas of intensive land use, there will be hunting preserves.

Chapter 2

HISTORY

Within my library is a book *Practical Game-Preserving*, written by William Carnegie in 1906,[4] and described as "a complete guide to the rearing and preservation of both winged and ground game, and the destruction of vermin." The book represents the state-of-the-art in 1906 and documents the rearing of gamebirds for sport hunting, a common practice in England in the 1800s.

The first American book on hunting preserves, *Upland Game Bird Shooting in America*, was authored by a number of sportsmen and published by the Derrydale Press, New York, about 1930.[1] This book dwelt on the raising of gamebirds and the care and handling of hunting dogs and touched on shooting equipment. This book was followed by *American Game Preserve Shooting*, written by Lawrence B. Smith and published by Garden City Publishing Co., New York, 1937.[15] Smith makes clear that he used the term "game preserve" *not* to denote a sanctuary or reservation, but rather a *shooting preserve*, whether private or state

owned, operated for the purpose of *sport* alone. His observations on hunting preserves in the 1930s were as pertinent then as they are now: "That there is room for both public and private shooting grounds there is no doubt, and the development of one can but benefit the development of the other. The supply of wild game is steadily diminishing and in some cases borders upon extermination. The blame for this condition must to a large degree be attributed to the advance of civilization as well as to the shooting public itself.

"The ever-increasing interest in the production of game birds and in the matter of posting land on which they are to be found is evidence enough that a great change has taken place in shooting in America. In the neighborhood of any large city one may travel for miles without passing a piece of cover suitable for bird shooting that is not posted against public shooting. In many places far from the cities the choicest covers are posted also. To anyone who has studied this problem with an open and unprejudiced mind it is evident that the day of open public shooting is over, or nearly so.''

A good working definition for a hunting preserve is ''an acreage of land owned or leased for the purpose of releasing pen-reared game-birds over a period of 3 or more months for the purpose of hunting under license of the state wildlife agency.'' It is an expression of private effort in action.

The concept has had many names: ''fee hunting,'' ''pay-as-you-shoot hunting,'' ''put-and-take shooting,'' ''shooting'' or ''hunting resort,'' and ''shooting preserve''. Between the late 1950s and mid-1970s when the sporting arms and ammunition industry was active in promoting hunting preserves, the general consensus of opinion settled on a single term, ''shooting preserve,'' to avoid confusion by the general public. It may not have been the best term, but ''shooting preserve'' was the first to be used [15] in keeping with its definition in the state of New York — the passage of the Bayne Bill in the New York State Legislature on June 26, 1911.[3, 6] The Millbrook Hunt Club, operated by C. Beverly Davidson in New York State in 1929,[2] is credited as the first hunting preserve to offer hunting for a fee.

The term ''shooting preserve'' didn't really fit. After all, such places were not preserving shooting; they were preserving hunting. So, the word ''shooting'' was dropped and ''hunting'' substituted. Some have gone further and refer to the preserve concept as a ''hunting resort.'' True, some are resorts, but many Private and Do-it-yourself Preserves are not; they are basically places to hunt. For the purposes of this book, I have settled for the term ''hunting preserve.''

The Hunting Preserve Concept

The early development of the hunting preserve concept was slow. Wild game was relatively abundant, and the majority of our population was rural. But as the nation grew and metropolitan areas expanded, the need for hunting preserves became more apparent.[13]

Hunters, generally, were not quick to endorse the hunting preserve concept.[6] They were suspicious of the idea and did not favor legislation to permit the operation of preserves. Game had always belonged to the commonwealth or state and was not to be sold. There was something un-American about the concept. Perhaps sportsmen felt it was a return to ''The European System.''

After World War II, however, this attitude began to change for several reasons:

1. An increase in the number of individuals purchasing hunting licenses (approximately 10 million in 1946 and 15 million in 1956), as 1 result of an expanding human population; a shorter work week and higher pay scales, providing more time and money for hunting; and an increase in the percentage of individuals of retirement age with time to spend in pursuit of hunting opportunities. These factors contributed to an increase in hunting license sales.

2. Mechanization of game propagation, improvement and control of the quality of game feeds, and development of effective medication for various game diseases made it possible to produce game at a lower cost per bird.

3. Ever-increasing restrictions on public hunting opportunities by wildlife agencies, in an attempt to provide for a harvest of game species within biological surpluses, restricted hunting seasons and limits to a minimum.

In 1933, Professor Aldo Leopold[10] pointed out that restrictive controls on hunting had ramified into infinite detail, while incentives for the production of game experienced only the most rudimentary development. With the exception of 1 or 2 states which passed ''shooting preserve laws,'' authorizing more liberal hunting privileges on land artificially restocked, there was not a single move toward the most obvious of all ways toward building incentive: allowing land ''sown'' proportionate privileges in ''reaping.''

In 1937, Seth Gordon, then Executive Director of the Pennsylvania Game Commission, writing in the foreword of *American Game Preserve Shooting* stated, ''The sportsman who has the desire for more shooting than is afforded by public administration and who has the means for developing better shooting should be given every reasonable aid. It can easily be done without affecting public game or public shooting. On the contrary, a substantial percentage of the birds and animals produced or liberated escape to adjacent areas open to the public.''

4. The willingness by various individuals to do something about increasing the opportunity of enjoying a day afield with dog and gun.

A Model Law

One of the early problems of the hunting preserve movement was obtaining suitable legislation that would permit the preserve operator to earn a profit and would also protect the natural wildlife resources from exploitation. In the early years, the attitude of wildlife administrators at the state level was a mixture of endorsement and resentment. In the State of New York there were many so-called preserves that were established to take advantage of an extended hunting season, since there were no requirements to stock any gamebirds. Michigan was another excellent example of inadequate legislation in the beginning. Later, hunting preserves were closed down in Michigan. It was not easy to legalize preserves a second time.

A model state statute for the establishment and operation of hunting preserves was developed by the Sporting Arms and Ammunition Manufacturers' Institute. This statute served as a guideline for state legislation throughout the nation.[8] It placed both minimum and maximum acreages, a minimum stocking of gamebirds to be hunted, a maximum percentage of native gamebirds that could be harvested, a longer hunting season, and a system of identifying gamebirds taken on a preserve along with a system of proper record keeping. The model law served as a draft of good legislation for many states.

Although hunting preserves first appeared in 1911 in the state of New York, there was limited growth. As late as 1954, only 22 states legalized this type of hunting, with 136 public preserves open on a daily-fee basis and 620 private preserves with a restricted membership, for a total of 756 hunting preserves. Yet, once SAAMI became interested in the concept, and hired field men to help promote the concept, expansion was

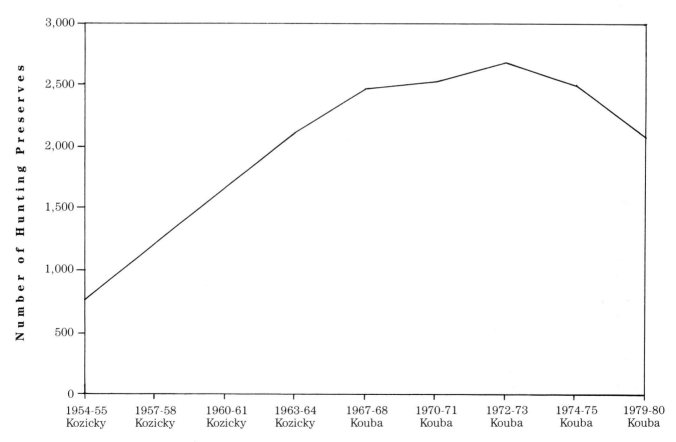

FIGURE 1: Number of Public and Private Hunting Preserves in The United States.

Table 1..Number of Hunting Preserves in The United States, Selected Years.

State	1954-55	1957-58	1960-61	1963-64	1967-68	1970-71	1972-73	1974-75	1979-80
Alabama	–	2	4	6	12	No data	17	15	13
Alaska	–	–	–	–	–	–	–	2	0
Arizona	2	1	4	1	4	3	5	4	2
Arkansas	1	3	9	17	14	29	22	22	14
California	73	121	154	189	202	203	212	186	142
Colorado	–	2	2	2	10	14	18	15	21
Connecticut	21	26	26	29	26	23	24	23	22
Delaware	1	3	1	3	3	4	3	3	3
Florida	2	4	44	80	93	80	79	71	66
Georgia	1	10	36	40	41	42	41	37	49
Hawaii	–	–	1	–	–	–	–	0	1
Idaho	–	–	–	–	–	–	–	–	3
Illinois	70	110	119	132	149	167	167	150	133
Indiana	–	6	14	28	31	40	41	30	41
Iowa	–	9	9	10	10	12	10	12	5
Kansas	–	15	15	19	26	27	29	24	22
Kentucky	–	11	10	14	11	14	22	21	19
Louisiana	1	2	4	6	7	3	3	3	5
Maine	–	–	–	–	–	–	1	1	0
Maryland	9	14	31	32	38	36	38	32	28
Massachusetts	–	–	–	–	10	9	9	11	11
Michigan	–	3	42	59	63	75	77	71*	51
Minnesota	4	7	11	11	17	30	30	28	21
Mississippi	2	4	4	19	34	55	54	43	23
Missouri	9	10	19	35	36	42	49	38	37
Montana	–	–	–	–	–	4	2	1	4
Nebraska	–	2	1	–	1	2	4	2	4
Nevada	3	4	4	8	9	10	7	7	11
New Hampshire	–	1	1	No data	2	3	3	2	1
New Jersey	115	124	173	229	322	305	315	314	304
New Mexico	–	–	2	4	12	15	6	11	7
New York	258	335	412	491	534	524	592	550	418
North Carolina	–	12	11	11	32	39	41	34	38
North Dakota	–	–	–	–	–	2	1	2	2
Ohio	16	48	60	61	49	45	50	54	38
Oklahoma	1	2	2	2	2	5	3	3	5
Oregon	–	–	2	–	–	1	3	2	1
Pennsylvania	80	134	172	190	199	212	208	197	169
Rhode Island	7	6	6	8	7	7	8	6	4
South Carolina	–	1	13	24	36	30	37	44	38
South Dakota	–	–	–	–	1	2	2	1	1
Tennessee	1	2	12	36	60	48	46	46	17
Texas	–	35	45	82	94	91	94	81	93
Utah	–	–	2	2	4	16	17	16	21
Vermont	–	–	–	–	2	1	2	0	2
Virginia	–	28	43	46	63	57	55	39	25
Washington	–	5	6	8	8	8	11	7	4
West Virginia	–	2	3	8	8	5	7	7	5
Wisconsin	79	103	134	177	176	179	197	220*	103
Wyoming	–	–	–	–	13	15	19	15	29
Totals:	756	1,207	1,663	2,119	2,471	2,534	2,681	2,503	2,076

*—1973-74 data for Michigan and Wisconsin.

rapid. In 1957-58, there were 338 public and 869 private preserves, a total of 1,207 (a 60% increase in the 3-year period). The increase in number of public and private preserves continued through 1972-73 (Table 1).[5] There was a decline in number of preserves in 1974-75, which continued through 1979-80 (Figure 1).[5] No statistics are currently available on the number of preserves in the United States, but the general consensus is that the number has leveled off. One of the major recent problems facing potential investors in the hunting preserve industry is the high cost of land. Also, when SAAMI stopped providing technical assistance with field representatives, there was a loss of promotional activity that undoubtedly contributed to a drop of interest.

General opinion within the hunting preserve industry today is that, even though there are fewer preserves, more birds are being harvested on individual commercial preserves, and for good reason. Twenty years ago a family-operated preserve could realize a profit by handling only 5,000 gamebirds in a season; that minimum number now has risen to 10,000. There has also been an increase in Co-op and Do-it-yourself Preserves which are not motivated by profit. The state of Illinois maintains records on the numbers of gamebirds harvested on all types of hunting preserves (Table 2).[12]

Madson,[11] writing in *Kansas Wildlife,* stated, "Many hunters are suspicious of the quality of pen-reared birds, and if there is anything that separates a really well-run preserve from its competition, it's the way the birds perform in the field.

"The key to having a good preserve hunt is finding a good hunting preserve. Preserves come

Table 2. Hunting Preserve Statistics for the State of Illinois, 1980-85.

Year	Number of Preserves	Birds Released	Birds Harvested
1980-81	126	195,073	128,895
1981-82	130	209,562	128,232
1982-83	132	204,829	135,084
1983-84	139	193,947	114,522*
1984-85	137	193,030	130,960

*Severe weather conditions during the preserve hunting season.

in 2 broad types, membership types and public areas where hunters pay by the day or by the bird. The kind of area you pick depends on what is available in your area and how much you are willing to spend. Top-flight preserves are placing their emphasis on the sport and esthetics of their hunt."

Wildlife Agencies and Hunting Preserves

The American Game Policy[9] of 1930 recognized that 1 of 2 ways to induce a landholder to manage for game in the United States is to compensate him directly or indirectly for producing a game crop, and for the privilege of harvesting it. The other way is to buy him out and become the landholder. The Policy further states that free public hunting is increasingly ineffective on farms because, as hunters increase, trespass becomes a nuisance, and posting follows. Closed seasons, posting, or both are the inevitable result on farmland.

Hunting preserves have proven to be effective in providing hunting opportunity to private individuals, and in letting those who enjoy and pay for the privilege do so.[10] Yet there has been all too little support of the hunting preserve concept within state wildlife agencies — beyond licensing. In the final analysis, there should be close cooperation between the 2 groups; they need one another.

Rajala[14] surveyed 43 hunting preserves across the nation by mail. One question was, "Do you believe that there are state or local laws governing public hunting preserves that should be repealed or changed?" Twenty-four respondents said there were state laws that they felt should be repealed or changed, and 18 checked "No" (1 questionnaire was unanswered). Dissatisfaction was expressed with the laws in 15 out of 22 states. Almost all of the dissatisfied operators were dissatisfied with more than 1 item of legislation.

Fifteen respondents expressed dissatisfaction with the law that requires the marking of all live birds released on a hunting preserve (a requirement not recommended in the Model Law). Nine were unhappy with the price of licenses to operate a public hunting preserve. Eight complained about fencing and posting requirements for hunting preserves, and an equal number about the Sunday Hunting Law. Other subjects of legislation receiving more than 1 complaint were length of the public hunting season and the price of out-of-state hunting licenses for preserve hunters.

On the state wildlife agency side of the coin, many preserve operators are not aware of their responsibilities. Towell,[16] in a talk before the North American Game Bird Breeders Association, outlined the conservation commission's role as he saw it in Missouri, "Our first concern is that game breeders in the state be properly licensed and controlled to insure that their activities are in no way detrimental to our native wildlife population. We cannot permit the introduction of undesirable species. We must avoid the introduction of new diseases, parasites, or insect pests. We must control releases of birds or animals that through breeding might weaken or destroy native wildlife.

"Expressed briefly, our policy is primarily one of responsibility to the resources entrusted to our care and secondarily to the citizens of Missouri that own and can benefit from these resources. A conservation department has major responsibilities for hunting preserves in the control of both their quantity and quality. We want this artificial hunting to be of the highest type possible. It is our obligation to the sportsman to keep it so. The only way this can be done is to make sure that the birds released are produced in hatcheries of quality — where only the best are raised and the operator gives attention to such items as size, behavior pattern, and physical condition instead of the dollar being the main goal. Too many game breeders are concerned mainly with profit and their product is a heavy, dull, tame, practically unexcitable bird, with edged or broken primaries, and often deformed bills. We are determined in Missouri that our preserves will provide quality shooting.

"There is a job to be done in the production of high quality birds for quality preserve shooting. The commercial bird breeder has an important function to fill — he can be of great value to the conservation department, but he must understand his role and not become a working force against sound game management. Hunting as an outdoor recreation must not be allowed to deteriorate through poorly operated hunting preserves and low quality gamebirds. It is the role of the conservation commission to maintain high standards of quality, to exercise fair and impartial control of operations, and to assist producers and operators in the performance of their necessary functions. As one conservation administrator, I pledge my cooperation and earnestly enlist your support."

Both state wildlife agencies and hunting preserve operators (exotic big game and gamebirds) must work together to develop minimum standards of quality hunting for preserves. The public expects the state wildlife agency to be the arbiter of hunting quality whether on or off hunting preserves, and like it or not, the agency must accept that responsibility. Through the cooperation of private enterprise, minimum quality standards have been set for preserves featuring exotic big game and gamebirds. The Exotic Wildlife Association in Texas has established a "Code of Ethics" and the North American Gamebird Association established a set of minimum standards for quality hunting on preserves in the 1960s, which is published in their annual directory. They are:

1. The area should look like good hunting country, with a blend of natural and planted cover.

2. Pheasants, quail, and chukars should be full-plumaged, more than 16 weeks of age, and of the same color and conformation as birds in the wild.

3. Mallards should be similar in weight and plumage to free-ranging mallards and capable of strong flight between release sites and the rest pond.

4. Well-trained dogs should be available for the guests to reduce the crippling loss of game.

Good preserve operators realize that a quality operation is the key to success. They know that a substandard operation is detrimental to the industry and to the future of their business. Sub-quality operators eventually go out of business, but they leave bitter memories of commercial operations with sportsmen and with the public if they receive attention from the media.

State wildlife agencies have side-stepped the issue of quality hunting on preserves by stating that they have no jurisdiction over exotic big game animals. This is a fine line which the public will not accept, nor should they be expected to accept. In the final analysis, hunting in any form is the responsibility of the state wildlife agency.[16] *The public will demand that neither the hunter nor the hunted be shamed in the act of hunting.* I am not aware of any state wildlife agency that has revoked a hunting preserve license for a sub-quality operation, although the Michigan Legislature, reacting to public demand, once closed all hunting preserves within the state for a few years.

There must be a closer partnership between state wildlife agencies and the hunting preserve industry, one of mutual understanding and trust rather than a cool tolerance. Every state wildlife agency should appoint a well-qualified biologist, who understands hunting preserve management, to work with the concept. This responsibility should neither be assigned to someone who lacks the ability or desire to work with private enterprise, nor should it be given to someone who just happens to be on the payroll but has shown little or no ability to do any other task within the organization. One good man is more important than three or four who are already overburdened with other duties, or who lack the proper attitude. Divided responsibility ends up with no one being responsible.

The man or woman chosen for this job should be in complete sympathy with the role of private enterprise in the field of hunting and see the future with the eyes of a Seth Gordon or an Aldo Leopold. That person should have complete backing within the agency and be willing to study and become knowledgeable on the management, promotion, and economics of hunting preserves and game breeding. It is a demanding task that currently is not appreciated by most state wildlife agencies.

One of the most useful services of such a person may be to discourage ill-conceived ventures in the gamebird breeding or hunting preserve industries. Such an individual can help the gamebird breeder and the hunting preserve operator with management problems and win their everlasting gratitude, as in Illinois. That coordinator can be the catalyst that brings about a close working relationship between the state wildlife agency and the hunting preserve industry.[7]

The North American Gamebird Association

The major organization serving the hunting preserve and game breeder industries is the North American Gamebird Association (NAGA). The value of both the NAGA and state associations is discussed under "Helpful Organizations" in the chapter on "Short Subjects." The early history of the development of NAGA and John M. Olin's involvement is outlined in the "Foreword." One year after the passage of the Bayne Bill in 1912, which authorized hunting preserves in the State of New York, the Game Conservation Society was formed. In the late 1920s the Game Conservation Society became "More Game Birds in America." About 1932, this group split into "Ducks Unlimited" and the "North American Association of Game Breeders." In 1960, the name of the organization was changed to the North American Game Breeders and Shooting Preserve Association, to provide for more visibility of the preserve industry. However, the name proved cumbersome, and it was again changed in 1980 to the North American Gamebird Association.

Contributors to the Preserve Industry

It would be impossible to credit properly the many outstanding individuals who have devoted time, money, and/or energy to the hunting preserve concept. However, I would be remiss not to recognize those with whom I have had a close association.

Max McGraw, industrialist and sportsman, developed the first hunting preserve in the state of Illinois and founded the Max McGraw Wildlife Foundation that is currently managed by Dr. George V. Burger. Under Dr. Burger's direction, the Max McGraw Wildlife Foundation continues active research into both gamebird rearing and preserve management. Since John M. Olin was an early member of McGraw's hunting preserve and a personal friend of Max McGraw, his hunting experience at "McGraw" had a profound influence on his decision to start Nilo Farms.

Max McGraw (1883-1964)

Glen Palmer, a Director of the Illinois Conservation Department, helped pioneer needed legislation for hunting preserves in Illinois, and developed the Illinois Association of Hunting Preserves. He appointed a knowledgeable individual from the conservation department to work with hunting preserve operators, and helped game breeders develop a better strain of gamebirds for hunting preserves.

Leo Whalen, Whistling Wings, Hanover, Illinois, developed an excellent strain of mallard ducks for hunting preserves.

John M. Mullin, Editor of *Wildlife Harvest*, was a pioneer in the development of Arrowhead Hunting Club, Goose Lake, Iowa. John faced many obstacles in the early years, but his determination and indomitable Irish ancestry persevered. The preserve industry and the North

American Gamebird Association have benefitted from his counsel and promotional efforts for more than 30 years.

On the East Coast, George Schellinger of Spring Farm, Sag Harbor, New York, pioneered in the operation of an outstanding game farm and hunting preserve. George and his family specialized in producing quality gamebirds and in offering quality hunting with a touch of class. The operation is now managed by George's son, Dave.

And last, but by no means least, my good friend and co-worker for 22 years, John Madson. John not only co-authored *Shooting Preserve Management — The Nilo System* with me, but he wrote many news releases promoting hunting preserves, provided wise counsel in the administration of Nilo, and was the "driving force" in the production of 3 movies promoting the hunting preserve concept by the Winchester Group, Olin Corp.

References

1. Anon. 1930. Upland game bird shooting in America. Derrydale Press, New York, NY.
2. Boehmer, P. 1986. Personal communication. Assoc. Ed., Wildlife Harvest, Goose Lake, IA.
3. Burger, G. 1962. Licensed shooting preserves in Wisconsin. Tech. Bull. #24, Wisconsin Conservation Dept. Madison, WI. 40pp.
4. Carnegie, W. 1906. Practical game-preserving. 3rd ed., Charles Scribner's Sons, New York, NY. 424pp.
5. Kouba, L. 1981. Geographical distribution of hunting preserves in the U.S. Wildlife Harvest 12(3):46-49. Goose Lake, IA.
6. Kozicky, E. 1958. Shooting preserves — private enterprise in game management. 20th Midwest Wildlife Conf., Columbus, OH. 5pp.
7. _____. 1975. The shooting preserve concept. 1st Gamebird Production Management Short Course. Columbia, MO. Oct. 3-4.
8. _____. and J. Madson. 1966. Shooting preserve management — the Nilo system. Winchester Group, Olin Corp., E. Alton, IL. 311pp.
9. Leopold, A. 1930. American game policy. 17th Ann. American Game Conference, New York, NY. Dec. 1-2.
10. _____. 1933. Game Management. Charles Scribner's Sons, New York, NY. 481pp.
11. Madson, C. 1981. The shooting preserve alternative. Kansas Wildlife 38(5):18-21. Kansas Fish and Game, Pratt, KS.
12. Musser, T. 1986. Personal communication. Illinois Dept. of Conservation, Springfield, IL.

13. Olser, P. 1958. Observations on the background and prospects for shooting and fishing in North America. Trans. N.E. Wildlife Conf. 1:366-373.
14. Rajala, J. 1973. Results of a survey of shooting preserves. Wildlife Harvest 4(10):17-21. Goose Lake, IA.
15. Smith, L. 1937. American game preserve shooting. Garden City Publishing Co., Garden City, NY. 175pp.
16. Towell, W. 1960. The conservation commission's role in game farm management. Ann. Meeting of the North American Game Bird Breeders Assoc., St. Louis, MO. 6pp.

Chapter 3

TYPES OF HUNTING PRESERVES

The basic types of hunting preserves are Commercial and Non-Commercial. Commercial Hunting Preserves have a single purpose: to provide a profit for the owner/operator who furnishes quality hunting to those willing to pay for it. They can be open to the public on a daily-fee basis or open to members only, or a combination of the two. Many Private, Commercial Preserves have an introductory hunt, which gives the operator and the hunter a chance to become acquainted.

Non-commercial Hunting Preserves are meant to provide quality hunting for a group of hunters on a non-profit basis. The hunters on such preserves may do all of the work or hire the personnel to do it.

All hunting preserves have a common goal: quality sport in safe, pleasant surroundings. Regardless of the type of hunting preserve you are contemplating, visit the state wildlife agency and become thoroughly familiar with the laws governing preserve operations. Some state agencies have personnel on their staffs who can

be of great help to you on the economics, management, and promotion of hunting preserves.

Read all available literature on hunting preserves. And visit several preserves, both commercial and non-commercial, and talk to the people who operate them. It is well to profit from the mistakes of others, and most preserve operators are willing to discuss their trials and tribulations.[3]

Commercial

Preliminary Considerations

Commercial Preserves require a firm personal, and a large financial, commitment. The large financial outlay is land; however, if you cannot afford to purchase the necessary land, perhaps you can negotiate a long-term lease (10 or more years) with either an estate, individual, or land-holding company. The land does not have to be prime agricultural land (see chapter on "Hunting Preserve Cover").

The next most important step is to analyze yourself. Do you like to meet and cater to people? (This may sound easy, but it isn't!) Is your family interested in the enterprise, and willing to work with you? The high cost of labor can spell the difference between failure and success, and most preserves are family managed.[4]

Next comes a market analysis. From where will your potential customers come? Are there enough people in your market area interested in patronizing a hunting preserve? If so, what type of preserve will they support? If a suitable market doesn't exist locally, how about nearby population centers (50–100 miles away)? The closer the preserve to the customer, the better.

Business volume is the key to a successful hunting preserve; hence, it is wise to survey a cross section of the people you intend to attract. To do so, one should prepare a prospectus of the proposed hunting preserve. Seek professional help in the layout of the prospectus. You can change the proposed clubhouse, dog kennels, fishing lakes, clay target facilities, picnic areas, etc. on a prospectus far easier than when it is a fixed asset on your preserve. Seek the advice of your prospects on the facilities, but only if they are willing to make a financial commitment as a member.

All-weather roads are an important consideration, especially if you will operate in the winter. What other Commercial and Non-commercial Preserves are nearby? In some instances, one can complement another. Is there some type of hunting, especially waterfowl, that attracts hunters to your area? If so, there will be days when hunting for wild waterfowl will be slow, and you will have prime prospects for a Daily-fee Preserve.

Are there any laws or ordinances that will hinder your operation? Can you depend on community support? Are there good overnight lodging facilities located near your proposed preserve? If so, you may not have to concern yourself with overnight guests and evening meals.

Prolonged periods of a week or more of snow and extreme cold are a detriment to the hunting preserve business. Consult weather records and find the average number of days in the fall and winter when there may be an inch or more of snow on the ground and/or the temperature may be below 20°F. Cancelled reservations mean lost business. You will be wise to discount the bad weather days in a 5–6-month preserve season. Longer hunting preserve seasons are not the answer. The weather may be too warm to hunt in September, and by late March gamebirds will be entering the breeding season. Once they do, the quality of the hunting becomes substandard.

The success or failure of a hunting preserve will largely depend on your planning and your personal interests, aptitudes, and skills. The hunting preserve operator must be a jack-of-all-trades and master of most. He must understand hunters and hunting, dog training and handling, the management of pen-reared gamebirds, farming, personnel management, public relations, business administration, and shotgun shooting.

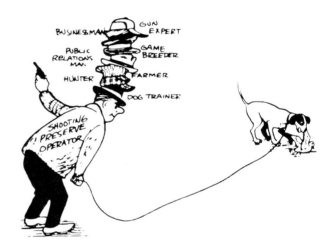

Few hunting preserves provide an adequate annual income. The successful operators are those who obtain a year-round income from a combination of seasonal activities, such as boarding and training dogs, game breeding, farming, camping, fishing, picnicking, and clay target shooting.[5]

Take a long look at the economics of the type of hunting preserve you plan to install. How much money will you have to invest in the necessary land, bird dogs, clubhouse, holding pens, bird handling and farming equipment, employees, and guides? Perhaps most important is the financial resources to operate in the "red" for at least 3 years. It takes time and effort to build the necessary volume of hunters, and it is the rare hunting preserve that is a profitable enterprise in less than 3 years. (Read chapters on "Profitability" and "The A-B-Cs of Successful Hunting Preserves".)

Financial help for hunting preserves is difficult. One should check not only with his banker but the local office of the U.S. Department of Agriculture. Government loans for qualified farm families have been available.[7]

As a final step before gambling one's finances and future in a hunting preserve venture, consider hiring a consultant — a person who has operated a successful preserve, of the type you have in mind, for 10 years or more. A list of consultants can be obtained from the North American Gamebird Association, P.O. Box 1368, Cayce, South Carolina 29033, or through the advertisements in *Wildlife Harvest*. The consultant will charge you a fee, but he may save your family nest egg. He will certainly think of many things that you have overlooked and could be the best investment you ever made.

Most operators who fail in the hunting preserve industry are people who tried to short-cut this tedious program of study, analysis, and self-examination. The human factors of work, management, and judgment are the greatest contributors to success — and the hardest to evaluate — in the operation of a commercial preserve.[2]

Daily-fee versus Private

It is quite common for a preserve to begin as a Daily-fee Preserve and eventually become a Private Preserve. The operator who can find enough members to start a Private Preserve is indeed fortunate. Even within a Private Preserve, the turnover rate of the average member is high (probably less than 10 years), and new members must be recruited. The age factor among members who can afford preserve hunting is the main reason for the turnover. Recruitment can either come through invitations of current members or through introductory hunts to non-members. Some hunting preserves have separate days of the week for members and other days for daily-fee hunts.

A Private Preserve has a number of advantages over a Daily-fee Preserve. The annual membership dues of a few hundred to several thousand dollars provide cash for the operator in the spring of the year and guarantee a certain amount of business in the fall. Some private preserves charge a basic membership fee, which only permits access to the preserve. Preston

A preserve hunter enjoying a hunt with his springer spaniel (courtesy Winchester Group, Olin Corp.)

Mann, Hunters Creek Club, Michigan, makes a good point on a basic annual fee for a Private Preserve, "Where else can you find an acreage of this size and beauty with facilities for hunting, fishing, picnicking, dining, clay target shooting, and dog training completely staffed for your outdoor enjoyment?"

Some of these preserves have their members order gamebirds in the spring for fall hunting. To induce members to do so, the operator will discount the birds, as compared to fall prices. Such an arrangement not only provides revenue to the operator in the spring, but he is in position to enter into firm contracts with game breeders for the necessary birds.

A Private Preserve becomes a team effort, with the members helping to recruit new members. Good sportsmen attract good sportsmen. Within a Private Preserve one can establish a membership committee to screen the membership and, if necessary, drop any member who acted in a dangerous or unsportsmanlike manner during the previous hunting preserve season.

When a member of a Private Preserve has made a commitment for a given number of birds for fall hunting, it is his responsibility to use the birds. There are no refunds.

In short, the Private Preserve has many advantages over a Daily-fee Preserve, but one has to attract hunters to his preserve and offer them a quality product at a fair price before "going private."

Non-commercial

Within the Non-commercial Hunting Preserves there are Private, Co-op, and Do-it-yourself hunting preserves. In 1984, in the State of Illinois, there were 35 Commercial preserves and 105 Non-commercial Preserves. Of the 105 Non-commercial Preserves, 5 were Private, 50 were Co-ops, and 50 were Do-it-yourself Hunting Preserves.[6]

Private

A Non-commercial Private Preserve is one owned by an individual, corporation, or foundation as a non-profit venture. A manager is employed to operate the preserve. The success of such preserves depends on hiring the right manager — a man who likes people, hunting, and shooting; knows how to train and handle hunting dogs; understands farming and farm machinery; and comprehends the management of pen-reared gamebirds on a hunting preserve. Too often, non-commercial operations hire an individual with only 1 or 2 of the above qualifications. When this happens, the members soon become disenchanted with the entire operation. The right manager is the key to a successful private preserve. Once a policy of management has been established by the owner or the board of directors, the manager must have the authority to run the club without interference by individual members.

Most Non-commercial Private Preserves offer a variety of outdoor activities, such as hunting, fishing, picnicking, clay target shooting, nature hiking, skiing, snowmobiling, bird watching, etc.

Co-op

A Co-op Hunting Preserve is usually operated by a group of organized sportsmen. This type of preserve is growing in number and replacing the smaller and more loosely structured Do-it-yourself Preserve.

The Pioneer Valley Gun Association in Illinois is a good example. This is an incorporated, non-profit group with elected officers operating hunting preserves on 3 different tracts of land. Currently, they have 60–75 members. Each member is annually assessed a basic charge of about $350, which permits him to harvest 16 pheasants per year. He will also be required to work a given number of days each year and attend meetings. Throughout the year, the Pioneer Valley Gun Association raises money to finance their Co-Op Preserves by holding gun shows, fish frys, wild game dinners, etc.

They use a travel trailer as a clubhouse. All the land on each preserve is leased, and the land-owner is paid extra for any cover plantings, space for the holding pens, and utilities for the trailer.

The Association contracts with a game breeder for biweekly delivery of ring-necked pheasants. Some game breeders are specializing in supplying Co-op Preserves and make weekly or biweekly runs to a series of them. Such an arrangement

Three generations of hunters and their springer spaniel at the Oak View Hunting Club, Prairie City, Iowa.

makes it profitable for the breeder and convenient for the Co-op.

Structured hunting is scheduled only on weekends and holidays. Members may hunt on other days of the week, but no birds are released. On the day of a structured hunt, 2 members of the Association are assigned to manage the hunt on a given preserve. They will arrive early at the pheasant holding pens, capture the necessary birds, and transport the birds in crates to release sites. They simply open the crates and let the birds walk out. Then, on the return trip to the clubhouse, they pick up all release crates. They open the trailer clubhouse, prepare the coffee, and are responsible for registering all hunters and recording their kill. Sometimes they know who is coming to hunt; sometimes, not. A typical pheasant release will be 25 birds on Saturday and 35 on Sunday. All members have an option for more pheasants than the original quota of 16. Extra birds are sold at cost to the Association. The main emphasis is on ring-necked pheasants

(about 1,500 annually), but they also release pen-reared bobwhite quail (about 250 annually). Hunting dogs are owned by individual members. The Association carries both liability and property damage insurance.

The concept of a Co-op Preserve is a good one for a group of sportsmen wanting to substitute labor for money in order to enjoy better hunting. They can organize as a separate entity whose sole purpose is to operate a hunting preserve, such as the Pioneer Valley Gun Association, or it can be composed of a segment of the membership of an established sportsmen's organization. It just takes a few ''sparkplugs'' within the club to organize the interested members, check state regulations on preserves, lease the proper land, contact the game breeders, erect the holding pens, and find a travel trailer for a clubhouse.

Do-it-yourself

The Do-it-yourself Hunting Preserve is more loosely organized than a Co-op. Such preserves are usually operated by a small group (10 or less) of sportsmen who band together to operate a hunting preserve. They do not have formal meetings or elect officers, but they do share expenses. Even though they may not elect officers, it takes a couple of ''sparkplugs'' within the group to organize and operate the preserve. Do-it-yourself Preserves either lease the necessary land or one of their members owns the land. They are incorporated for the protection of the members and they carry liability and property damage insurance.

A lease agreement is reached with the landowner with the option to renew for the preserve's acreage, holding-pen space and, if available, a building for a clubhouse. Do-it-yourself Preserves may or may not have structured hunts, such as a Co-op. Being a more loosely organized group, they are more likely to have a number of non-structured hunts. The individual members catch and release their own birds, sign the registry, record the numbers of birds released and killed, and hunt with their own dogs. At the end of the season they get together to settle the finances of the group and make arrangements for the next year. In some areas of the country they may want to consider plans for a dove hunting field.

Guidelines for Co-ops
and Do-it-yourself Preserves

There are common management guidelines for both types of preserves. Once a group of sportsmen has decided to organize to improve their hunting, the group has the option of either type of preserve. However, if there are more than 10 members, they should give serious consideration to a Co-op Preserve. Both groups should be incorporated as a non-profit corporation with appropriate liability and property damage insurance for the protection of the members of the club and the landowner.[1]

The first problem is finding 200–300 acres of land with a good supply of natural cover for releasing and holding pheasants (see chapters on "Hunting Preserve Cover" and "The Ring-necked Pheasant"). If such cover is not available, can it be developed? Then, there is the problem of whether or not the landowner will lease the land for preserve hunting, plant the necessary cover or permit the preserve members to do so, and permit the erection of a holding pen for pheasants. It is a fortunate group of sportsmen that can find such a landowner within their own organization.

The ring-necked pheasant is ideally suited for amateur management. The bird does not domesticate under the influence of man, it is readily available from many game breeders, and it requires a minimum amount of attention and care. Anyone can learn to stock pheasants properly, and the bird is a sporting trophy that is unexcelled on the table. Other species of gamebirds, such as the chukar partridge, bobwhite quail, and gray (Hungarian) partridge, are best left to professional management. If bobwhite quail are a serious consideration by the members, the Smith-O'Neall Stocking System (see chapter on "The Bobwhite Quail") is the best approach for amateur management, providing that food and cover are available for holding quail throughout the preserve hunting season. The new technique for flighting mallards (see chapter on "The Mallard Duck") has possibilities on a Co-op Preserve. The 2 main requirements are a suitable layout for quality pass-shooting of mallards, and personnel to manage the sanctuary pond on a daily basis and conduct the shoots.

You can write to your state wildlife agency for a list of game breeders within your state. You will also find advertisements in *Wildlife Harvest*, Goose Lake, Iowa 52750. You should satisfy yourself that the game breeder has a reputation for the production of good, strong-flying pheasants with the conformation and coloration of wild ringnecks. Avoid hobbyist game breeders and game breeders who brail their birds.

Draw up a contract with the game breeder to assure that: (1) the birds have been reared, without brailing, in large outside pens from about 8 weeks of age; (2) the coloration and conformation of the birds approximates wild ringnecks; (3) the number, age (16 weeks or older), and sex ratio of the birds; (4) the price per bird based on the delivery schedule; (5) the charges for transportation, if any; and (6) the right to refuse delivery if the birds are not of suitable quality. Be sure that the pheasants' bills have not been debeaked to the point that the birds cannot pick grain; however, better breeders will not have such birds in their pens. Some breeders will use "specs" on birds to reduce cannibalism in their pens, and will remove them prior to shipment. The price of adult pheasants varies with regions of the country and the supply of birds.

To keep birds in good flying condition, which includes their plumage, it is essential to build a good holding pen. It is a major investment, but a good holding pen should only require minor repairs in a 10-year period. A pheasant holding pen suitable for about 150–200 pheasants is described in Appendix A. If you crowd more birds into the pen, you may have an outbreak of cannibalism, which is a vicious problem with confined pheasants. It is advisable to construct a shelter with sheet-metal roofing on 1 end of the holding pen. During rainy spells, the shelter will help to keep birds dry for stocking, and the shelter area will facilitate the use of a catch box (see chapter on "The Ring-necked Pheasant," Appendix A). Pheasants can be caught with a poultry net or by hand, but they are subject to far more injury than if they are herded into a catch box. The pen should have automatic watering devices or large pans of available water and large-capacity feeders. It is advisable to feed the birds the same formulation as did the game breeder. If possible, it is also helpful to introduce the birds (with an extra feeder) to the grain that they will encounter on the hunting areas.

One end of the pen should be large enough to admit a garden tractor, and the soil should be plowed at the end of the season; wind, rain, and sun are good sanitizing agents. Plant grain sorghums in the spring for pen cover. In the early fall it is advisable to check the pens every day for any dead birds. The carcasses of dead birds should be removed from the pen; otherwise, the birds in your pen are prime candidates for botulism (see chapter on "Gamebird Diseases").

There are always some members who want the operation to rear its own pheasants or quail. *DON'T DO IT.* This can easily take the fun out of a preserve venture. The rearing of quality gamebirds is best left to the professional game breeder.

The main responsibilities of members of Do-it-yourself or Co-op Preserves are the construction of a holding pen for pheasants, crates for transporting birds, a vehicle to transport birds to the field (3-wheelers have become very popular on all hunting preserves as a stocking vehicle), and a clubhouse. A travel trailer with utilities can make an excellent clubhouse.

Rules will have to be established on safety, hours and days for hunting, use of dogs, the clubhouse, compliance with state regulations on preserves, and the wishes of the landowner.

With the right group of men, a Co-op or Do-it-yourself Preserve can offer nearly half a year of uncrowded, quality sport at modest cost — not to mention the satisfaction of using your own energy and ingenuity to solve the universal problem of having a good place to hunt.

References

1. Dickey, C. 1962. How to have more pheasant hunting. Nat. Shooting Sports Found., 1075 Post Road, Riverside, CT.
2. Kozicky, E. 1964. Private enterprise in outdoor recreation. Jour. Soil & Water Conservation 19(2):57-60. Soil Conservation Soc. of America, 7515 N.E. Ankeny Road, Ankeny, IA.
3. _____. 1965. Before you recreationalize your ranch. Western Livestock Jour. 43(31):36-38. Nelson R. Crow Publ., Inc., 326 Livestock Exch. Bldg., Denver, CO.
4. _____. and Madson, J. 1966. Shooting preserve management — the Nilo system. Winchester Group, Olin Corp., E. Alton, IL. 311pp.
5. McLaurin, E. 1964. Shooting preserves. Florida Wildlife 17(9):12-15. Florida Game & Fresh Water Fish Comm., Tallahassee, FL.
6. Musser, T. 1985. Personal communication. Illinois Dept. of Conservation, Springfield, IL.
7. Shanklin, J. F. 1963. Federal assistance in outdoor recreation. Jour. of Soil & Water Conservation 18(2):75-80. Soil Conservation Soc. of America, 7515 N.E. Ankeny Road, Ankeny, IA.

APPENDIX A

Co-op or Do-it-yourself Pheasant Holding Pen

The pen shown is 144 feet long and 24 feet wide, or 3,456 square feet. It is suitable for holding 150–200 mature ring-necked pheasants.

A spacing of 12 feet between poles will adequately support a 2-inch nylon netting roof. Nine-gauge wire is suitable for top bracing between poles.

Around the sides of the pen, start with 18-gauge, 1-inch mesh wire galvanized before weaving, 3 feet wide. Plow a furrow around the outside perimeter of the pen about 6 inches deep and 6 inches wide. Bend the lower foot of the 1-inch mesh wire into the furrow in a 90-degree "L" shape and cover it with dirt to help keep predators out. For the remainder of the sides (5 feet) of the pen use 2-inch mesh, 18-gauge wire galvanized before-weaving, and hog ring the 2 strips of wire together. Cover the top of the pen with 2-inch nylon netting. Do not stretch the wire or nylon netting too tight. If the wire is loose, it will help absorb the shock of flying pheasants, and a loose nylon netting on the top of the pen will stretch with the weight of snow. The posts should be about 10 feet high; set them 3 feet deep, which will give you an inside height of 7 feet in your holding pen. Use braces to hold the outside posts upright, especially the corner posts.

The sides and top of the shelter area should be sufficiently braced with wood boards to attach plywood and/or sheet-metal or aluminum roofing. The front part of the shelter area (the side inside the holding pen) should be covered with 1-inch poultry netting except for the lower 30 inches. The bottom of the 30 inches should be a swinging gate operated by ropes to admit pheasants into the shelter. When pheasants are needed, the birds are herded into the shelter, and the gate is dropped. Pheasants within the shelter area can either be caught by hand or with a poultry net. A better technique is to construct a catch box on the outside of the shelter area (see chapter on "The Ring-necked Pheasant") and connect the two with a sliding door.

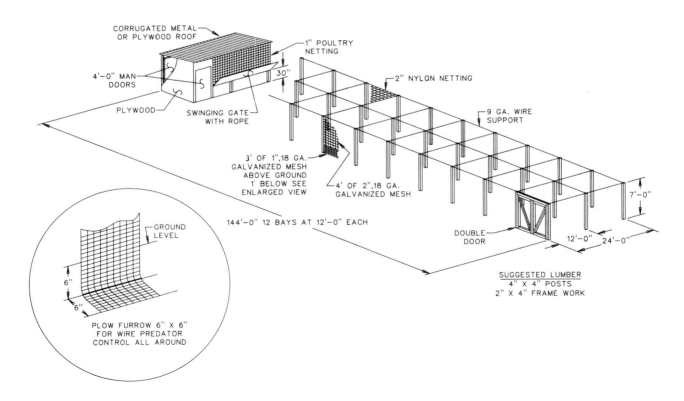

CORRUGATED METAL OR PLYWOOD ROOF

1" POULTRY NETTING

4'-0" MAN DOORS

30"

2" NYLON NETTING

PLYWOOD

SWINGING GATE WITH ROPE

9 GA. WIRE SUPPORT

3' OF 1",18 GA. GALVANIZED MESH ABOVE GROUND 1' BELOW SEE ENLARGED VIEW

4' OF 2",18 GA. GALVANIZED MESH

144'-0" 12 BAYS AT 12'-0" EACH

DOUBLE DOOR

7'-0"

12'-0" 24'-0"

GROUND LEVEL

6"

6"

PLOW FURROW 6" X 6" FOR WIRE PREDATOR CONTROL ALL AROUND

SUGGESTED LUMBER
4" X 4" POSTS
2" X 4" FRAME WORK

Chapter 4

THE A-B-Cs OF SUCCESSFUL HUNTING PRESERVES

From fall 1984 through fall 1985, I visited 17 successful hunting preserves that had been in business for 8 or more years and had excellent reputations among hunters. These successful preserves were scattered from Florida to Minnesota and from Pennsylvania through Texas (see "Acknowledgements").

Successful hunting preserves are no accident. They all have a common thread of management that make them successsful.[2] Through marketing research or fortuitous circumstances each determined the customers in a given area, built and managed a hunting preserve to satisfy the needs of the customers, set prices accordingly, and provided services commensurate with their prices. They differed as to clubhouse and overnight accommodations, services, hunting routines, regulations for hunting guests, and facilities. But an analysis of the "common thread" indicates 3 broad categories of similarity, with a decreasing rank of importance as one progresses from category A through B and C.

Category A

Good birds, good hunting dogs, good guides, and good vegetative cover (natural and planted) constitute the basics of *every* successful hunting preserve. All four are essential in providing quality hunting in natural surroundings. Quality hunting on a preserve simulates the wild hunting of gamebirds so closely that the hunter does not perceive the difference. This is understandable, since good hunting for wild gamebirds is a combination of a good gamebird population, dog work, and "birdy" cover.

Good birds — ring-necked pheasants, bobwhite quail, mallard ducks, chukar partridge, gray partridge, or wild turkeys — must be mature birds (at least 16 weeks of age), fully feathered, and capable of strong flight. The birds should not have off-color plumage or misshapened bills.

Successful preserves also specialize in providing the highest quality hunting for at least 1 species of gamebird. North of the Mason-Dixon

Line, that bird is the ring-necked pheasant; south of the Line, the bobwhite quail. In short, they specialize and excel in top-quality hunting and "hunting atmosphere" for a given species — pheasant hunting in corn or milo fields, cattail marshes, or weedy fields; or hunting bobwhites under stately pine trees with good ground cover, such as wire grass and feed patches, in the South. Other gamebirds, mainly chukars and mallards, are usually available as supplemental gamebirds, if desired by the hunters.

West of the Mississippi River, hunting preserves are not prone to the same degree of specialization as they are in the East. In Texas some hunting preserves specialize in pheasants, others in bobwhite quail. But they will offer other species of gamebirds to satisfy their clientele. In California the ring-necked pheasant is the "king-pin" on hunting preserves.[3]

Sportsmen want to hunt birds that resemble their wild counterparts and will examine the birds for coloration and conformation. A good guide doesn't hesitate to call attention to the beauty of the birds, especially during a field photo session.

If it is a rainy day or snowing and the preserve operator cannot cancel or reschedule the hunt, he informs his guests what to expect as to the field performance of the birds. The same is true of late-season (March and April) hunting, espe-

cially ring-necked pheasants, which are then more interested in mating than survival. The cock birds are prone to run more or be oblivious to an approaching hunting party.

Next in importance is good vegetative cover on the hunting courses. Cover influences the behavior of the birds when encountered in the field, as well as the dog work and the enjoyment and the success of the hunter. How? For example, pheasants will not remain for any length of time in cover that does not provide a good overhead canopy, and bobwhite quail will run under tall overhead cover that is open at ground level, as opposed to grassy cover, and the birds will not flush as a covey.

The vegetative cover should also permit a good view of the hunting dogs. Hunters, whether on foot or in a hunting vehicle, enjoy watching good dog work. Since most guests on a hunting preserve have hunted either pheasants or bobwhite quail in the wild, it helps to have the hunting courses look like "birdy cover."

The vegetative cover also should be of such height that the hunters have a good chance to kill game on the initial flush and also on the second flush, such as bobwhite quail and chukar partridge. If the birds fly into a wooded swamp or exceedingly rough terrain after the initial flush, the hunters have little to no chance of pursuing the birds. Good bobwhite hunting

Guides with clean hunting vehicles waiting for their hunting parties, Riverview Plantation, Camilla, Georgia.

courses, especially in the South, are laid out with this in mind.

Good dog work is an important segment of quality hunting on a preserve. The hunting dog should have the conformation of its breed and be well-conditioned and free of any injuries. The dog must be obedient, have a good nose, and be force-broken to retrieve all birds to hand. Hunters appreciate a stylish, obedient dog that forms an effective team with the guide.

The guide is the fourth factor. Hunting is a great American tradition, and one either enjoys a guide or never wants to see him again. There doesn't seem to be a middle ground. Strangers can become good friends on a single hunt. The guide should be a hunter who likes to take people hunting, be friendly by nature, likes his work, be dressed like a dog handler — with all of the tools of the trade — and wear clean clothes.

Cader Cox of Riverview Plantation, Georgia, believes so strongly in the importance of the guide that he furnishes each guide with an instructional manual on their responsibilities. Jeff hughes of Wild Wings of Oneka, Minnesota, holds a guiding seminar each fall prior to the hunting season for all of his guides.

Category B

Category B of successful preserves includes the manager, hunter freedom, grounds and equipment, buildings and signs, and hunter safety.

The manager, above all else, must like people and be a Pollyana. Every group of hunters wants to be greeted, catered to, and even bid farewell by the manager. The best managers make it a point to do all three. As Preston Mann, Hunters Creek Club, Michigan, says, "Managing a hunting preserve is a 'hands on' business."

Regardless of weather conditions or personal problems, the manager must be optimistic and develop a hunting plan to make the most of each day. Hunters can have a grand time afield under the most miserable weather conditions — good managers turn disasters into a memorable hunt.[4] They are living examples of the power of a positive mental attitude (PMA).

The manager must be dressed to look the part. Good quality outdoor clothing worn by the manager helps to create the illusion of 1 hunter talking to another, and helps to break down any mental barriers between the manager and his hunting guests. He must have the complete respect of his employees, and never lose his "cool" with the guests, or with employees in front of guests.

The manager tries to treat each hunting party as special guests. He doesn't mix hunters from 2 different hunting parties in the field. If possible, he may even serve them separate meals or arrange private quarters for their social hour.

The better managers are good judges of the physical limitations of their guests, their shooting ability, their financial limitations, and the type of hunt — length, dogs, guide, terrain, and cover — they enjoy, and plan accordingly. In short, good managers help the hunter maintain a "macho" image and avoid either personal or financial embarrassment.

Above all else, good managers love the sport of hunting and understand quality hunting and its components — gamebirds, dogs, guides, and cover. But they also are businessmen, good promotors, and have pleasant personalities — the attributes of a good salesman. They are the kind of folks that attract hunters like honey attracts bees.

Hunter freedom is an intangible, but it is part of a quality experience by hunters on a number of successful hunting preserves, especially club operations.

In the final analysis hunting is a classical exercise in personal freedom, and only free men enjoy the sport of hunting. Hence, the appeal of some preserves is a minimum of restrictions — no guides unless you want one, use your own dog, hunt where you like and as long as you like, and shoot as many birds as you like. Richmond Game Fields, Illinois, and Squash Hill Shooting Preserve,[1] North Carolina, epitomize this type of operation, and they are highly successful hunting preserves.

The less regimentation and "don'ts" on a hunting preserve, the better. The tempo on a hunting preserve should be one of relaxed outdoor recreation with the hunter setting his own pace. On other preserves, however, especially where a member is entertaining a group of guests, there does have to be a given amount of regimentation and scheduling of activities.

The grounds and equipment must be clean and neat. All employees should be responsible for picking up litter. Expended shotshells and cigarette butts are the 2 worst offenders, and their presence on the ground should be kept to a minimum. All equipment should be clean and free of litter. Tools of the gamebird trade — catch and release paraphernalia, holding crates, and/or pens — should never be seen by hunting guests.

Buildings and signs are the first impression that a hunter receives of a hunting preserve. Above all else, they should be attractive, freshly painted, and landscaped if possible. They need not be elaborate.

The clubhouse should be clean, especially the kitchen. Both the clubhouse and the kitchen should be designed for ease of cleaning. There are days when mud and sand will be tracked into the clubhouse by hunters. Some preserves have special facilities, such as "mud rooms" where hunters can wash off their boots before coming into the clubhouse.

Mr. Norman Thomas at the attractive entrance to his hunting preserve, Norman Park, Georgia.

Most successful preserves serve a noon meal — a house specialty, such as fried chicken, pheasant or chukar potpie, etc. Don't overlook the importance of a good, home-cooked meal. "Pop" Lehner, former owner of Wild Wings of Oneka, Minnesota, said it best years ago, "Once in awhile everything goes wrong on a hunting preserve — weather, dogs, birds, or all three. When this happens, you have to make it up with the biscuits."

Most successful preserves provide a clean, spacious, and comfortable clubhouse for their guests. They also serve good meals on a reservation basis, especially breakfast and lunch. Dinners are also served on special occasions, ranging from meetings to weddings. A scheduled meal time for hunting guests gives the manager and his guides an opportunity to organize either the morning or afternoon hunt (number and species of gamebirds to stock, hunting areas, dogs to use, etc.).

The dog kennels are part of your showcase and will be visited by hunters. A number of successful preserves board, train, and sell hunting dogs to supplement their income; such operators are well aware of the importance of clean and neat kennels. Dog kennels should be designed for a complete washing down at least twice a day.

Hunter safety should always be uppermost in the manager's mind. A Private or Do-it-yourself Hunting Preserve may require less hunter safety than a Daily-fee Preserve or a hunt wherein a host is entertaining a group of guests. In the latter group, chances are that there are individuals who have not hunted with others of the group, or some who have not hunted in years. In such instances, after consultation with the host, a 5–10-minute talk on proper shotgun handling and field etiquette is not only in order but is deeply appreciated by all members of the group. Each member of the group is concerned that their hunting partners receive the full message.

If hunting guests are arriving on a given afternoon to hunt on the following day, some preserves offer clay target shooting or trout fishing for the early arrivals. Stocked trout will survive, even in the South, from late fall through the winter months. The trout pond and the clay

The interior of the Nilo clubhouse (courtesy Winchester Group, Olin Corp.).

target facilities are usually located within walking distance of the clubhouse. The purpose of clay target shooting is not only to familiarize the hunter with handling a shotgun but to help him shoot effectively in the field. All efforts are made to keep a guest from being embarrassed with his poor shooting in the field — even to the extent of matching a good shooter with a poor one.

Category C

Category C includes the care, cleaning, and packaging of dead birds and communicating with members. All dead gamebirds should be treated with respect. The birds should be hung on cooling racks in the shade after a hunt. Ducks can be laid out in a neat row on their backs by the guide on a duck shoot. Under no circumstances should the birds be thrown into a pile. At a minimum they should be spread out on the ground in the shade for quick dispersion of body heat.

The cleaning and packaging of gamebirds should be done on a daily basis, as quickly as possible following a hunt. Of great importance is that the picked and eviscerated birds be kept overnight, in a chill tank (ice water) and then placed on a draining rack in the morning prior to being placed in an air-tight plastic bag and frozen. Otherwise, when the bird is thawed prior to cook-

ing, there will be considerable bloody water in the package. The package should be plainly marked as to contents and, if possible, each hunter should be given the gamebirds that he shot. These little niceties are deeply appreciated by the cook and are usually conveyed to the hunter.

Most successful hunting preserves remain in contact with their hunters with either a monthly, quarterly, or semi-annual newsletter, or by using postcards or flyers for special events — continental shoot, clean-up hunt, championship hunt, field days, dog-training sessions, etc. Jeff Hughes, Wild Wings of Oneka, Minnesota, believes that communication with his membership is all-important. If business is slow after the first of the year and the snow is deep, Jeff and his wife Sue will organize and publicize some type of special event for their members. It works.

Summary

Like the successful flighting of gamebirds on a hunting preserve, there is no single answer or panacea to the successful management of a hunting preserve. Both efforts require constant attention to many details.

The primary requisites for a successful hunting preserve are top-quality gamebirds, hunting dogs, vegetative cover, and guides; feature the traditional gamebird in a given area; and strive to provide hunting of that species so close to wild conditions that you have to blink your eyes to tell the difference.

Of secondary importance are a congenial manager, hunting freedom, a comfortable clubhouse, good food, and clay target facilities. Overnight accommodations are only needed if not available within a convenient driving distance. But, if they are available, they should be high quality.

All successful preserves clean gamebirds for their hunting guests and establish a line of communications — newsletters, special events, postcards, etc. — with their hunters throughout the year.

References

1. Jones, S. III. 1979. Squash Hill Shooting Preserve. Wildlife Harvest 10(5):4-8. Goose Lake, IA.
2. Jordan, H. 1979. Practices of hunting preserves. Pennsylvania Game Bird Bull. 12(6):5. RD 2, Hegins, PA.
3. Klingle, Jack and Georgette. 1973. The story of Hastings Island Hunt Preserve. Wildlife Harvest 4(10):15-16. Goose Lake, IA.
4. Mann, P. 1978. Hunting preserve management. Wildlife Harvest 9(10):17. Goose Lake, IA.

Chapter 5

THE PRESERVE OPERATOR'S ROLE

A hunting preserve operator or manager should be a hunter and should be knowledgeable in the training and handling of hunting dogs and sport hunting. Sportsmen come from a wide variety of backgrounds, but when two of them meet, they are quick to judge and build trust in one another on their respective knowledge of hunting.

Besides being a hunter, a preserve operator must be a jack-of-all-trades, and a master of most. He must understand quality gamebirds and their maintenance, the training and handling of dogs, hunting, farming, preserve management, promotion, administration, and shotgun shooting. The better preserve operators, as explained in the chapter, ''The A-B-Cs of Successful Hunting Preserves,'' are such people. Also, in the same chapter, the overall importance of quality hunting in natural surroundings was emphasized as the most important factor in the successful management of a hunting preserve. This chapter stresses the day-to-day routine of handling preserve hunting guests.

A Good Host

From the operator to the guides, all personnel of the preserve should be friendly and interested in hunters. Every guest should feel that the entire operation has been geared to his visit.

A warm bond of welcome and a sunny disposition should prevail, regardless of personal moods, and the operator and his guides must maintain that outlook for a 5–6-month season. The preserve operator is in the outdoor recreation business, and he must never forget that the objective of his preserve, his birds, his cover, and his guides is to provide outdoor enjoyment of high quality.

When hunters arrive at the preserve, the operator should be the first to meet them. Bring the hunters into the clubhouse, and while they are enjoying hot coffee, check their hunting licenses, and register them into the preserve log book.

The main room of the clubhouse should be decorated with hunting pictures and photos of

A preserve operator greeting hunting guests on arrival (courtesy Winchester Group, Olin Corp.)

guests. There should be a guest register and literature about the preserve. Each hunter should be made to feel at home among friends, in *clean* and *pleasant* surroundings.

It is important for the operator to judge the physical condition of the hunters, and to learn from artful questioning the kind of hunt each would like. Does the hunter want a maximum of shooting with a minimum of physical exertion, or does he want to tramp the fields behind a good dog for half a day or more?

Discretion should be used by the preserve operator in learning how long each hunter wants to hunt, and how many birds he and his party would like to shoot. Try to expose each hunting party to about as many birds as they can afford; don't tempt them with an excessive number. Shooting birds is like eating popcorn — it's hard to stop. Tailor the hunt to your hunters' finances and general fitness, and try to avoid embarrassing them on either count.

One of the best ways to solve many of these preliminaries is to serve a hearty breakfast at the preserve. This gives the operator time to talk to the hunters, and to alert his guides on any changes in the hunting plans for a given group. Weather conditions at reservation time can be drastically different on the day of the hunt and — when it is — the operator must be up-beat and optimistic. The operator should check to ensure that everyone in the group is equipped with the proper ammunition and offer advice on appropriate clothing and footgear.

One hunting group should never be forced to join another. If several groups of hunters are scheduled for the day, their hunting should be planned so that they overlap as little as possible. Even 1 stranger in a hunting party can dampen the enthusiasm of the group.

When the hunting party is ready to go afield, the operator should introduce the hunters to their guide. If there are new hunters in the group, the operator should explain the preserve's rules on hunting safety and etiquette (see chapter on "Hunting Safety").

Regimentation and Artificiality

Avoid unnecessary regimentation like the plague. Your hunters have come to escape regimentation and schedules of daily life; they want to relax and enjoy themselves. It's your job to help them do so.

Some operators have a tendency to speed up hunting activities and "process" the guests, working on the theory that the faster turnover of hunters means faster profits. This is a mistake and a management pitfall. Such "processing" means regimentation, and what should be fun and relaxation may become the worst type of "canned" hunt. Guests should be permitted to set their own hunting pace within the limits of morning and afternoon activities.

In the chapter on "The A-B-Cs of Successful Preserves," freedom from regimentation ranks only below quality hunting. The watchword for the management of hunting guests should be "relaxation," and regimentation of any type should be avoided whenever and wherever possible.

Another management pitfall in the diabolical tendency to "process" hunters is to drift away from natural hunting to artificiality.[1] The more artificial the hunting, the better the recovery of gamebirds and the higher the profits. The more artificial the hunting the less work the operator has to do. More artificial hunting means less expenses incurred in feed and cover, stocking, and handling. It also means more birds can be shot in a shorter period of time. Even the hunters

tend to pull the operator towards artificiality, for a few of them will not only put up with artificial hunting but will proclaim that they enjoy it. It is a natural human trait for the operator to take the easy road and convince himself that *all* hunters will accept artificial hunting. When this happens, the operator will soon be out of business, and the whole hunting preserve industry suffers. *Experience has proved time and time again that only sporty hunting survives.*

Food and Leisure

Mothers tell their daughters that the way to a man's heart is through his stomach. Well, mother knows best, and her advice is just as appropriate for hunting preserve operators. Serve hearty meals of home-cooked food and develop several preserve specialities — pheasant or chukar potpie, fried chicken, or steaks. At Nilo we always had freshly baked biscuits at the noon meal, and this little wrinkle helped put a smile of satisfaction and contentment on many a hunter's face.

Provide as much privacy as possible for your hunters in clean and pleasant surroundings for the noon meal. At the end of the hunt, they should have some privacy in which to exchange hunting experiences, relax, change into their dress clothes, and enjoy refreshments. Hunters should never be rushed on a preserve. If they want to sit and talk long after the hunt, let them.

Cleanliness

Cleanliness is next to Godliness on a hunting preserve. The entire hunting preserve should be clean and neat, but not give the impression of being a manicured country club. It must appear to be a natural area for all forms of wildlife. All signs of previous use, such as empty shotshells or cigarette butts near the entrance to the clubhouse, should be removed on a daily basis. Order and cleanliness are essential to all parts of the hunting preserve accessible to the guests, and this is particularly important in the kitchen and dog kennels.

The operator's personal dress, as well as that of the guides, need not be elaborate, but always

Joe Zerkowsky, a former Nilo chef, preparing his famous pheasant potpie.

clean. Hunting vehicles should be cleaned every day.

The entrance to the hunting preserve, the roadway to the clubhouse, and the dog kennels should be tastefully landscaped. Signs should be freshly painted each year. These are the areas where first impressions are made by visitors and hunters; let these impressions be good ones.

Teaching and Diplomacy

Sooner or later you are going to be asked to help a hunter with his shooting. Let him know that you are a willing instructor. The best approach is to slip off with him to the clay target range and give him your undivided attention. Chances are that his confidence is badly shaken, and all you need to do is to restore it. You may even have to teach a guest hunter how to load and operate a shotgun. For other novices, you may have to explain the difference between pointing and flushing bird dogs, or else instruct the guide of the hunting party to do so prior to the hunt.

All holding pens for gamebirds should be well hidden. Hunters don't come to see birds in the pens; they come to hunt. At their best, holding pens are not aesthetic — and they don't get any prettier as the season wears on. If you cannot move your pens to an area not frequented by visitors, at least plant vegetation around them and/or construct a picket fence to hide their presence.

Have a stock excuse ready for hunters who ask to visit the bird pens. For instance, you might say that strangers cause your fine, sporty birds to batter themselves against the wire.

Releasing gamebirds should never be done in the presence of hunters unless someone who is paying on the basis of released birds wants to be present. Bird crates and other "tools of the trade" should never be displayed or visible. The best time to release gamebirds is when the hunters are in the clubhouse or shooting clay targets.

Guides should be non-commital about when the birds were released, or how many were released, except to the host of the hunting group (and then only when he is paying for birds on a released basis). Let the host inform the other members of his hunting group, if he so desires.

Isolation of hunting areas is important. If there is a constant commotion or traffic through a hunting area, the spell of being afield with hunting companies and bird dogs is broken. The hunting area should not be cluttered with sightseers. No one relaxes when shooting before a gallery. Don't allow non-hunters to watch, it is dangerous *and* distracting to the hunters. People get paid to stage exhibitions. Arrange for non-hunters to enjoy the clubhouse or visit the kennels.

Management

Managing a hunting preserve is a business to the operator and a source of relaxation and recreation for his hunting guests — and never shall the twain meet. The operator needs to constantly check on the flow of business, the quality of hunting, the supply of birds, promoting, analyzing costs, and income statements on every phase of his operation and the overall enjoyment of his hunting guests. It pays to be a good listener.

Every preserve operator should visit his game suppliers to check on the quality of their gamebirds and to establish mutual trust and friendship. Preserve operators and game breeders need one another.

Don't let outside obligations or office work keep you from visiting with your hunters. Be on hand to greet them, listen to their comments, and

A group of hunters at the Max McGraw Wildlife Foundation, Dundee, Illinois, enjoying a break with their guide, Rudy Wendt.

bid them farewell. Operating a hunting preserve is a "hands on" business.

Condition your hunters to make reservations for hunting, meals, and other activities as far in advance as possible, and for good reason. You must not only have the desired gamebirds and hunting areas available for them but the necessary personnel. Good business practice would dictate a reasonable cancellation fee with less than 24-hour notice.

Good, part-time help is always a problem. However, guides can be found among sportsmen who own good hunting dogs, especially 40-hour-a-week shift workers. Extra kitchen help is available, mostly from middle-aged women who no longer have children at home. Help to process shot gamebirds, feed game, clean dog kennels, etc., can be found among high-school teenagers after normal school hours and on weekends. And, if all else fails, there is always your family.

Summary

The preserve manager must guard against the day-to-day monotony of routine, and a very human tendency to relax from the extra effort that a top-quality hunting preserve demands. Once the first slip in good management occurs, the remainder follow in quick succession. It requires constant attention to small details that make the difference between a mediocre and a quality hunting preserve. After all, the word "quality" is the summation of all things on a preserve — both tangible and intangible — that make a hunt a happy memory for your hunters.

References

1. Dickey, C. 1962. Sport mallard shooting. North American Game Breeders and Shooting Preserve Assoc. Meeting, Chicago, IL. January 14-16.

Chapter 6

GAMEBIRD BEHAVIOR

One area of knowledge that needs more appreciation by both game-farm and hunting preserve operators is gamebird behavior or ''wildness.'' We in the industry have a tendency to consider all pen-reared gamebirds as being equal. They are not. There is a vast difference in inherent wildness in gamebirds not only between species but within pen-reared stock of a given species. Unless the hunting preserve operator is aware of these differences, he will be confused and frustrated with the field behavior of his gamebirds.

Gamebirds that exhibit ''proper behavior'' or wildness in the field do so based on the influence of genetics and environment. In most game-farm species, wildness is essential for proper field performance; in other species (chukars) we have developed hunting techniques that assure a quality field performance despite a lack of wildness.

Gamebird Propagation

Over the years, the game-farm operator had

a tendency to select the best layers and the most docile and fertile gamebirds as breeding stock. In essence, he was also selecting for the most domestic strain of the birds. The wilder the strain of gamebirds, the less fertility and egg production and the greater the cannibalism problem. So, in many instances, we are flighting gamebirds, such as the chukar, that have lost their inherent wildness except for the ability to fly. But we are able to flight chukars successfully on hunting preserves by using flushing-type dogs, or pointing dogs, that are trained to flush on command. Further, the vast majority of patrons on a hunting preserve have never hunted chukars in the wild, so their expectations are not bound to tradition. All we need to produce is a fast-flying bird. On the other hand, bobwhite quail hunting traditions demand that the birds hold for a pointing dog and flush as a covey when approached by the hunter. Most game-farm bobwhites have domesticated to the point where they do not perform satisfactorily in the field — they run out into the open, have no apparent fear of approaching hunters or bird dogs, do not rise as a covey, give short flights (5–15 yards) when flushed as singles or pairs, and have poor, if any, survival.

Patrons at hunting preserves have a right to expect pen-reared gamebirds to approximate the field behavior of their wild counterparts. These birds are expected to exhibit strong flight on their initial flush, have the same color and conformation as wild birds and be fully feathered and not grossly debeaked. Preserve operators and game farms have made progress in the last 30 years, especially with quality ring-necked pheasants, and more progress can be expected in the years ahead as the industry grows and matures.

In the final analysis, we must start with a gamebird that has the necessary genes to transmit a basic wildness to its progeny, and then rear the progeny in an environment wherein the birds, upon maturity, will provide a consistent quality field performance shortly after being released for hunting guests. Since the bobwhite is the most difficult gamebird to flight successfully on a hunting preserve, I will go into greater detail on environmental factors influencing the behavior of this species. However, to varying degrees, these same environmental factors will influence the field behavior of all gamebirds.

Bobwhite Quail

The king of native gamebirds in the South is a sensitive gentleman compared to the ring-necked pheasant. And it is this very sensitivity that must be understood by both the game-farm and hunting preserve operator.

We are still seeking ways to provide consistent, strong-flying bobwhites on the initial flush in the field. We are aware of a number of environmental details, but do not understand their relative importance, nor do we have assurance that we are aware of all the factors affecting field performance of bobwhites. All we can do is report on the state-of-the-art as we understand it.

Quality bobwhite hunting starts with quality pen-reared birds. There are game-farm operators who refuse to discuss their management techniques — because of pride, competition, or selfishness. So be it. This reminds one of the Scottish game keepers years ago who only handed down the "mysteries" of ring-necked pheasant production on game farms to their sons. All hunting preserve operators who flight quail should visit their supplier and check out the field performance of his or her quail. Don't buy birds on hearsay or by pen inspection. Further, only buy quail from a producer who pledges you complete cooperation, should you encounter a problem. And, unless the bobwhites are handled properly at the hunting preserve, a good flyer can become a poor one in a few days. Certain management techniques and environmental factors for quality bobwhites have emerged through the years and are worthy of discussion.

Wildness

Wildness in pen-reared bobwhites can be improved by back-crossing to wild birds, especially wild male birds. The success of such back-crossing requires isolation of the breeding pairs from all disturbance. The superiority of the progeny of such crosses has been documented for bobwhite by the efforts of state game farms in Illinois and Ohio.[1] As yet, we do not know how often such back-crossing is necessary for quality bobwhites, but the rumor in the South is every fourth generation.

How much wildness needs to be introduced into a given strain of bobwhites is an art rather than a science. Back-crossing pen-reared birds to wild birds can be overdone. The wilder the bird, the less egg production and fertility and the greater the cannibalism problem. However, remember that the objective is to produce pen-reared bobwhites that hold well before the dog, flush as a covey, are capable of strong flight on the initial, and second flush, and do not run out of cover into the open.

Isolation

Isolation of pen-reared bobwhites from disturbance by man or dog is not only important to the successful breeding of wild cocks to game-farm hens, but it is also important throughout the rearing and holding stages of bobwhites at the game farm and the hunting preserve. The Burnette Quail Farm,[2] Tecumseh, Missouri, was isolated to the point where the only human beings that the birds ever saw were the Burnettes, who even wore neutral-colored clothing when attending the birds. No visitors or dogs were permitted around the pens. Isolation is not a half-way measure. You either practice strict isolation, or you don't. The importance of isolation in rearing quality bobwhites seems to have concurrence throughout the gamebird industry.

Flight Pens

Flight pens, *per se*, are not the solution to quality bobwhites. Once bobwhites have become docile and have accepted man, flight pens have little, if any, influence on their field behavior. On the other hand, flight pens are not known to be detrimental. Such pens do provide an ample opportunity for the birds to exercise and strengthen their wing and breast muscles. Some folks insist that they are beneficial. The difference of opinion could well be related to the genetic background of the bobwhites. The Burnette bobwhites were never in a pen larger than 8 feet by 28 feet, and only 3 feet in height — the standard game-farm holding pen for bobwhites.[2] After all, bobwhites are small birds compared to a ring-necked pheasant, and the Burnette bobwhites received all of the exercise they apparently needed to be strong flyers.

It does not appear advisable to provide any type of perch in a holding or flight pen. If you do provide perches, such as rafters, the birds will have a tendency to fly onto tree limbs upon being flushed in the field, an escape substitute for the rafters that they used in the holding pens.

Rearing on Ground or Wire

Whether to rear or hold bobwhites on the

Quail pens isolated from human disturbance with both natural and artificial overhead cover (courtesy Winchester Group, Olin Corp.)

ground or on wire has been a subject of great discussion. It certainly is more natural to rear and hold birds on the ground rather than on wire; however, the disease problem, especially ulcerative enteritis, in many areas of the United States precludes holding birds on the ground. In the South many bobwhites are held on sandy, well-drained soil or on pine shavings, and the birds are given a prophylactic medication of bacitracin in their feed. Again, the Burnette birds were held on 1/2-inch hardware cloth until released in the field.

Overhead Cover

Overhead cover, either natural or artificial, appears to be important to the proper field behavior of pen-reared quail. One cannot expect bobwhites that have been reared under the open sky through their lives to remain in vegetative cover upon release. Such birds are going to seek open areas. Hunters encountering bobwhites in the open are going to be disappointed, and the birds are "easy pickings" for avian predators. Overhead cover for holding pens can either be natural or artificial. At Nilo we used sheet-metal roofing to provide such cover for the Burnette birds after the frost defoliated the trees above the holding pens. The Burnette Quail Farm was in a heavily timbered area with a canopy of large oak trees that towered 50–70 feet above the quail pens.[2]

Darkened Holding Pens

Some hunting preserves hold their bobwhite quail in darkened rooms and are pleased with the behavior of their released birds. At least they believe the quail provide a better field performance than the same birds held in open pens. The darkened room serves 2 purposes. Darkness in any phase of holding, transporting, or transferring bobwhites sedates the birds, and they are easier to handle. Also, in a darkened room the birds may well develop an aversion for full sunlight and will tend to remain in cover upon release for hunting purposes.

Exposure to the weather is important in the proper development of the oil gland, which provides weather-proofing for the feathers of bobwhites. If the birds are not weather-proofed, they will not fly well as soon as any moisture penetrates the flight feathers. Moreover, a bird soaked with moisture stands little chance of survival in cold weather. Charles Baehr, Elkhorn Lake Shooting Park, Ohio, actually sprays water on his bobwhites every day. Some game farms fog their quail with water to help develop the oil gland and to hold down the dust, especially if the birds are held on litter.

Food, Water, and Dusting

"We are what we eat" applies to people and to gamebirds. Hunting preserve operators should try to feed the same rations as did the breeder, or at least the same formulation. If you try to switch rations on bobwhites, they may lose an ounce or .more before they accept the new rations, and a good flyer can become a poor flyer in a couple of days. Jerry Waters, Hawkeye Hunting Club, Texas, is a firm believer in the necessity of providing fresh feed and an abundance of feeders to avoid competition at the feeder. He only buys small quantities of feed at a time and insists that the feed supplier grind fresh feed for his birds. Jerry also likes to keep a new shipment of quail for a week or more and give the birds a chance to recover from the shock of shipment, to settle down in their new quarters, and to regain their strength prior to stocking the birds for hunting.

Water is essential and should be provided daily, regardless of temperature. Dusting areas (pans of dry soil in a sheltered location) are essential to the general welfare of bobwhites, especially if the birds are held on wire. The Burnettes were also firm believers in supplying shocks of grain, such as golden millet, to keep adult birds occupied and to help adjust the birds to feed found on the hunting areas.

Shipping

Shipping time for bobwhites is important — the less time, the better. As with other gamebirds, bobwhites should not be crowded in a shipping box. The number of birds in a compartment depends on the size of the compartment and the ambient air temperature. Ed Morris, Morris Quail Farm, Florida, likes to use cardboard shipping boxes designed for poultry chicks. Also, with allowances for air circulation, the darker the environment inside the box, the better. Bobwhites are less nervous to outside stimuli in a darkened environment. Jerry Waters, Hawkeye Hunting Club, Texas, will not purchase bobwhites from a breeder who requires more than 12 hours of delivery time.

One should not mix bobwhites from different quail farms. Bobwhites have strong social ties and establish a peck order within a given flock, and there is unrest when bobwhites from different pens or flocks are brought together. Unrest, like so many other environmental factors, can place the quail under stress, which makes the birds prime candidates for the quail disease, ulcerative enteritis (see chapter on "The Bobwhite Quail"). If possible, have the game-farm supplier mark all shipping crates from different holding pens so that you can maintain the integrity of a given flock with separate holding pens at your preserve.

Summary

As yet no one has developed an environmental influence that will reverse the tendency for bobwhites to domesticate in captivity. All of the above techniques, with the exception of backcrossing to wild birds, are environmental measures to delay domestication or to influence the field behavior of pen-reared bobwhites. However, with the passage of time, exchange of information, and the help of state universities and state wildlife agencies, the art of producing quality pen-reared bobwhites for hunting preserves will become more of a science, just as today's large-scale production of ring-necked pheasants has emerged from the trade secrets of the Scottish gamekeepers.

Currently, quality flighting of bobwhites on hunting preserves requires attention to many details, far more than for any other gamebird. Hunting preserve operators will tend to "cut corners" but, when they do, their hunters will be disappointed and the preserve operators will be frustrated.

There are no bargain quail. You can expect to pay more for good birds, and you can expect to charge more. You may even have to educate your hunters to the difference and let them make a choice. The greatest mistake that the hunting

preserve industry can make, especially in the South, is to be satisfied with status quo and not strive for better quality bobwhites.

Ring-Necked Pheasant

Today, ring-necked pheasant game farms catering to hunting preserves consistently produce high-quality birds. Good game farms produce pheasants that look and fly like wild ring-necked pheasants. No longer does one see bob-tailed, bare-backed, off-colored, grossly debeaked ring-necked pheasants, at least not on quality hunting preserves. There is a good reason for this. Better hunting preserve operators will not tolerate such birds on their preserves, and the game-farm operator knows it. Such was not the case 30 years ago.

Why the change? There is no longer a mystery in producing ring-necked pheasants on game farms. A number of game-farm operators have specialized in producing a quality bird for hunting preserves and take justifiable pride in their product.

Fortunately for the hunting preserve industry, the ring-necked pheasant is wild by nature and doesn't tame in captivity. Wildness in the ring-necked pheasant is largely inherited from 1 generation of game-farm birds to the next. The environment in which the pheasant is reared plays only a small part in its behavior upon release, providing the bird has not been brailed, and has been given large holding pens in which to exercise. For the sake of comparison, one could say that wildness in pheasants is 75% inherited and 25% (or less) the environment in which the bird is reared, whereas in the bobwhite quail the ratio is probably reversed.

The Chinese (blue-backed) strain of ring-necked pheasant, crossed with Mongolian, Formosan, and/or Korean strains, appears to be an ideal bird for hunting preserves. They are not as large as other crosses of ring-necked pheasants, but they are strong flyers and just don't "cool down" in captivity.

Game-farm operators have learned the importance of proper feed for good feathering, large holding pens for space and exercise, and the use of "specs" to reduce cannibalism. Also, the ring-necked pheasant has a high resistance to most poultry diseases and can be reared and held on the ground throughout the United States.

The ring-necked pheasant is a large gamebird compared to bobwhite quail and can endure stress for a greater length of time and absorb more physical abuse. In the 1940s, the Pennsylvania Game Commission conducted winter stress-tests with a climatometer that was capable of duplicating temperature, wind, and moisture conditions the birds encountered in the field. Under severe stress, pheasants could exist for about a month; bobwhite quail lasted for about 7 days.

The ring-necked pheasant is a wild, rough, tough, hard-flying gamebird that never loses his love for freedom and refuses to acquiesce to man's wire pens and "free lunch." Little wonder that this exotic gamebird is dearly loved by hunters north of the Mason-Dixon Line, his adopted home in the wild. The pen-reared ringneck — more than any other gamebird — was responsible for the initial success of hunting preserves by providing quality hunting with a minimum attention to management details on the part of the preserve operator. The vast majority of successful hunting preserves north of the Mason-Dixon Line feature ring-necked pheasant hunting and use other species, such as chukar partridge, mallard ducks, and/or bobwhite quail, as supplemental gamebirds.

Chukar Partridge

The pen-reared chukar partridge is largely a domesticated gamebird that has little in common with the behavior of its wild counterpart except in looks, conformation, and the ability to fly.

By the time chukar partridge were flighted on hunting preserves, the birds were largely domesticated. Yet, unlike bobwhite quail, hunting preserves have found the domestication of the bird to be of advantage.

The domestication of the chukar has made the bird relatively docile and prone to remain where released unless disturbed by a predator. Hence, even on rainy days, chukars which were kept dry overnight can be stocked for hunting purposes. If released in pairs, they usually remain in the immediate area for several hours. Whereas ring-necked pheasants, although released as dry birds, are restless with their newfound freedom and will run through the vegetation and become water-soaked, offering less-than-desirable flight characteristics for sporty hunting.

Two systems are used for hunting chukars on preserves. The birds can be disoriented by a slight shaking of the head, put down in grassy cover, short sorghum patches, or stubble fields and hunted successfully with flushing-type hunting dogs — springer spaniels and Labrador retrievers — or by using a point dog trained to flush but *not* catch chukars on command.

Some hunting preserve operators like to hold their chukars in a darkened building (this technique is discussed in the chapter, "The Bobwhite Quail"). Such operators believe that their chukars so held are less prone to leave cover and seek open areas. Flight pens and isolation from human activity do enhance the field performance of game-farm chukars.

The survival rate of chukar partridge in the wild is about nil. The birds seem completely lost when released and are prime targets for every predator on a preserve.

Chukars like the company of other chukars, and very often are attracted back to the calling of the chukars in a holding pen. They also are less cannibalistic than ring-necked pheasants, and can be hunted into March and April; whereas male ring-necked pheasants are pugnacious in establishing breeding territories in late winter and are far more interested in procreation than survival.

Mallard Ducks

Of all species of waterfowl, the mallard duck is the easiest to rear in captivity. Further, mallards in captivity seem to retain a degree of wildness, providing their ancestors were not too many generations removed from the wild. By law, captive mallards must be at least 2 generations removed from wild stock.

Good flying mallards on hunting preserves are restless during the fall months. It is quite common for the birds, if disturbed, to take wing. Sometimes they appear to fly just for the joy of flying. One could easily deduce that the urge to migrate still remains but, fortunately, the urge is not strong enough for the mallards to leave their "free lunch." By January, these same mallards are less restless and will actually become rather sedentary unless forced to fly between feed and water.

The large breeders of mallard ducks know how to manipulate their breeding stock to maintain quality birds for hunting preserves. Besides genetics, proper feed has considerable influence on the development of flight feathers and, of course, the flying ability of the duck.

Occasionally, some hunting preserve operator will buy local, domesticated mallards at a bargain price. It's a mistake. Such birds do not fly well, if at all. Stick with mallard game farms that have proven track records of supplying good-flying mallards for hunting preserves.

Gray (Hungarian) Partridge

The gray partridge ("Hun") is wild by nature and does not do well in captivity. The very wildness of this gamebird makes it difficult to rear in captivity — compatability of breeding pairs, egg production, and fertility are some of the problems. A few game breeders are trying to overcome these problems — problems inherent in gamebirds where wildness is largely controlled by genetics rather than environment.

One game breeder, Carl Patterson of Buffalo, Missouri, overcame production problems by spending considerable time with the breeders and getting the birds accustomed to him and the pens. But the progeny of these birds were kept isolated from human disturbance and retained their basic wildness.

If gray partridges can be produced in quantity at a reasonable price and are hunted to take

advantage of their sporting attributes, the species holds great promise as an excellent gamebird for hunting preserves in the future. Currently, the Max McGraw Wildlife Foundation, Dundee, Illinois, is devoting considerable time, money, and manpower to the problems of rearing the gray partridge in captivity. Hopefully, they will be successful in their efforts to solve the problem of rearing these birds on a volume basis at a reasonable price without the loss of inherent wildness.

Wild Turkeys

Game farm wild turkeys, either Eastern, Rio Grande, Merriam's, or a mixture thereof, have little in common when compared to their wild cousins except for their coloration. Rearing wild turkeys on game farms quickly removes the basic wildness of this great gamebird. The main emphasis on hunting preserves that feature wild turkeys is to have the bird fly when encountered during a hunt. Hence, game farms tend to emphasize a smaller strain of birds to enhance their flying ability.

The future of wild turkeys on hunting preserves is as a supplemental bird to either pheasant or quail hunting. No preserve has found a way to duplicate the thrill of hunting wild turkeys with their pen-reared counterparts. Years ago, Bill Bonnette, Bonnette Hunting and Fishing Club, Florida, tried with a separate hunting area complete with turkey blinds and guides as callers, but his members were not impressed with the project, and the effort was terminated.

Regardless, there continues to be a demand for turkeys on hunting preserves, especially during the months of November and December. So, a number of hunting preserves offer turkeys as supplemental gamebirds to either pheasants or bobwhite quail hunting. In the final analysis, the successful hunting preserve operator must be closely atuned to the demands of his clients, and turkeys provide an additional source of income with very little added expense (a holding pen) to the operator.

References

1. Eversole, R. 1983. Reproducing ''native quail.'' Wildlife Harvest 14(11):28. Goose Lake, IA.
2. Kozicky, E., and J. Madson. 1966. Shooting preserve management — the Nilo system. Winchester Div., Olin Corp., E. Alton, IL. 311pp.

Chapter 7

THE RING-NECKED
PHEASANT

Of all the gamebirds in the world, the ring-necked pheasant is most able to stand the indignities of artificial propagation and yet perform like his wild cousins when released in the field. As a hunting preserve bird, "The Chink" is *almost* foolproof.

He is a big, rugged bird that isn't spoiled by the modern gadgets of game breeding and the "free lunch;" he reverts to the wild as soon as he can slip the bondage of wire netting. At heart he is a wild creature, and he stays wild. His sense of survival among men has been honed razor sharp through centuries of living in the hills, fields, and rice paddies of teeming Asia. He has thrived where less hardy birds have perished.

Other gamebirds have a tendency to domesticate in captivity, but not the gaudy Chink. All he asks is enough living room so that he is not crowded, and a chance to exercise his wings and legs for his break with captivity. There is nothing that man can offer him that is more precious than his freedom.

As a transplant from China in the late 1800s, he has won the hearts of American sportsmen, especially on the West Coast and the states of the Upper Midwest. He is not an easy target; yet, he is not the most difficult. He is a bird that the hunter can proudly bring home "in feather" to his family. The more you know about this regal gamebird, the more respect you have for him in the wild, at the hunting preserve, or on the table.

Pheasants comprise the great share of gamebirds harvested on hunting preserves, and there is every indication that their popularity is on the increase. The ringneck is the "bread and butter" bird for hunting preserves, and the only gamebird that will perform with a high degree of satisfaction for the Do-it-yourself or Co-op Preserve.[6]

Although the ring-necked pheasant is the easiest gamebird species to handle, he should not be taken for granted by preserve operators.[4] His demands are few, but they cannot be denied. To do so will mean the loss of hunting quality.

The ring-necked pheasant — the backbone of the preserve industry (courtesy Winchester Group, Olin Corp.).

What Strain of Ring-necked Pheasant?

Every breeder seems to have his own pet theory of the ideal strain of pheasant. Some favor the heavier types, such as the blackneck and Mongolian, whereas others prefer the Chinese strain.

The preserve operator must assure himself that a given game breeder is interested in rearing birds for hunting preserves and not for the meat market. Birds weighing more than 3 pounds usually are slower to fly and more likely to run. Regardless of what the game breeder may claim, the preserve operator should be suspicious of the quality of the pheasants if the breeder does not have long, covered flight pens with an abundance of vegetation in late summer. Pheasants need such pens for exercise, green feed, insects, and weather conditioning. By late fall the plant cover in a pheasant pen will be gone.

Pheasants on hunting preserves should have the time-honored white ring around the neck

that has resulted in the name "ring-necked" pheasant. Avoid off-color birds; they belong in an aviary, not on a hunting preserve. Hunters want to hunt pheasants that look and act like wild birds.

In the last 25 years, much progress has been made in the rearing of pheasants. Today we have a number of game farms that specialize solely in the production of pheasants for hunting preserves. The predominant strain of good ring-necks on hunting preserves seems to be the Chinese, with varying amounts of Mongolian blood lines. But there still is a difference of opinion among breeders and preserve operators on the ideal bird. Much depends on the needs of preserve operators. For instance, Jack Campbell, Duck Creek Game Farm, Texas, has developed a cross of Chinese, White-winged Afghan, and Korean pheasants that he believes is more adaptable to food and weather conditions in Texas[5]. Ole Oldenburg, Max McGraw Wildlife Foundation, Illinois, prefers a 50-50 cross of Chinese and Mongolian pheasants. Every year he selects the blue-backed males to cross with the lighter-color hens.

Also, some preserve operators find that their hunters prefer large, heavy birds. But, the heavier the bird, the more difficult it will be for the bird to fly — simple physics.

Rear or Buy Your Birds?

The average operator likes to think of rearing his own pheasants from the egg to the mature bird — rearing animals has a certain appeal to our sense of husbandry. However, unless you have cheap labor, enough acreage to separate the rearing area from the hunting preserve, the knowledge and ability to rear pheasants, and are thinking in terms of 5,000 pheasants or more per year, you will be better off buying your pheasants. Leave the rearing to the professionals who can usually do the job better and cheaper than you.

The good game breeder with modern incubation techniques and automated feeding and watering equipment can produce large numbers of pheasants of a better quality and sell them at a profit for less money than the average operator would spend producing a few thousands birds on his own. Also, if the preserve operator should encounter a problem, such as severe cannibalism, he is ''stuck'' with poor quality birds to open the season. It does happen. Hunting preserve operators are specialists in the outdoor recreation business, not in gamebird husbandry. There are a number of game farms that have supplemented their income with a hunting preserve, but they are large-volume breeders who have had years of experience. However, incubators, brooders, and rearing and holding pens do not enhance the landscape of a hunting preserve.

The best way to buy pheasants is to contract early in the year for adult birds to be delivered during the hunting season. Written contracts constitute good business and help to avoid misunderstandings.

The delivery schedules should be set up to give the pheasants about 2 weeks in which to settle down after delivery to the preserve. The process of trapping, crating, handling, and shipping is a shock to the pheasants.[3] Give the birds a chance to recover from the shock, and adjust to their new surroundings. The recovery rate of released birds means money to the operator — the more settled the bird, the greater the chances that he will remain in the vicinity of the release cover until a hunter has a chance to flush him.

Good game breeders do not crowd birds in shipping crates; they know the importance of good tail feathers. When you receive the birds, check the tail feathers on the birds. If there are a few who have lost parts of their tail feathers, give them a chance to regrow the feathers. This may take 6–8 weeks, but it is worth the wait. A bob-tailed pheasant is an eyesore on a hunting preserve.

Good game-farm operators have shipping crates that give the birds ample ventilation and are designed to expedite release, and to prevent the birds from piling on top of one another while in transit.[9, 12, 13, 14] The crates may vary in width and length to accommodate the bed of the hauling vehicle, but they usually are not more than 7 inches in height to prevent the birds from climbing on top of one another.

Hunting preserve operators should visit their supplier of gamebirds for 2 reasons. The preserve operator needs to assure himself that the pheasants are being reared in large, covered pens where they have a chance to exercise and develop their wing muscles. He needs to develop a good working relationship with the game-farm operator because problems do arise, in shipping and holding pheasants, that need the cooperation of both parties. The preserve operator should also know what type of feed the game-farm operator is feeding the pheasants, and the type of feeders and waterers, and try to duplicate the same in his holding pen(s).

By all means, avoid purchasing pheasants that have been brailed (strapping a wing in a folded position so that it cannot be used). Some game farms use this technique to rear pheasants in open-top pens, but the practice is less prevalent today than 20 years ago.

Holding Pens

One of the most common complaints of game-farm operators is that too many hunting preserves do not have adequate holding pens to maintain the high quality of their pheasants. And, with the exception of game farms that also operate a hunting preserve, the complaint is all too often legitimate. Good holding pens are essential for good field performance by pen-reared birds, including the pheasant.

Since space (''living room'') is necessary to avoid cannibalism in penned pheasants,[16] one should plan on about 25 square feet for each bird. The use of blinders, ''specs,'' ''peepers,'' etc., can reduce the necessary square feet per bird to about 15, but the blinders should be off birds when a shipment is received from a game breeder. The birds need time to adjust their eyes to 180-degree vision, as compared to only 90 degrees.

Ideally, pheasants should be held in pens about 50 feet in width, 150–200 feet in length, and about 7 feet in height. Also, there should be a minimum of 2 such pens with ground space available for additional pens (Appendix A). Two pens permit the separation of new shipments of birds and the separation of hens and cocks at the onset of the breeding season. Alleyways should be constructed at 1 end to permit the transfer of birds from 1 pen to another, or the herding of birds from either pen into a shelter and/or catch area.

Holding pens should be on a slope to improve drainage, and the more porous the soil, the better. Disease organisms proliferate in damp or wet environments. Also, muddy conditions in holding pens can cause the loss of tail feathers in pheasants. If the pen must be placed on flat ground, one should install drainage tile.

The construction of such pens is diagrammed in Appendix A. Many game farms and hunting preserves use nylon netting to cover their holding pens instead of 2-inch poultry netting. Nylon netting has advantages in being flexible and not subject to collapse under the weight of wet snow. Adrian Pratt[15] discusses the use of nylon netting and 2-inch poultry wire for covering pheasants pens, as well as a ''collar'' design to raise and lower nylon netting. In southern states,

The Nilo pheasant holding pens. Note the general construction and guy wires (courtesy Winchester Group, Olin Corp.).

such as Texas, the sun tends to make the nylon brittle and subject to tearing.[5] One should check with the manufacturer of nylon netting for the tops of pheasants pens prior to using nylon.

Buying cheap materials is false economy. Use good wire, nylon netting, and sound lumber; your main expense is in erecting the pens.

For predator control, bury at least 1 foot of 1-inch poultry netting 6 inches deep and extending 6 inches at a right angle away from the pen. String 2 "hot" wires around the pen: one where the 1-inch poultry netting meets the 2-inch wire, and the other 6 inches from the top. These wires should be checked daily and kept free of debris.

Perch poles should be provided in the pen. Such poles enable pheasants that are being harassed to escape their tormentors.[8] Shelters for feeders can serve the same purpose. Old Christmas trees placed in small piles are also useful.

Each pen should have a gate large enough to admit a tractor with agricultural implements. Each spring, the grounds in the pens should be plowed and planted to sorghum or other food patch mixtures, preferably the mixtures used in your food patches on the hunting areas. Some preserves just let natural cover volunteer in the pens; however, the plowing operation will bury all refuse from the previous year and enhance the growth of volunteer or planted cover.

Before placing pheasants in the pen, walking paths should be mowed through the vegetation to facilitate the movement of birds and a daily search for any dead pheasants, which should be promptly removed. In late summer and early fall, dead pheasants — like dead ducks — can be the focal point of botulism, a disease that can devastate a flock of pheasants.

Food and Water

The pheasant is easily kept, for it is basically a rugged, wild chicken. However, there are some guidelines that should be followed.

1. If possible feed the same food or feed formulation as the game breeder. Gamebird finisher feed is usually about 17% protein.

2. Store only limited quantities of feed in a clean and dry area. Dampness can cause the development of toxic molds.

3. Use feeders that have a deep trough, wide lip, and provide protection to the feed from wind and rain.

4. Don't fill the feeders over one-half full. Birds will waste feed.

5. Have an abundance of feeders. Aggressive birds can force timid birds away from feeders.

6. Crumbles and pellets cost more, but they are not easily wasted and prevent ingredient separation.

7. Mature birds can be fed grain. This reduces the protein intake, gets the birds used to whole grain, and helps to prevent cannibalism.

Feeding field corn on the ear is a good supplement and gives the birds something to pick besides each other. However, the energy intake may have to be restricted if excess fat is a problem. This can be accomplished by restricting feed intake to 80 – 90% of normal. Baled alfalfa, especially late in the preserve season, keeps the birds occupied, and satiates their eternal quest for "greens."[1,11]

Water needs are most acute in late summer and early fall. Waterers should be available in several areas in a given pen. They should be kept clean and washed, and refilled daily, or more often in warm weather. If the water being used is not from a public supply system, it should be tested for pathogenic organisms, such as Salmonellas, and for dissolved minerals, salinity, and temperature. Birds like "cool" water in summer and "warm" water in winter. Since birds consume 2–4 times as much water as feed, the quality of the water is important.[1]

Catch Pens

There was a time when a typical pheasant holding pen contained an inner catch pen, 24 feet by 12 feet, that was wired off with 2-inch poultry netting. The pen had an access door large enough to permit the easy handling of stocking crates. The door was opened and the pheasants were herded from the far side of the pen. The door was then closed and the birds were either caught by hand or with the help of a poultry catch net. Needless to say, the birds would panic and were subject to great stress and physical injury. Physical injury was a 2-way affair — sometimes the bird and sometimes the catcher. Good gloves were a necessity.

Today, a number of preserves have built shelter houses (Appendix A) on 1 end of the holding pen. The shelter house provides a dry area for holding pheasants during rainy periods and for capturing birds. (Never handle wet pheasants, for wet feathers pull out easily.)

The birds are herded into the shelter house the night before they are to be released, and kept there overnight. Don't overcrowd the shelter house with pheasants, or you will have a cannibalism problem by morning. The shelter house may be just poultry netting on 1 side; but the best are enclosed shelters so that they are semi-dark inside. The darker the area, the quieter the birds will be. When pheasants are needed for stocking, they are herded into a catch box, which adjoins the shelter house. The catch box can be as long as the shelter house. The catch box is usually 18–24 inches wide and 12–14 inches high. The outside of the catch box is covered with 1-inch poultry netting and the floor is plywood. The top is covered with overlapping rubber (stretched inner tubes from truck tires). The catch pen should be sectionalized at 4-foot intervals to facilitate the installation of the overlapping rubber and to permit the insertion of 1/4-inch plywood boards as dividers to keep the birds from piling up on top of one another.[9] As the plywood dividers are inserted, a canvas flap can be dropped over the outside of the catch box off the overlapping-rubber roof to darken the box.

Then, the operator reaches through the overlapping rubber, grasps a pheasant by quickly inserting the thumb under the base of the wing and the first and second fingers over the base of the neck. With a small amount of pressure the bird becomes immobilized.[2] When the bird is removed from the catch box, the bird's legs are grasped with the other hand. The operator checks the bird for body and tail feathers, and either places the bird in a stocking crate or back into the holding pen.

Releasing

Crates

Everything from burlap bags to poultry-hauling crates have been used to release pheasants. However, the birds should be subjected to as a little stress as possible, and their feathers should remain intact. Charles Baehr, Elkhorn Lake Shooting Park, Ohio, says that pheasants will perform well even on rainy days if they have been weather-conditioned in open pens and their feathering is not ruffled in the process of catching and releasing. Birds should not be allowed to pile up on top of one another. Hence, the releasing crates should only be about 7 inches in height. One can design releasing crates modeled after the hauling crates used by game farms. They are semi-dark with adequate ventilation and will take considerable handling. The size of the crate depends on the bed of the releasing vehicle.

If pheasants are to be released as singles or pairs, it would be advisable to use overlapping rubber for the top. If they are going to be mass released, then the regular hauling crate with a sliding top or side panel is ideal.

At Richmond Game Club, Illinois, pheasants are released throughout the day, depending on the volume of business. The whole bed of a 1-ton truck constitutes the releasing vehicle. The birds are herded up a ramp from the shelter house into a truck. The holding area on the truck is semi-dark, about 14 inches in height, and has a release gate on the curb side at the rear of the truck. The gate is opened out of the sight of any hunters, and the birds fly directly into the cover. The pheasants are moved from the front of the truck to the rear with the help of board attached to a long pole that extends from the rear of the truck to the front. The board is only an inch or so less in width and height than the inside dimensions of the holding area on the truck.[7]

Techniques

Pheasants should be released on the day of the hunt, preferably about an hour before the hunt begins. Properly conditioned birds of the right stock will perform like birds reared in the wild as soon as they become oriented to their newfound freedom.

The 2 most common methods of release are letting pheasants fly from different locations on the hunting area, or "disorienting" a bird and placing it in good holding cover.

Mass releases work well on some preserves with good stopping cover — woody fencerows or islands of woody or brushy cover. This technique also seems to work better in good natural pheasant range with ideal late-fall and winter cover for wild birds, such as sloughs and cattail marshes. A preserve operator should approach this technique with caution in trying to stock large open fields, even with sorghum patches. Pheasants have a tendency to fly to woody cover upon release.

The most common releasing method is to "disorient" each bird. The Nilo technique of "disorienting" is to hold the bird in 1 hand — the palm of the hand over 1 wing, the thumb hooked behind the wing, and the tips of the fingers over and under the thigh. The neck of the bird is gripped lightly with the other hand and the head is rocked until the handler feels the bird beginning to relax. The bird is then placed in holding cover with a quick rearward departure by the handler. This technique permits a good distribution of pheasants over the hunting area.

"Pres" Mann, Hunters Creek Club, Michigan, never stops the releasing vehicle. The releasing crew consist of 2 hunting guides. One drives and the other rides the rear of the truck with the bird crates. Each pheasant is slightly disoriented and pitched into good holding cover. At the end of each food patch on Hunters Creek Club is a section of tall sorghum. When the pheasant is pitched by the guide, the tall sorghum cushions the fall of the pheasant to the ground. When the bird hits the ground, it is in ideal holding cover. Within a few minutes the bird is completely oriented and may walk into adjoining cover. It does not take long to release game birds in a sizeable hunting area by this method, and the guides rotate their responsibility on the areas they are assigned to hunt. The guide then knows where the birds were released,

A pheasant grasped in the proper manner, 1 hand over the bird's wing and the fingers over and under the thigh. The other hand is free to gently shake the pheasant's head and disorient the bird for release into hunting cover (courtesy Winchester Group, Olin Corp.).

and he cannot blame the releasing crew if he has difficulty in finding the birds.

"Disorienting" a pheasant is an art. It is possible to disorient a bird so that it will not recover for several hours. The whole objective is to get the bird out of your hand and into the holding cover in such a way that the bird does not fly off.

Holding Cover

Ideal pheasant cover provides birds with enough security after their release so that they do not fly away, and yet is hardy enough to withstand weather and the tramping of hunters and dogs through the long season.

The basic purposes of holding cover are to keep released birds within a limited area until found by the hunting party, and to keep the birds on the area if they escape the hunters. Ideal holding cover — hybrid sorghum patches for example — also offers a good opportunity for the hunters to kill a pheasant when it flushes.

Birds that escape hunting parties will drift into holding cover, such as wooded areas; clumps of honeysuckle, multiflora rose, or brush; cattail marshes; or stands of evergreens. Such cover provides excellent overhead protection, yet permits high mobility for pheasants at ground level. Holding cover becomes very important in keeping pheasants on a hunting area in the winter months. You may have to cut paths or do some pruning in large blocks of holding cover to facilitate hunting, but without it your overall recovery of released birds by hunters will suffer.

All wild gallinaceous (chicken-like) gamebirds eat green vegetation — clover, alfalfa, and winter rye or wheat. We still do not fully understand the importance of green vegetation in the diet of gamebirds, but it always seems to be present in their crops throughout the year. Holding cover, along with green vegetation and feed, such as corn or milo, will help to keep released birds on a preserve.

Pheasant Hunting

The general rule among hunting preserves is a party of not more than 4 hunters with a guide. The guide is in charge of the hunt and usually places 2 men on each side of him to walk abreast through the cover following the dog. The guide sets the pace for the hunt and watches for safe handling of shotguns and keeps the hunters abreast of one another. Safety is a prime consideration in all hunting (see chapter on "Safety").

The average middle-aged hunter wants to tramp after pheasants for at least an hour but for not much more than 2. The day's hunt should be a pleasant experience and not a physical endurance contest. However, the guide should be in good physical condition and both willing and able to accommodate the wishes of the hunters.

When the pheasant is flushed, the 2 hunters on the right or the left of the guide shoot, depending on the direction in which the bird is flying. Hunters should be cautioned about shooting too quickly; someone has to eat the bird. They also have to be told to shoot hens as well as cocks.

There has been much talk about the best dogs for pheasant hunting — flushing dogs or the pointing breeds. My choice is pointing dogs, especially for novice hunters. It is a thrill to watch a dog go on point, and it adds to the enjoyment of the day afield.

When a dog goes on point, some hunters become mesmerized. They want to watch the dog, and have to be urged to walk in and flush the bird. These are the moments of excitement that make for a memorable hunt. Sometimes the guide will station the hunters, and he will flush the bird. Flushing should be done by the guide with a flushing whip but never with the toe of his foot.

The German shorthaired pointer and Brittany spaniel are excellent dogs for a hunting preserve. By nature they are obedient and have a tendency to work close to the guide. The guide knows the general areas where the birds were released. All he needs is a helping nose to pinpoint the pheasants for the hunters.

Flushing dogs, such as springer spaniels and Labrador retrievers, offer more of a shooting challenge to the hunter. They will indicate by their actions that they are tracking game, but it is impossible to tell when the bird will flush, and the hunters must remain alert. This type of dog has more appeal to some hunters. Flushing dogs have their greatest value when the pheasant

Nash Buckingham, Writer, Sportsman, Field-trial Judge, and Southern Gentleman, admiring a Nilo pheasant (courtesy Winchester Group, Olin Corp.).

cover is unusually thick, in deep snow, or whenever the birds are likely to run. The general consensus of opinion among hunting preserve operators is that pheasants have a greater tendency to run ahead of a hunting party on cold, hot, and/or windy days.

No preserve operator can afford the luxury of a dog with a poor nose or a lack of hunting instinct. The hunting dog assigned to each party should be a specialist on pheasants — a "meat" dog in every sense. A good pheasant dog is actually worth his weight in gold if able to find pheasants under all types of weather conditions, *and* if he is an obedient, top-notch retriever. A good pheasant dog and guide mean happy hunters, a high recovery rate of released birds, and repeat bookings by the hunters. Hunters will express a preference for a certain dog and guide, which tells the preserve operator he has a winning combination.

The recovery rate by hunters of released

pheasants should approach 70% or better. There are a number of factors that affect recovery: time and method of release, quality of the holding cover on the hunting areas, shooting ability of the hunters, quality of the hunting dogs and the guides, and the frequency of hunts on the hunting preserve. One cannot judge the recovery rate by any given day. Weather conditions play an important role in the behavior of pheasants. On some days the birds are more prone to run than to flush. Cover, especially early in the hunting season, may be so rank as to inhibit good scenting conditions. However, the operator should calculate the recovery on a monthly and seasonal basis. If it is not approaching the 70% level, he should be finding out why.

Shot birds should be treated with respect. They should not be thrown in a pile. It is essential to dissipate their body heat as rapidly as possible, and this can be done by laying the birds out neatly on a bench or rack above the ground

An English pointer retrieving a ring-necked pheasant, Sun Hunting Preserve, Salina, Kansas.

so the air is free to circulate around the individual bird. The bench or rack should be in a cool area where there is shade.

Some hunting preserves build a special rack with the name of the preserve clearly painted on the rack. A rack is ideal for hanging birds until they are processed, and offers good shots for photos for personal mementos or for advertising the hunting preserve

As soon as possible, the birds should be cleaned and packaged for the table. No day on a hunting preserve is finished until all shot birds have been processed for table use. Some preserves gather shot birds during a hunt to expedite the cleaning process.

Deep Snow

Some of the best hunts occur when there is a soft, fluffy, 6-inch snow. The birds fly well, and the hunters enjoy the outing and "reading" the bird signs in fresh snow. But, if the snow gets deeper than 7 or 8 inches, or is very wet or crusted, it may be necessary to have a "pitch shoot."

"Pitch shoots" are usually conducted from the top of a timbered hill above a deep ravine, where the hunters are stationed. The shoot is governed by the operator who stands behind the shooters (where he can see the personnel at the top of the ravine but the shooters cannot). The operator will have a couple of retrievers to pick up all shot birds. When the shooters are stationed at their shooting posts, the operator will tip his hat or blow a whistle as a signal to the personnel on top of the hill, who then pitch live pheasants over the tree tops towards the shooters. They may throw 1 bird, or 3 or 4, from different locations along the top of the ravine. Depending on the shooting, the operator will rotate the shooters among the shooting stations so that all the shooters have a chance to enjoy the better stations. When the downed birds are retrieved and the shooters are positioned at their stations, the operator will again tip his hat or blow a whistle for the next release.

Although "pitch shoots" leave much to be desired as sporty hunting, they do provide an answer on how to handle guests when weather will not permit hunting in the field. The actual shooting may often be more difficult than field shooting since the birds are overhead shots through timber. With a good thrower, a pheasant can reach a high rate of speed in a short distance.

Continental Shoots

Continental shoots for pheasants are gaining in popularity. But it takes the right terrain and timbered area, good flying pheasants, a bit of showmanship, personnel that are able to throw pheasants, and, if possible, the help of a local retriever club. All of these salient features are included in one of the oldest and best continental shoots in the country: Spring Farm, Sag Harbor, Long Island, New York, operated by the Schellinger family.[10] It was my privilege to participate in one of Spring Farm's classical continental shoots, and I was impressed with the event.

The continental shoot at Spring Farm is laid out on a timbered hill in a circle of 12 stations with an option of only 10 stations. An overview of the shoot would resemble a large wheel with the hub being on top of the hill at the spot from where the birds are thrown. The shooting stations are laid out along the rim of the wheel. The spokes of the wheel are clearings around the hub where the timber has been opened up to facilitate the launching of pheasants by the bird thrower. However, these spokes are not apparent to the shooters on the rim. The trees are 40–60 feet high, and by the time the pheasants reach the rim of the wheel (about 40–45 yards) they are under "full throttle." If the distance is more than 50 yards between the release point and the shooter, a pheasant will probably be sailing downwards.

Each station on the rim is separated from the adjoining station by about 50 yards. The safety rules for the shoot are as follows: no birds can be shot below a 45 degree angle; the actions of guns are either broken or open at all times, except when at a shooting station; and the "hunter's horn" is blown to start the hunt. If any safety rules are violated, the violator is asked to leave the shoot.

At no time does a shooter see the area from which the birds are being thrown. The bird thrower wears safety glasses and operates from a shallow pit. Pheasants are thrown underhand and are held by the right wing and right thigh. Each shooting station is clearly marked with a numbered post. A shelf on top of the post will hold 1 or 2 boxes of shotshells. The walking path between the stations is well groomed. As

Schellinger says, "We like to project the image that each group of shooters is the first group there."

Shooters draw for their starting stations, and a dog handler with a retriever is assigned to work every 2 stations. After the shooters are positioned, a "hunters horn" is sounded and the shooting begins. When 20 birds have been flighted on a 240-bird shoot, the "hunters horn" is again sounded. All shooters unload their shotguns and leave the action of their guns either open or broken. The shooters at odd-numbered stations move 2 stations to their left (clockwise). The shooters at even-numbered stations move 2 stations to their right (counterclockwise). By moving 2 stations at a time, and rotating even- and odd-numbered stations in the opposite directions, everyone moves around the stations faster and everyone meets on the walking trail through the timber. Halfway through the shoot, the "hunters horn," blown from the release site, will signal a break in the shoot. All hunters walk to a picnic area for refreshments — delicious sandwiches and a traditional drink of hot consommé and white sauterne wine (5 parts to 1). The picnic is a leisurely affair in a beautiful outdoor setting complete with picnic tables. The picnic break also gives the bird throwers a rest and a chance to organize for the second half of the shoot. A local retriever club helps with picking up all downed birds. They enjoy the outing and a chance to work their dogs. Both the Labradors and handlers are top quality.

In the second half of the shoot the odd-numbered shooters in the first half become even-numbered shooters. Consequently, at the end of the shoot, every shooter has shot at each of the 12 stations. All signals to start the hunt, change stations, the picnic break and the end of the hunt are given by the "hunters horn." Both the shooters and the dog handlers are hosted to a fine lunch at the clubhouse. Mallard ducks can be used with ring-necked pheasants if desired by the shooters.

The difficulty of the shooting is reflected in the percentage of the released birds that are killed — the average is around 50%. Unless the shooting is a challenge, such as a timbered area, a continental shoot can rapidly deteriorate into a "crate shoot." (When that happens everyone loses, including the hunting-preserve industry.) At Spring Farm the birds that escape restock the hunting areas. Charges for the shoot are based on the number of birds thrown for the shooters.

The whole shoot is conducted at a leisurely pace with excellent flying pheasants and/or mallard ducks. The relaxed pace and the camaraderie among shooters, the Schellingers, and the local retriever club make this a "class operation."

References

1. Adams, A. 1973. Feeding management of gamebirds. Wildlife Harvest 4(9): 6-10. Goose Lake, IA.
2. Anon. 1976. How to catch pheasants. Game Bird Bull. 10(3):12. RD 2, Hegins, PA.
3. Burger, G. 1959. Release technique and survival of pheasants on shooting preserves. Modern Game Breeding 29(11):6-7.
4. _____. 1960. Problems of pheasant management on shooting preserves. Modern Game Breeding 30(12):18-19.
5. Campbell, J. 1984. Personal communication, Duck Creek Game Farm, Spur, TX.
6. Kozicky, E., and J. Madson. 1966. Shooting preserve management — the Nilo system. Winchester Div., Olin Corp., E. Alton, IL. 311pp.
7. _____. 1984. Richmond hunting club. Wildlife Harvest 4(9):30-32. Goose Lake, IA.
8. Mauldin, J. 1984. "Peck order" in gamebird flocks. Wildlife Harvest 15(2):13. Goose Lake, IA.
9. Mullin, J. 1977. Catching the critters. Wildlife Harvest 8(6):24-25. Goose Lake, IA.
10. _____. 1977. Spring Farm hunts. Wildlife Harvest 8(12):10-17. Goose Lake, IA.
11. _____. 1978. Gamebird propagation. Arrowhead Hunting & Conservation Club, Goose Lake, IA. 194pp.
12. _____. 1978. Hauling crates. Wildlife Harvest 9(1):19-19. Goose Lake, IA.
13. _____. 1979. Crating and hauling. Wildlife Harvest 10(2): 36-37. Goose Lake, IA.
14. _____. 1981. Catching, hauling and releasing gamebirds. Wildlife Harvest 12(10):25. Goose Lake, IA.
15. Pratt, A. 1983. Indiana state game farm. Wildlife Harvest 14(7):4-6. Goose Lake, IA.
16. Woodard, A. 1984. Cannibalism: its cause and control. Game Bird Bull. 17(1):17,23,27. RD 2, Hegins, PA.

APPENDIX A
Pheasant Holding Pen, Shelter Area, and Catch Box

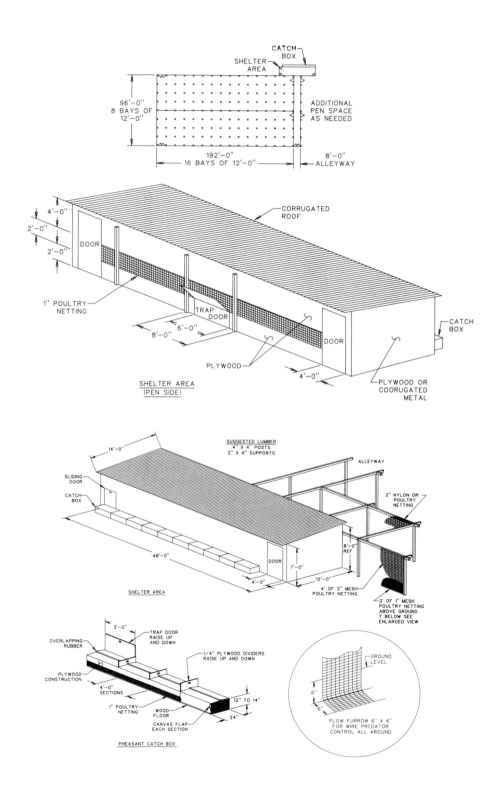

Chapter 8

THE BOBWHITE QUAIL

Rich men have bought southern plantations for the sole purpose of hunting bobwhite quail, and men of less affluence have bargained their very souls for good quail hunting. There are few things more precious to a bobwhite quail hunter than a crisp autumn day, an abundance of quail, a pair of well-broken pointers or setters, and a good hunting companion.

The "moment of truth" for the hunter comes when the dogs are locked up on point, one backing the other, and he and his companion walk abreast on either side of the dogs with every nerve in their bodies on edge awaiting a covey rise. When the "explosion" does come, the shooting is quick and, hopefully, accurate. No other type of upland gamebird hunting is bound with as much tradition — good birds and dogs, the covey rise, and shooting etiquette. A dedicated bobwhite quail hunter understands the comment of Ortega Y Gasset[9] who wrote, "Man does not hunt in order to kill; on the contrary, one kills in order to have hunted."

The bobwhite quail is so famous and beloved in Dixie that he is simply referred to as "The Bird" by southern hunters. "The Bird" can never really be appreciated by men or women who have not hunted him.

On hunting preserves, though, the bobwhite has a flaw. He will domesticate in captivity unless a number of management details are followed to retain the bird's wildness. The semi-domesticated bobwhites found on some hunting preserves are only pale shadows of their wild cousins.

Wildness in any gamebird is the sum of heredity and environment. And, although the ring-necked pheasant doesn't seem to be greatly influenced by his environment, the bobwhite quail is (see chapter on "Gamebird Behavior"). As the quail adjusts to the ways of man, and learns to accept him as a friend, he loses all sense of wariness and degenerates into domesticated poultry; therein lies a problem for the future of bobwhite quail hunting on preserves.

State-of-the-art

The objective on a preserve is to provide consistent quality hunting of bobwhite quail with birds released 30–60 minutes before hunting. The key words are "consistent" and "quality."

Consistent means that one can expect the same field performance under the same weather conditions throughout the hunting season. Too often we hear that the quail performed well 1 day and not the next. What happened? In many instances we do not know. But it is a fair assumption that some detail(s) of management for quality quail hunting has been overlooked. The operator, looking for a scapegoat, is prone to blame the breeder. But if the birds were good flyers at the time of purchase, the answer lies in either the shipping or the management of the birds on the preserve.

Quality bobwhite quail are of the same color and conformation as their wild counterparts, fully feathered, not noticeably debeaked, and 16 weeks or more of age. They hold well for a point-

A covey of bobwhite quail busy feeding (courtesy Missouri Conservation Dept.).

ing dog, and fly 40 or more yards on the first and second flushes. The brood stock of quail used by the breeder is important; like begets like.

Quality bobwhite quail for hunting preserves are not an accident. They result from attention to many details by both the game breeder and the hunting preserve operator. Consequently, it is essential for the breeder and the preserve operator to form a close alliance.

Rearing quality quail is not for the amateur or the hobbyist. It takes a breeder who has dedicated himself to the production of quality quail for hunting preserves, and there is a growing number of such quail producers in the South.

The preserve operator must visit quail breeders with whom he intends to do business. He needs to check on how the birds are being reared — isolation of the birds from man and dogs, holding pens, weather conditioning, overhead cover, and feeding and watering techniques. However, the most important reason for the visit is to check on the field performance of the breeder's quail. Dr. J. Richard Cain[2] has shown that, to date, we cannot judge the field performance of pen-reared quail by the most common anatomical or physiological variables — rectal temperature, heart rate, body weight, wing measurements, head width, breast width, keel length, shank measurements, or toe or leg length. If the breeder will not allow you to test his quail with dog and gun in the field, find another quail breeder. If he does show you a flighty, top-quality product, prize him like gold! You have found your "silent" partner.

Many quail breeders are more interested in quantity than quality, and a few are learning how to produce both quality and quantity. Don't look for bargain quail; look for quality. It takes dedication, time, space, and effort to produce pen-reared quail of high quality.

Within the hunting preserve industry we are aware of many details that affect the field performance of bobwhite quail, ranging from heredity to weather conditions. We are still struggling with the relative importance of management details. But we are learning. More studies, such as the one conducted by Dr. Cain are needed. It is only through such efforts that we are going to separate fact from opinion. The dearth of facts is also why we have so many opinions on what is, and what is not, necessary for consistent, quality field performance by bobwhite quail on hunting preserves.

There is no doubt that the southern plantation-style hunting preserves are the leaders in quality bobwhite quail hunting, and for good reason — it is their specialty. Many other hunting preserves manage bobwhite quail as a gamebird secondary to ring-necked pheasants. They also have a tendency to manage bobwhites in much the same manner as ring-necked pheasants, and suffer the consequences of substandard quail hunts. However, it must also be recognized that some hunters will accept substandard quail hunting, or give the preserve operator the impression that they will. If a successful hunting preserve offers substandard quail hunting, their overall success is mainly based on superb ring-necked pheasant hunting, and any quail hunting they do is mainly to appease their pheasant hunters.

Since the state-of-the-art on offering quality bobwhite quail hunting on preserves is still unfolding, I shall start with my experience at Nilo with Burnette quail[4] and my tour of quail hunting preserves in the South. Then, I shall discuss quail dogs, quail hunting, influence of weather on hunting, care of shot quail, call pens, pen-reared and wild quail, and quail diseases; and close the chapter with suggestions for Co-op and Do-it-yourself Preserves and state-of-the-art guidelines for quality quail hunting.

The Burnette Quail

The policy at Nilo under John Olin's direction was not to flight any pen-reared gamebirds whose field performance called for an apology. Hence, we didn't flight pen-reared quail at Nilo until we found Mr. and Mrs. Clyde Burnette, Tecumseh, Missouri, in the early 1960s. Their pen-reared quail were a source of great pride at Nilo until the Burnettes retired from the business. Unfortunately, the Burnettes would never discuss the source of their brood stock or their rearing techniques. However, they convinced me that pen-reared bobwhite quail are capable of consistent, high-quality field performance.

I visited their quail farm many times, and a

number of their management efforts were obvious. These included strict isolation from man and dogs, plus overhead cover, and small holding pens. The Burnette quail are discussed in the bobwhite section of the chapter on "Gamebird Behavior".

Tour of Southern Quail Hunting Preserves

No 2 hunting preserves in the South follow the same procedure for managing quail. There is also much secrecy, warranted or not, by some southern quail-preserve operators. It is also apparent that no 1 preserve has all of the answers, and for good reason — each shipment of quail, even though from the same game farm, is unique, and the quality of the birds can vary from 1 shipment to the next. Different preserve operators may express high praise or strong criticism of the quality of birds from the same quail breeder. One has the feeling that any substandard quail hunting, which can occur on a given day on the best of preserves, is overcome with the food, accommodations, plantation atmosphere, and southern hospitality.

Supply of Quail

All of the successful preserves I visited purchase their quail from more than 1 breeder. Individually, they seek out quail breeders who concentrate on producing quail for hunting preserves. Some of these breeders have even started to specialize in weather-conditioned quail. Such birds bring a premium price and are the salvation of preserve operators on rainy days, or when the vegetation is wet.

Since bobwhite quail are subject to stress through crating and shipping, preserve operators like a source of birds close to their preserve. Prompt and reliable delivery of birds is expected. Also, the preserve operator expects the cooperation of the breeder in analyzing any problem that may occur in flighting the birds.

Holding Pens

Holding pens on southern quail preserves are usually large — 60–100 feet long, 6–20 feet wide, and 6–10 feet high. At 1 end of the holding pen(s) a shed is constructed to hold birds out of the

Holding pen for quail on a preserve in southern Florida. Note the abundance of large-sized feeders and waterers and space per bird.

weather and in semi-darkness. The birds are herded into the shelter, and a portion of the flock is trapped within the shelter by swinging gates attached to ropes. Placing a number of birds in the shelter each day facilitates the trapping of birds for the next day's hunt and keeps them dry. Most of the preserves hold birds on the ground, but the ground is basically sandy and well-drained.

The holding pens are usually in isolated areas away from human disturbance. In some cases the holding pens are shielded from either man or dogs by solid wooden fences. In other cases, the lower portion of the holding pens is covered with sheet metal roofing for the first 2–3 feet above the ground. None of the holding pens are under trees or artificial cover, but some preserves are contemplating the use of camouflage netting over the tops of their holding pens.

Dr. Cain states that a preserve operator should allow 4–5 square feet per bird in holding pens if the birds are on the ground. When operators provide such space, their problems with cannibalism and disease will be minimal. Dr. Cain likes such pens to be at least 100 feet long and planted to sorghums down the middle. Walking paths are needed to check for sick and dead birds. If the birds are held on wire, only 2 square feet per bird is needed; however, the general opinion is that birds on the ground are more resistant to disease and survive better on hunting areas.[1]

One large quail preserve not blessed with good drainage and sandy soil has its holding pens on wire. Each pen is 100 feet long, 16 feet wide, and 10 feet high. The pen is isolated from man and beast, and no visitors are allowed. One man does all the feeding and watering of the birds. The tops of most holding pens are covered with loosely stretched 1-inch nylon netting.

The length of time birds should be in a holding pen depends upon the condition of the birds when they arrive at the preserve. Some large-volume preserves will use birds in good physical condition the day that they arrive from the breeder. Other preserve operators like to keep the birds in holding pens separate from the rest of their birds for a week or more and give the quail a chance to recover from the shock of handling and transportation. The appetite of the birds is perhaps the best barometer on their health and general well-being.

Feeding, Water, and Medication

Most hunting preserves are careful to follow the same feeding, watering, and medication routine as the breeder — including, if possible, the same types of waterers and feeders. The importance of fresh feed cannot be overstressed. Jerry Waters, Hawkeye Hunting Club, Texas, is a firm believer in fresh feed for his quail, with an abundance of waterers and feeders. Feed starts to deteriorate as soon as it is formulated, especially the vitamins, which will start to oxidize. Feed for bobwhite quail should not be stored for more than about 2 weeks, and storage should be in a dry place on pallets off the ground or on concrete. Rodent control around feed storage areas is essential.[7]

Jerry Waters also believes in the importance of pans of dry soil to serve as dust baths for his quail. Sevin mixed into the soil will help control external parasites. Jerry also introduces his new quail to cracked corn, which is used at times as supplemental feed on his hunting areas. Cracked corn helps to condition the birds to the feed that they will find when released.

Catching Quail

The wilder the pen-reared quail, the more care must be exercised in their capture and handling to minimize stressing the birds. Conversely, with semi-domesticated, pen-reared quail, it could well be that "rough" handling within limits will improve field performance. But in "rough" handling, birds are injured, and a quail with a physical injury probably will not fly well. One no longer sees the capture of bobwhite quail by poultry nets on the better hunting preserves. There is too much danger of injuring and stressing the bird.

Most southern quail preserves try to minimize stressing their quail when capturing and releasing birds to hunting areas. They usually drive enough birds for at least the next day's hunt into a shelter, where they are supplied with feed and water and held overnight. The next day they will herd the birds from the shelter into a catch box, located either on the outside or the inside of the pen. The box size will vary. The catch box may be 6–10 feet long with sliding dividers inserted to keep the birds from piling on top of one another. The width and height of the box varies. Some are 18 or more inches in width and 12–16 inches in height. The height is important; the less height, the less chance of birds piling on top of

one another, but one has the problems of getting the birds to enter the box on their own will. The sides are usually covered with 1/2-inch hardware cloth, and the top consists of 2 pieces of overlapping rubber.

The best approach would be to locate the catch box on the outside of the pen. The quail enter the catch box through a sliding door on the shelter. With such pens, the sides of the box can be solid and only the end of the box needs to be covered with 1/2-inch hardware cloth to admit light. Our catch box at Nilo was a portable box, 10 inches wide, 12 inches high, 30 inches long, and it held 25–30 quail with ease. If more quail are needed, use more catch boxes. Catch boxes on the outside of the pen reduce the disturbance of the birds remaining in the holding pen.

Birds in the catch box are transferred to release equipment. The transfer is accomplished by reaching through the overlapping rubber strips on top of the box and capturing a quail by grasping the bird with its neck between your first and second fingers, enclosing the body with your hand. This method prevents the bird from fluttering and allows the legs to hang free. If the bird does not feel strong to the operator, or is thin, he will either sacrifice the bird or place it in another holding crate for possible recuperation. However, large-scale operators believe that a mature bird that does not feel vigorous in the hand is a liability, and they will sacrifice the bird.

Besides the condition and strength of the bird, the outer primaries of the bird will be checked for wear, especially late in the hunting season. The outer primaries will wear down on bobwhite quail from contact with the wire on pens to the point where the bird cannot fly well. Some operators, if they have the time, will pull the outer primaries on such birds, place them in a separate pen, and the bird will grow a new set of outer primaries in 6–8 weeks; other operators will sacrifice the bird for table use.

Releasing Quail

Every hunting preserve seems to have its own technique for releasing quail on hunting areas. Techniques range from flying quail out of a wire cage into hunting cover, using release boxes, grasping 3 or 4 quail by the legs and disorienting the birds, or using wire baskets or cloth and paper sacks. The cloth and paper sacks force the birds on top of one another, and the plumage on some of the birds is going to be ruffled. All of the weather conditioning of the birds by the breeder and the preserve operator can be greatly impaired until the bird has a chance to rearrange his feathers in their proper order.

My choice of the best technique is the one used by Ed Norman, Quailridge, Georgia. He uses light plywood boxes with air vent holes for each covey of 4–8 birds. The covey boxes are 16 inches long, 16 inches wide, and 5 inches high. The top of the box is covered with 2 strips of overlapping rubber to facilitate transfer of the birds from the catch box. The bottom of the covey box is a sliding piece of plywood that is secured in place for transportation to the field. When he has found the right cover to release the birds on a hunting area, he places the box on the ground and slowly pulls out the floor of the box. Then, in 1 quick motion he lifts the box off the birds and backtracks away from the birds. If the pen-reared quail are exceptionally wild, it may be well to rock the box back and forth while enroute to the release cover. Nothing is left in the field but the birds, and they have been transferred from the catch box to the field with a minimum of physical abuse. The darkened box also sedates the birds.

Steve Johnson, Red Bank Ale & Quail Club, California, flies his quail from small wire cages into hunting areas. On many hunting preserves the birds would fly into brushy or wooded areas where hunting would be difficult. Weber[13] found that pen-reared quail will fly a greater distance on the initial flush when released in open fields with distant tree lines.

Hunting preserves in the South avoid releasing quail where they will be exposed to the sun. They try to find a shady spot. If they do release the birds in a sunny area, there is a good probability that the birds will fly before the hunting party arrives.

The importance of selecting the proper vegetative cover for releasing bobwhite quail is discussed in the chapter on "Hunting Preserve Cover."

Quail Dogs

Either the English pointer or setter are the traditional dogs to hunt quail, especially coveys. Other pointing dogs can be used, but they usually have a flaw if one is interested in a covey rise by released quail — they are over-cautious.

The over-cautious dog provides too much opportunity for the birds to run ahead of the hunting party, whereas a fast-moving, bold dog will surprise the birds, and they will usually react by "freezing" on the spot — a natural trait of quail when in immediate danger. Such coveys offer a better chance of flushing as a covey, compared to birds that start to run and become scattered. On the other hand, there are a growing number of hunters who pay for the birds released, and who are not interested in covey shooting and would rather have their quail flush as singles and pairs.

Hunting dogs should always be handled into the wind as much as possible. Otherwise, they may stumble into a covey of quail before scenting them. In summary, the breed of dog, his training, and wind direction all influence the field performance of pen-reared bobwhite quail.

Weather Conditions

Dr. Cain has shown that weather conditions will affect the flight performance of pen-reared quail. Higher air temperature and relative humidity were negatively correlated with field performance of quail. In short, quail flew best on cool, dry, and breezy days.[2]

All upland gamebirds are reluctant to fly in wet weather. If pen-reared quail are not weather conditioned and properly handled in the releasing process, it doesn't take long for the birds to become water-soaked and unable to fly. A rainy day may be a good time to have a "clean-up" hunt for birds that are still on the preserve from previous hunts.

When snow covers the ground, quail often light in trees and are very difficult to flush. Actually, the bird is highly frightened and doesn't want to leave the security of the tree and fly into the open. When a quail takes refuge in a tree, the best thing is to ignore the bird. Or, if the guest insists, have him shoot it out of the tree. The real circus will start, to your embarrassment, if you try to make the bird fly by throwing objects at it.

If it is necessary to flight quail under snowy or rainy conditions, explain to your guests what to expect and let them make the decision. It beats making excuses after the hunt.

Hunting Quail

There is something personal, and rather private, about quail hunting. Crowds shouldn't be part of the scene; it is something to be enjoyed with a companion and good dogs.

Havilah Babock, in his book, *I Don't Want to Shoot an Elephant*, wrote, "There are many things that three men can do together. They can golf together, bet on a horse race, grub a sassafras bush, or maybe shuck a pile of corn. But three men cannot hunt birds together. Like a honeymoon, bird hunting is built for two. When three men hunt together, one is a stranger."

Because of the bobwhite's great game value and tendency to do the unexpected, quail hunting reaches the epitome of sport when 2 hunters walk in to flush a covey. This 2-man technique also has inherent safety features never found in a larger hunting party.

When 4 men are assigned to a hunting area with guide and dogs, only 2 hunters should be permitted to shoot at a given covey, and any singles that may be marked down after the covey rise. After these 2 covey shooters have hunted their singles, they retire and their 2 companions move up to hunt the next covey.

Quail are tricky, unpredictable flyers, and it is essential that every hunter know the exact location of all other members of the party when the covey is flushed. Quail are fast on the wing, and a clean hit demands split-second timing.

Aside from safety, it's difficult to tell who scored on a quail when there are 4 guns in action. Something of the quality of the sport is also lost. There is a certain dignity to this great game-bird that calls for hunters to meet him on a man-bird basis, and not with a fusillade from 4 automatic shotguns. Ideally, quail are hunted with a 20-gauge, improved cylinder, double-barreled shotgun, using #7 1/2 or #8 shot in light field loads.

Quail should be hunted with a pointing dog. Without a dog, it's not really a quail hunt. The guide, the cover, and the field behavior of the quail are half the preserve operator's show. The style and proficiency of his quail dogs are the other half, and should not be overlooked or underrated.[4]

Care of Shot Birds

Shot quail should be handled with respect by the guide. The occasion, especially the first birds shot, calls for a bit of showmanship on his part, and it will be appreciated by the hunters if not carried to extremes. Quail are beautiful birds and the hens and cocks are marked differently. He can also show the hunters how to age a quail.

The shot birds should be put in a cool place, preferably where air can circulate around them. At the very least they should be separated and not allowed to be in contact with each other when laid on a table or in a dog wagon.

The birds should be processed for the table as quickly as possible. At 1 time all bobwhites were picked; nowadays, the tendency is to skin the birds. It's faster and permits even a 1-day hunter to leave the preserve with the birds he shot.

Call Pens

The temptation to recover quail that have not been shot on a hunting area is a valid one, but the implementation of the practice depends on the legality of the technique in a given state and the availability of time. Some states do not permit the use of call pens to trap quail.

Call or release-recovery pens are widely used by bird dog trainers, and such pens are manufactured and sold by the Georgia Quail Farm, Savannah, Georgia (see chapter on "Short Subjects").

Large quail hunting preserves in the South do not use call pens. As 1 operator told me, "All released birds are stressed, and I don't want a stressed bird in my quail holding pens." Stress is considered a precursor to an outbreak of ulcerative enteritis in quail. Sounds like good advice!

Pen-reared and Wild Quail

Many novice operators are hopeful that their pen-reared quail will integrate with coveys of wild quail on the preserve. It does happen, but it is the exception rather than the rule.

Coveys of wild quail are distinct social units. Even in the wild, 1 covey will defend its territory against the intrusion of another. Quail have a recognized home range. They may tolerate the presence of another covey on certain parts of that range and not on another. Two or 3 coveys may even come together where corners of their ranges coincide and seem to recognize the others' territories. Pen-reared quail released to the wild are strangers there and are not always welcome. Val Lehmann[5] points out that a covey of quail may or may not accept unattached quail. For 11 days a wild, marked male quail on the King Ranch tried without success to join a group of 10 quail. Hopefully, the unshot birds will band together in a covey, and they will adjust to the feed found on your hunting areas. L. J. Shields[11] studied the integrity of quail coveys with radio telemetry at Tall Timbers Research Station, Tallahassee, Florida. He attached transmitters to nearly 60 bobwhite quail that were members of several different coveys living in the same general area. During the late winter of 1983 he located these birds more than 1,000 times and did not find a single instance in which a quail moved from 1 covey to another.

Strong social ties among the members of a wild bobwhite covey explain why the covey rises as a unit when encountered in the field. The lack of a chance to develop strong social ties by pen-reared bobwhite quail, especially when individual birds of a released covey are from different game farms and/or holding pens, helps to explain the tendency of the birds to flush as singles or pairs rather than as a covey.

Diseases

Although there is a chapter in the book entitled, "Gamebird Diseases," cannibalism and ulcerative enteritis (quail disease) are the 2 diseases that the preserve operator is most likely to encounter.

The best cure for cannibalism is space. There is always the temptation to crowd birds into a pen rather than building another pen. When you do, you can expect 2 problems — cannibalism and ulcerative enteritis. Dr. Cain recommends 4–5 square feet per bird for holding pens on the ground and 2 square feet per bird for holding pens on wire. Cannibalism within a flock of quail will stress the birds, which, in turn, leads to ulcerative enteritis.

Twenty years ago ulcerative enteritis was the bane of pen-reared bobwhite quail both on the game farm and the hunting preserve. Today, with good husbandry and the use of preventive medication such as bacitracin, the incidence of the disease has been greatly reduced.

The general opinion is that outbreaks of ulcerative enteritis are caused by stress. Stress can be induced in quail in many ways — moving or handling the birds; overcrowding in holding pens; shortage of food or water (even for 1 day); poor sanitation; or disturbance by predators, dogs, or man.

One cannot overemphasize the importance of quick diagnosis and speedy treatment of ulcerative enteritis. A postmortem should be conducted on every dead quail found in the holding pen. It doesn't take long to recognize diseased from healthy tissue. If you are suspicious of a disease outbreak, seek out the nearest poultry disease diagnostic laboratory as quickly as possible. Once ulcerative enteritis starts in a pen of quail, it's difficult to stop. But don't start to medicate the birds before you know what the disease is. You could be doing more harm than good.[3]

Co-op and Do-it-yourself Preserves

The Co-op and Do-it-yourself Preserves, groups of sportsmen banding together to share expenses and work, are gaining momentum in a number of states (see chapter on "Types of Hunting Preserves"). Such preserves are not large volume and do not feature daily hunting. Hunting is usually restricted to 1 or 2 days a week. Further, some of the members have the time and interest to do the necessary work of feeding and caring for game prior to and during the hunting season. Such hunting preserves have been successful in providing quail hunting through the Smith-O'Neall Stocking System (Appendix A).

The State of Illinois has been successful in establishing coveys of quail on their field-trial areas using the Smith-O'Neall Stocking System. They have also found that the successful transformation of pen-reared quail to the wild varies greatly with the genetics of the bird. Their "gene improved" quail, (a cross between a wild cock and a game farm hen) required only 10 days to adjust, whereas their reconditioned breeders (quail that had been on the game farm for 1 year or more) required 21 days (3 times as long) if they survived at all.[8] Southern plantations, especially with a poor crop of wild birds, have used the Smith-O'Neall Stocking System or a version of it.[10]

Studies initiated at the Tall Timbers Research Station, Tallahassee, Florida, revealed that spring stocking of pen-reared quail with feeders and shelters was not successful; however, fall stocking on quail hunting plantations did contribute to the total bag of birds. Of 7,000 birds released on Merrily Plantation, Thomas County, Georgia, in October of 1981 and 1982 onto pre-selected sites, the pen-reared birds comprised 53% of the total kill of quail (pen-reared and native) on the plantation.[6]

The general opinion in the South is that the best time to stock quail with feed and shelters is between mid-August and mid-September. The birds should be between 8 and 12 weeks of age, since younger birds seem to adapt to the wild faster than older birds. The quail should be released on the same day they arrive from the game farm in coveys of 20 to allow for attrition. The release of the birds is accomplished along the same lines as the Smith-O'Neall Stocking System — a gentle release in protective cover with a feeder and a source of water. Sometimes the coveys will shift their territories from the original release area, especially with intense hunting pressure. The best time to restock coveys with additional mature, pen-reared birds is immediately after a hunt, while the birds are still scattered and calling.[12]

The Smith-O'Neall System of stocking pen-reared quail will work if the birds are of a good quality and released in habitat suitable for a covey of quail, including natural food, cultivated grain (corn, milo), and necessary cover. For the first couple of weeks the condition of the call bird and the supply of food and water must be checked. However, this system will not support daily hunting pressure on a large volume preserve. The coveys should only be hunted once every 7–10 days, which is fine for a Co-op or a Do-it-yourself Preserve or a southern plantation, but not for a commercial operation.

Guidelines for Quality Quail Hunting

The subject of providing consistent, quality pen-reared bobwhite quail hunting on preserves is still in a state of limbo, with more opinions than facts. We are still learning through the process of trial and error. What works for 1 strain or source of birds may not work for another. Also, there are many details of management that influence the field performance of pen-reared bobwhites, and it is the attention to many details that separate the do-it-yourself or amateur preserve operator from the professional.

The hunting preserve operator cannot wait for the necessary research to provide all the answers on how to provide consistent quality hunting with pen-reared birds. He needs the best guidelines to help him with daily decisions. It is with this in mind that I have drafted a set of guidelines based on my experience and observations.

Source of Birds

Visit a number of established breeders of bobwhite quail to observe their quail and operations (isolation, holding pens, shipping, etc.), check the field performance of their quail, and establish the degree of cooperation that you can expect with shipping and management problems. Don't even consider flighting bobwhite quail until you have found at least 1 (preferably 2 or 3) good source of birds.

Shipping

Shipping time is important, but not as much as the quality of the birds. Birds have been shipped by air from Florida to California. Ask that each shipping box be marked as to whether or not the birds are from the same holding pen on the game farm. The number of birds per shipping box depends on the weather and shipping time. Don't overcrowd the birds for the sake of cutting shipping costs. Release the birds into holding pens upon arrival at your preserve. Those birds that came from the same holding pen at the game farm should be kept together. The best time to introduce birds to your pens is at night, when they are less likely to injure themselves. Feeders, waterers, and dust baths should be full prior to arrival of the birds.

Holding Pens

All holding pens should be isolated from man or beast even though the location may not be convenient to your other gamebird pens. Isolation is not a half-way measure with quail.

Unless the soil is sandy and has excellent drainage, build holding pens on wire (Appendix B). Each pen is capable of holding 100–125 birds, so construct a series of them for your current needs and leave room for expansion. Enclose the entire holding-pen area with a 6-foot fence of either chicken or welded wire. Plow or dig a trench (6 inches deep and 6 inches wide) around the outside of the fence, bury 1 foot of 1-inch mesh chicken wire in a 90-degree, "L" shape fashion, and hog ring the chicken wire to the 6-foot fence. Install 2 "hot" wires, one about a foot above the ground and the other 6 inches from the top.

If possible, place the holding pens in a wooded area. Such a site would have an overstory of mature timber with an open understory. Otherwise, cover the tops of the pen with used sheet-metal roofing. Even in a timbered area, you may have to cover the holding pens with sheet metal roofing as soon as the frost has removed the leaves. With sheet-metal roofing, you only want shade, not protection from rain.

Feed, Water, Medication, and Dust Baths

Follow the same procedure as your supplier of quail, including, if possible, the same types of waterers and feeders. Above all, make sure that the feed is freshly formulated and don't store more than a 2-week supply. Supply the birds with fresh water on a daily basis. Be sure to have an ample supply of waterers, feeders, and dust baths in each pen.

Permit only 1 individual to feed and water the birds. He should be required to wear neutral-colored clothing when working around the birds.

Follow the same procedure of preventive medication as the breeder. Also, with the help of your veterinarian, be prepared for an outbreak of ulcerative enteritis. Speedy treatment is essential to control the disease.

The dust-bath pans should be located in the sun porch area of the pen, and the soil within the pans should be changed on a regular basis. At least 1 feeder in each pen should contain the grain (milo, corn) to be found on your hunting areas. If possible, give the birds some green vegetation. Baled alfalfa is fine; however, the supply should be changed every few days.

Catching Quail

Although one should give a new shipment of quail about 3 days to recover from shipping and adjust to their new environment, it all depends on the condition of the birds. If they are alert and eating well, they probably are ready. If in doubt, try a few in the field.

Quail should be caught from a holding pen with a catch box on the end of the shelter or the sun porch from the outside of the pen. Don't overload the catch box; it's better to use additional boxes.

Releasing Procedure

Remove the catch box(es) from the vicinity of the holding pen. Reach through the overlapping strips of rubber and catch a quail with your hand. If a given bird does not offer resistance and does not have a good firm body, sacrifice it. Late in the season check the outer edges of the birds' primary feathers. If they are worn too much, don't place the bird in the release box. Avoid mixing quail from different holding pens in the same release box. Use the Ed Norman release box. The box will hold 8 quail comfortably.

Release the quail in appropriate bobwhite quail cover (see section on bobwhite quail in the chapter, "Hunting Preserve Cover"). After you have found the spot where you want to release the quail, place the box on the ground and slowly slide the floor out of the box. Pick up the box and floor and retreat to your vehicle. Allow a minimum of 30 minutes before hunting for the birds to adjust to their new-found freedom.

If you are having problems getting good covey rises, reduce the number of birds being released as a covey. However, the release of single quail will induce excessive bobwhite calling on a release area and distract from the quality of the hunt.

Quail Dogs

Use stylish pointers or setters that are staunch on point, steady to wing and shot, and obedient to commands. Hunt the dog(s) into the wind as much as possible.

Strive for the quail to flush as a covey. It will not always happen, in spite of your best efforts.

Hunting

Permit only 2 hunters to shoot on each covey flush, including the pursuit of singles. Insist that the guide use a flushing whip to flush quail — never the toe of his boot.

Weather

When it is raining or a wet snow is falling, try to reschedule quail hunting parties. If not possible, tell them what they can expect in the way of field performance by the birds. Let them assume the responsibility for the quality of the hunt.

Summary

Quality hunting of bobwhite quail on your preserve requires strict attention to many details. Unless you are willing to commit yourself to such details, consider only flighting the easier species to manage — ring-necked pheasants, chukar partridge, and mallard ducks.

The hunting preserve operator and quail breeder who pays attention to management details will not only be successful but will take great pride in his operation. Such men are emerging on the scene, especially in the South, and are helping to unravel the mystery of quality quail hunting with pen-reared bobwhites. I salute their commitment and effort.

A stylish setter locked on point (courtesy John B. Madson).

References

1. Cain, R. 1985. Personal communication. Texas A&M Univ., College Station, TX.

2. _____. 1974. Proceedings of game bird management short course. Extension Service. Pennsylvania State Univ., Univ. Park, PA.

3. Eleazer, T. 1981. Ulcerative enteritis. Wildlife Harvest 12(7):16-18. Goose Lake, IA.

4. Kozicky, E., and J. Madson. 1966. Shooting preserve management — the Nilo system. Winchester Group, Olin Corp., E. Alton, IL. 311pp.

5. Lehmann, V. 1984. Bobwhites in the Rio Grande Plain of Texas. Texas A&M Univ. Press, College Station, TX. 371pp.

6. Mueller, B. 1984. Final report — banding study. North American Gamebird Assoc. Ann. Meeting, Daytona Beach, FL. Jan.

7. Mullin, J. 1983. Importance of fresh feed. Wildlife Harvest 14(1):8-9. Goose Lake, IA.

8. Musser, T. 1984. Personal communication. Illinois Dept. of Conservation, Springfield, IL.

9. Ortega y Gasset, J. 1972. Meditations on hunting. Charles Scribner's Sons, New York, NY. 152pp.

10. Phillips, J. 1978. From the pen to the wild. Wildlife Harvest 9(5):12-14. Goose Lake, IA.

11. Shields, L. J. 1985. Are quail faithful to their coveys? Covey Rise 4(5):1,4. P.O. Box 550, Edgefield, SC.

12. Vezey, S. A. 1986. Personal communication. Co-op Ext. Ser., Univ. of Georgia, Athens, GA.

13. Weber, J. 1977. Selected aspects of commercial game bird management. Unpublished M. S. Thesis, Poultry Science Dept., Texas A&M Univ., College Station, TX. 37pp.

APPENDIX A

The Smith-O'Neall System for Stocking Quail

(Adapted from an article by John O'Neall, Jr., *American Field*, Dec. 6, 1969, pp. 649-653, and *Wildlife Harvest* 14(12):34-37. Dec. 1983.)

The Smith-O'Neall System of stocking bobwhite quail in the fall to supplement wild birds has worked successfully in many locations, and has been used by the Illinois Department of Conservation to supplement wild quail populations on state game areas. The basis of success with this stocking system is the effective use of a *call bird*, a single quail caged and left, in an elevated position, at the intended feeding station for a newly released covey. The preferred sex is a male bird, but a female quail will also work. The main thing is that the bird be lively, vigorous, and selected from the group of birds to be released. The coveying instinct among quail is an overriding inherent impulse that makes the system work.

Quail have a language all their own. When the freshly released birds wander away from the intended feeding station, as they are prone to do, or, when they are disturbed and fly away, the "bird talk" starts as soon as all is quiet. Slowly but surely they start to get together as a covey. But 1 plaintive and insistent voice gets no closer — it is the call bird in the cage. He begs; he pleads — and sure enough, all the others inevitably gravitate back to the spot from where he is calling. When they do they find food, shelter, water, and protection.

You start by finding a spot adjacent to or within good protective cover and natural food for quail. Hopefully, the spot will have 3 young trees in a triangle about 8–10 feet apart. If not, 7-foot, steel, T-posts can substitute for young trees. Within the center of the triangle an area about 3 feet by 3 feet is raked clear of debris, and a quail feeder is installed and filled to capacity with coarse (not fine feed, because it packs) corn, millet, milo, or a mixture thereof. Handfuls are also scattered on the ground in the clear area along with some grit. For water cut a car tire in half along the center of the tread and bury the half tire so that the edge of the tire is at ground level. Then, fill it with water. Either the 3 steel posts or trees are surrounded with field (hog-wire) fence, 36 – 48 inches in height, upside down, so that the large holes are at the bottom and the small holes at the top. The large holes at the bottom permit easy entrance and exit for the quail. The wire is either stapled to the trees or tightly wired to the steel posts.

Cut a good supply of lower limbs from nearby trees, using pine if available, until you accumulate a large brush pile. Climb into the fenced area, pull the brush over a limb at a time and start covering the quail feeder and the cleared area, thrusting the ends through the woven wire as a means of holding the brush in place. Make sure the brush is tight to the ground but leave a tunnel effect so the birds can run freely under and through the brush pile. When about half of the limbs are used, lay a piece of black plastic (polyethelene), 8 feet by 8 feet, over the brush and then pile the remaining limbs on top. You have produced a "home" for the new covey, and it will remain relatively dry at ground level. If rats become a problem, feed them "D-con" under the feeder.

The next task is to build a holding cage for the call bird that will protect him or her from the weather and predators. You can build a sturdy wire cage about 24 inches by 12 inches by 12 inches with a solid plywood top and wrap the top, bottom, and sides with clear plastic, leaving one-third of the cage to the open air. Also, provide the bird with a short plywood floor in the protected end to stand on. Include a quart-size, plastic feeder and a waterer, such as used for baby chicks. They are about 12 inches high and will just fit into the call cage. You will need to build a door on 1 end of the cage to insert the call bird and to refill the waterer and feeder. The open end of the call cage should face to the south.

Drive 2, 7-foot, steel T-posts about 12 inches apart near the brush pile, to a depth of about 3 feet and mount the call cage between and near the top of the 2 posts.

When your release sites are prepared and ready, the next step is to introduce a covey of quail at each site. Make arrangements to pick up each covey of quail (16–20 birds) in individual, cardboard boxes from the game breeder. Ask the breeder not to mix quail from different holding pens. Be sure to minimize the amount of time between picking up the quail and releasing them at the individual covey sites. You are going to lose some birds after release, and it is essential to maintain a respectable covey size, so don't try to release less than 16–20 birds at each site.

With a knife cut 3 sides of a big hole in 1 end of the box. Carefully reach into the box with your hand and grasp a single quail, male or female, for the call cage. Secure the hole in the box with tape until you have placed the single quail in the call cage. Then, ease the box of quail under the brush pile and open the hole in the end of the box. As soon as you do, leave the site as quickly as possible. The birds will be hungry and will start to eat when they emerge from the box, especially if your quail breeder has been feeding the birds some free choice grain of the same type as in the feeder.

The woven wire fence keeps out livestock and provides just enough protection from predators so that the birds can run to the opposite side, slip through the fence, and fly to safety. The large brush pile obscures the view of 4-legged predators and provides protection from avian predators.

The call bird should be checked every 3–4 days. Feed, grit, and water should be ample for a week or more, but you need to check the condition of the bird more frequently. If he or she is listless, give the bird its freedom and replace the bird with a fresh one. Regardless, the call bird should be replaced at the end of a week. As a rule, the second call bird can be freed at the end of his or her week or 10 days. By this time, the released covey should be acclimated to its new home. If the area has an abundance of natural cover and feed, the covey will visit the release site less and less, but the feeder and waterer should be kept filled and checked at regular intervals.

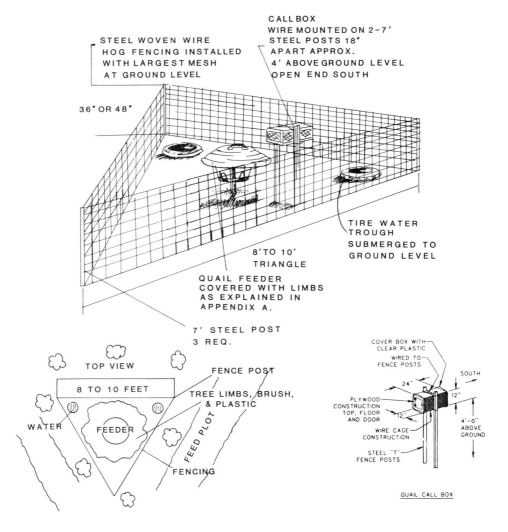

APPENDIX B
Bobwhite Quail Holding Pen

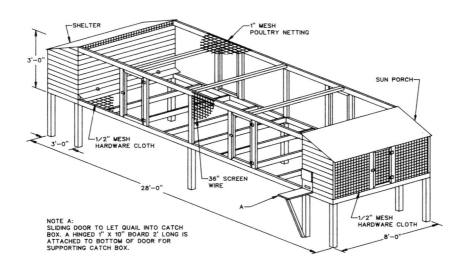

SHELTER

1" MESH
POULTRY NETTING

SUN PORCH

3'—0"

1/2" MESH
HARDWARE CLOTH

3'—0"

36" SCREEN
WIRE

28'—0"

A

NOTE A:
SLIDING DOOR TO LET QUAIL INTO CATCH
BOX. A HINGED 1" X 10" BOARD 2' LONG IS
ATTACHED TO BOTTOM OF DOOR FOR
SUPPORTING CATCH BOX.

1/2" MESH
HARDWARE CLOTH

8'—0"

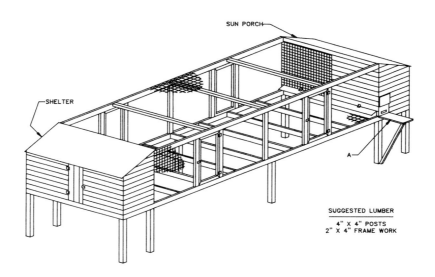

SUN PORCH

SHELTER

A

SUGGESTED LUMBER

4" X 4" POSTS
2" X 4" FRAME WORK

Chapter 9

THE MALLARD DUCK

The mallard is the most popular species of waterfowl, and the easiest to rear in captivity. The colorful drake and his squawking "susie" have thrilled hunters for generations, and there is every reason to believe they will be around for generations to come.

In the wild, the mallard is a "smart" duck when compared to a redhead or scaup. However, in spite of a mallard's innate wisdom, a pen-reared mallard becomes so attached to a pond and a feed hopper that he does not join his wild brethren on their fall migratory journey. Hard for a confirmed duck hunter to believe, but true. The wily greenhead is a fall guy for social security.

Of all wild ducks, the mallard is the easiest to propagate. In addition to his ability to adapt to pen conditions, the adult mallard is relatively free of disease and requires a minimum of shelter in the most severe weather.[2]

Regulations

Over the years there has been confusion between pen-reared and wild mallards. It has not been possible in all instances to distinguish between the two, and this dilemma has resulted in problems with the enforcement of regulations on seasons and bag limits for wild mallards.

In 1921, the U.S. Biological Survey (now the U.S. Fish and Wildlife Service) ruled that mallard ducks more than 2 generations removed from the wild were domestic poultry and not under its jurisdiction. On paper this ruling was fine, but in the field it proved to be a headache. Some violators of waterfowl regulations found a loophole and insisted that the mallards in their possession were pen-reared. How could law enforcement agents prove otherwise? After all, hunting preserve operators must offer mallards that look like their wild counterparts. Off-colored birds are oddities that lack the appeal of a true mallard to hunters.

Biologists within the Bureau tried to find some characteristic that would distinguish the pen-reared from the wild mallard, but finally came to the conclusion that they could not determine any plumage or physical characteristic that would be accurate under all conditions.

After many public hearings and meetings between game breeders, hunting preserve operators, retriever fanciers, and bird hobbyists, a miscellaneous amendment to the Migratory Bird Treaty Act resulted and was published in the August 19, 1966, issue of the *Federal Register.* Paragraph 16.16, "Acquisition, without a permit, of captive-reared mallard ducks," stated as follows:

"Captive-reared and properly marked mallard ducks, alive or dead, or their eggs, may be acquired, possessed, sold, traded, donated, transported, exported (but not imported), and disposed of by any person without a permit, subject to the following conditions, restrictions, and requirements: (a) Effective March 1, 1967, all such live mallard ducks then possessed in captivity without a permit, shall be physically marked by the removal of the hind toe from the right foot within 60 days, and all such ducks hatched, raised, and retained in captivity thereafter shall be so marked prior to reaching 4 weeks of age.

"(b) When so marked, such live birds may be disposed of to, or acquired from, any person and possessed and transported in any number at any time or place.

"(c) When so marked, such live birds may be killed, in any number, at any time or place, by any means except shooting. Such birds may be killed by shooting only in accordance with all applicable hunting regulations governing the taking of mallard ducks from the wild: PROVIDED, that such birds may be killed by shooting, in any number, at any time, on premises operated as a shooting (hunting) preserve under state license, permit, or authorization; or they may be shot, in any number, at any time or place, by any person for bona fide dog training or field trial purposes.

"(d) At all times during possession, transportation, and storage until the raw carcasses of such birds are finally processed immediately prior to cooking, smoking, or canning, the marked foot must remain attached to each carcass: PROVIDED, that persons, who operate game farms or shooting (hunting) preserves under a state license, permit, or authorization for such activities, may remove the marked foot when either the number of the state license, permit, or authorization has first been legibly stamped in ink on the back of each carcass or on the container in which each carcass is maintained, or each carcass is identified by a state band on leg or wing pursuant to requirements of his state license, permit, or authorization. When properly marked, such carcasses may be disposed of to, or acquired from, any person and possessed and transported in any number at any time or place.

"These regulations shall become effective March 1, 1968."

The problem was solved at the Federal level by the simple expedient of removing the right hind toe of a mallard duckling before it is 4 weeks of age. However, every preserve operator should contact his state wildlife agency on the legality of flighting pen-reared mallards. Not only does each state license and control hunting on preserves, it also sets the season during which mallards may be harvested on preserves.

Some concern has been expressed from time to time on the propriety of permitting preserves to flight mallards on a wild flyway. In the final analysis, however, all water areas are likely to attract wild waterfowl during the fall and spring migrations, but, in my 26 years of experience at Nilo, the occasional wild duck(s) that joined our pen-reared mallards on the sanctuary pond quickly departed as soon as someone approached.

Mallards on Hunting Preserves

The popularity and use of mallards on hunting preserves is not keeping pace with other gamebirds, such as the ring-necked pheasant or the bobwhite quail. There are probably several reasons for this:

1. The strain of mallards flighted were poor flyers.

2. The terrain on some hunting preserves is too flat and/or the lack of trees makes it difficult to offer sporty pass-shooting of mallards.

3. Pass-shooting of mallards is not as traditional as calling and hunting over decoys.

4. The old management effort of rearing young ducklings and training them to go between a holding pen and a sanctuary pond was time

consuming, demanding, and costly to the operator.

5. Hunters tend to burn out on mallards — it is shooting rather than hunting.

6. Mallards on preserves are only considered supplemental gamebirds to either the pheasant or the quail. With a few exceptions,[4] the operator has not used his imagination in how to make mallard shooting more attractive.

Mallards — high, fast, and handsome — over a Nilo duck blind.

Preserve operators with the proper terrain and timber need to take a second look at the mallard. Mallards have much to offer a preserve operation and have a number of advantages:

1. The flighting of mallards does not require a large acreage and can utilize portions of a preserve not suitable for upland hunting.

2. Mallards can be flighted for a shoot almost regardless of weather conditions.

3. The overall demands on the preserve operator's time have been greatly reduced with new management techniques.

4. Mallards offer another dimension to preserves that only offer upland hunting.

5. Mallards can be used with pheasants on a continental shoot.

Strains of Mallards

In the last 25 years, there has been a great improvement in the quality of mallards offered to preserve operators by game breeders. Credit for the improvement goes to the game breeders who specialize in producing mallard ducks for hunting preserves. We no longer need flight towers at release sites to help get the birds airborne.

All pen-reared mallards are not of the same quality, even though they may look the same. There is a great difference in not only the ability but the willingness of some strains of pen-reared mallards to fly. It is important that the preserve operator know the quality of the mallards he plans to use on his hunting preserve.

Beware of bargain mallards from hobbyists or breeders specializing in the production of mallards for the table. Seek out a game breeder known for producing quality mallards for hunting preserves. In the past year, 1 preserve operator who couldn't resist a bargain had to butcher his whole flock prior to the hunting season. The ducks did not want to fly; and, if they did, it was only for a short distance. He learned his lesson the hard way. But he was intelligent enough to sacrifice the birds rather than try to flight them for his hunting guests.

The Layout

The layout of a duck shooting area is important. The most natural layout would be to shoot ducks over water with decoys and a blind, but special precautions are necessary. It is illegal to use live decoys, and if some of your pen-reared ducks are on the water within shooting distance of a blind, it could be interpreted by a game agent as shooting over live birds. Federal agents do not have to prove that a wild duck was shot over so-called "live" decoys; the intent, or the possibility, is enough for successful prosecution. Don't risk your investment. The solution is to devise a system that eliminates the possibility of any violation. The most foolproof layout is to simulate the pass shooting of ducks between a release site and the sanctuary pond.

A good mallard pass-shooting layout makes use of terrain that is of little value for upland hunting or cultivation. The features that render such land ''worthless'' for farming make it ideal for mallard shooting. Wooded areas in rough terrain with a small brook or a spring for drainage offer some of the best sites.

A sanctuary pond is essential. The first steps in considering a duck flighting layout are to find a site with a reliable source of water and to test the suitability of the soil for dam construction. Local representatives of the U.S. Soil Conservation Service are experts on the subject.

Trees add to the difficulty of the shooting, and steep terrain enables the ducks to gain maximum speed in a short flight distance and increases the sport of the shooting. The object is to simulate pass-shooting of ducks in the wild, in such a way that the hunters do not know when the ducks are coming or where they are coming from. Because of this, the path or road to the blinds should not pass the release site(s) or the sanctuary pond.

Study the prevailing wind direction during the preserve season. The best pass-shooting layouts provide a tail wind for the ducks between the release site and the sanctuary pond.

The duck-flighting operation should be in a remote part of the preserve that isn't affected by other activities or neighboring landowners. A sanctuary pond and its environs are not very picturesque. Ducks are messy and quickly eat all green, herbaceous vegetation within their reach. Like holding pens for pheasants, a sanctuary pond should be off limits to hunting guests. The pond is strictly for the ducks — a true sanctuary.

The Sanctuary Pond

After the soil of the proposed sanctuary pond has been tested and found capable of holding water at the dam site, other features of a good sanctuary pond have to be considered.

There is no strict formula on how many ducks can be kept on a body of water. Much depends on the accessibility of bank space, shade trees, depth of the water, rate of evaporation, flow of fresh water, seepage, and time of the year. A ''guesstimate'' would be a minimum space of 1 acre of water for each 1,000 ducks, assuming that either springs or rainfall are sufficient to assure a flow of water, especially in late summer. Botulism is a potential problem with ducks on stagnated water.

Pond depth is important for 2 reasons. During periods of extended cold weather (below freezing), one must maintain open water holes. A flock of ducks on the pond can usually keep

Mallards on the sanctuary pond, Richmond Hunt Club, Richmond, Illinois.

some water open, but the operator may have to help by installing an aeration device or by chopping a hole early in the morning. The other consideration relating to water depth is to have a portion of the pond (the upper end) where the water depth is 18 inches or less. Mallards are dabblers, and they must have a place to dabble — it's the nature of the animal. If they don't have a place to dabble, they will move up the watershed until they find one, and the upper part of the watershed could be where your hunting blinds are located.

Mallards will dabble along the banks of the pond and at the dam site. The best protection against the deterioration of the bank, where necessary, is riprap with rock or used concrete blocks. The pond face of the dam should be protected with fencing (chain-link is ideal) staked flat against the dam, with 1 edge extending down into the water for about 2 feet. Fencing the pond face of the dam will also protect it from muskrats.

Shade trees on the bank are essential. Ducks will seek shady areas during the day. If no shade trees are available, artificial shade can be provided by shelters 3 or 4 feet in height and open on all sides.

If at all possible, install a large drain valve in the sanctuary pond. As previously stated, ducks are dabblers, and the accumulation of silt and muck needs to be at least partially removed every year. The least expensive way is to open the drain valve at the end of the preserve season and flush out the pond. The valve only has to be closed again in time to fill the pond with water prior to releasing ducks on the pond for the next preserve season.

Ducks do spend considerable time on the banks of a pond; hence, the slope of the surrounding land should not be greater than 2 to 1. Land surrounding the sanctuary pond should not be planted with any type of grain. If it is, the birds will be attracted to it and you will have a hard time controlling them.

Don't try to manage a sanctuary pond for both ducks and fishing. You may initially have even good fishing on a large pond or lake for a few years, but eventually the fishing will deteriorate. Besides, if possible, you should drain the pond every year.

Fencing the sanctuary pond is optional with adult ducks but necessary with young ducks. Fencing will tend to hold the ducks in a given area, offer some protection from stray dogs and other 4-legged predators. The ratio of the bank area to the water is about 3 to 1.

The most common perimeter fence, supported with wooden or steel posts, is 1-inch mesh, 18-gauge galvanized after weaving, poultry netting, in 6-foot widths.[1] The lower 1 foot is bent into a 90-degree, "L" and burried — 6 inches deep and 6 inches out from the perimeter of the fence.

Flighting Mallards

Until recently, preserve operators were under the impression that one had to train ducklings to travel between a holding pen and a sanctuary pond. And the training had to be initiated prior to the age when the ducks could fly. Or, they could place adult ducks directly on the sanctuary pond; and by moving the feeders a little farther away from the sanctuary pond towards the holding pen every day, train the ducks to return to the holding pen every night for their feed. The holding pen was usually 400–500 yards from the sanctuary pond. Either of these techniques required considerable time on the part of the operator and his employees. However, a holding pen does provide a certain amount of security for the ducks from predators during the night, and the birds do not have to be physically handled on the morning of a shoot.

New Technique

Now, with a good strain of flying mallards produced on open water for hunting preserves, we can release adult mallards (18 weeks of age or older) on a body of water, provide feed, and start hunting within 1–2 weeks.[7] The nightly chore of putting the ducks in the holding pen is no longer necessary. However, it should be kept in mind that the mallards employed in this new technique were reared on open water and have been fully exposed to the weather and predators. One does need to construct a catch pen for the ducks adjoining the sanctuary pond (Appendix A).

Mallards are released directly from the delivery truck onto the sanctuary pond. After being caught, crated, and shipped their only thought is water. Feed is supplied for the first few days on the banks and in the bulk feeders. During the week the birds are slowly trained to find all of their feed in the open catch pen.

At the end of 1–2 weeks, especially in the fall months, good ducks will be taking flights on their own during the morning and evening hours. They are getting acquainted with their surroundings and new home. It's exactly what you want, and time for the operator to trap some of the ducks and to start experimenting with good release sites. The first such sites should be in full view of the sanctuary pond.

The distance from which ducks can be released from the sanctuary pond can vary greatly. It helps if the ducks can see the sanctuary pond once they have cleared the trees and the ducks on the sanctuary pond are calling. Dave Schellinger[5] has a good suggestion. When you are at the release site, hold a hen mallard in your hand until you hear the ducks on the sanctuary pond calling. When you do, turn her loose, plus some of the other ducks, and she will lead the flock back to the sanctuary pond. It may take a few minutes, but be patient. One would suspect that about 400–500 yards, or calling distance, would be the maximum for the final release sites. If the distance is too great, the ducks are apt to circle and come into the pond at a different angle than desired. Also, they may be attracted to other bodies of water.[6] It may be advisable to withhold feed and water from the birds used to experiment with release sites.

If possible, try to establish more than 1 release point. Then, one can release ducks from a given site to take maximum advantage of a tail wind for the ducks. Further, different release points allow for changes in the flight patterns of the ducks over the blinds. However, the release sites should not be known by or be visible to the hunters. Trees and/or rolling terrain help to achieve this management objective. About 50 feet in front of the release site one should have a semicircle of 3-foot high, 2-inch poultry netting staked to the ground to trap any walkers (crippled ducks that cannot fly).

This new technique has many advantages, especially for the preserve flighting less than a couple of thousand ducks. The labor involved in training a limited number of mallards is almost as great as a large number. Compared to buying, rearing, and training a limited number of day-old ducklings for a period of 3–4 months, the price of 18-week-old mallards is a bargain.

The catch pen at the sanctuary pond need not be elaborate. It doesn't have to be at the edge of the pond. If it is, one may want to build a ramp of 1/2- by 3/4-inch rubber-coated wire from the lake to the pen. The catch pen recommended by Whalen[7] is shown in Appendix A.

The catch pen can also double as a holding pen if the feeding is done in the evening. All one has to do is enlarge the catch pen to hold the ducks by allowing 2 square feet of space for each duck.

When mallards are needed for a shoot, the feeding on the previous evening is done in the shelter area of the pen, and a swinging gate operated by ropes is shut when enough birds for the shoot are within the shelter. Then, the feeders on the outside are filled for the rest of the ducks.

The ducks within the shelter should remain dry overnight. If the floor of the shelter is wet, straw should be added to help keep the ducks dry. Early in the morning of a duck shoot, the mallards in the shelter area are either herded into a large crate on a trailer or caught and placed in poultry crates. Herding the ducks onto a trailer requires less labor.[3] All one needs is a sliding door that can be opened either directly to the large crate on the trailer or to a ramp leading to the trailer. But the use of crates facilitates the releasing of mallards from more than 1 site.

The importance of keeping the ducks' wings dry is crucial; otherwise, their flight will be impaired. Straw or hay may also be necessary during wet weather in the trailer or in poultry crates, as well as the shelter area of the catch pen.

Holding Pen Technique

If the operator chooses the older holding pen method, the pen is usually located 400–500 yards from the sanctuary pond. It should be large enough to permit a minimum of 2 square feet of space for each duck. The top of the pen on 2 sides should be covered with sheet-metal roofing for about 10 feet. This provides a shelter area under which to feed the ducks in rainy weather and to keep some of the ducks dry. The operator may also want a separate section of the shelter area to hold new birds for a few days. These sections of the pen should have necessary inside wiring and gates to offset them from the rest of the pen.

Proper drainage is very important. The floor of the pen should be tiled to help with drainage. Even with natural and tile drainage, duck feces are rather impervious to water after they have matted and dried, and pools of water do collect. These puddles may cause mud to accumulate on the feathers of the ducks, reducing good flyers to poor ones.

The holding pen must have a large door to admit a tractor and also to admit the ducks in the evening. A smaller swinging gate is necessary for the release of ducks during a shoot.

The construction of a holding pen for 2,000 ducks is shown in Appendix B. The holding pen is constructed of 1-inch poultry netting galvanized after weaving, 18-gauge, for 3 feet above the ground, with 1 foot buried in a 90-degree, "L" shape below the ground. The top 4 feet can be 18-gauge, 2-inch poultry netting, galvanized before weaving. The top of the pen can be covered with the same 2-inch poultry or nylon netting.

Electricity will ward off predators. This can be done with 2 "hot" wires, one about 12 inches from the ground and the other 6 inches from the top of the pen.

Training: With a holding pen you have a choice of starting with young ducklings (8–10 weeks of age) and walking them to the sanctuary pond[2] or releasing adult birds (flyers) directly on the sanctuary pond from the delivery truck.

If you release adult flyers directly on the sanctuary pond, you will want ample feed scattered along the shore, the banks, and in bulk feeders. Then, after a couple of days, you start the process of moving the bulk feeders back towards the holding pen; eventually all feeding is done in the holding pen.

Mallards will seek feed in the holding pen shortly before darkness, which can range from 9 PM in late summer to 5 PM in late fall. The birds should be accustomed to some noise when it is

time to bring them off the pond — the horn of an automobile, a duck call, or human voice. It helps to train the ducks to some sort of "chow call" from the holding pen at dusk. The effort will save many man-hours and eliminate much frustration throughout the preserve season.

At Nilo we found it best to keep the holding pen closed until all of the ducks were at the pen. If the doors are opened in advance, some of the flyers will decoy on top of the pen where it is almost impossible to retrieve them. Such ducks are prime targets to become a feast for a great horned owl, fox, or raccoon.

Wild Wings of Oneka, Minnesota, has used an automatic trap (Appendix C) for years. The ducks can enter the pen for food but are trapped in the pen when they do.

Every morning the mallards are released to fly back to the sanctuary pond. On the morning of a duck shoot, the birds are released as singles, pairs, or small flocks until the shoot is completed. To avoid any cripples walking through the area where the blinds are located, stake a semicircle of 2-inch poultry netting, 3 feet high, about 50 feet in front of the release gate.

After the shoot is over, and only when the hunters are returning to their vehicles, you can release all of the ducks in a spectacular show of airborne waterfowl that is bound to stir any duck hunter.

Feeding: Follow the directions of the breeder. He knows what the mallards should be eating at various times of the year to assure good flyers. One must watch the weight of adult ducks. If the ducks are getting overweight, oats can be substituted for some of their basic rations. However, if the ducks are not fed enough, they will leave the sanctuary pond in search of feed. If you are getting reports of hunters finding mallards in upland hunting areas, you undoubtedly have a problem of not enough feed for the ducks. Some field corn is fine in cold weather but, in the fall months, the birds should be fed a basic ration of about 17% protein.

Sanctuary Pond Management

Check the sanctuary pond and its perimeter every day. Remove any dead ducks and dispatch all cripples. If you are finding more than a normal number of dead ducks, take the carcasses to a poultry diagnostic laboratory as soon as possible.

Watch for signs of predation. You are likely to have problems with raccoons, hawks, owls, foxes, stray dogs and cats, coyotes, mink, etc. As soon as you have identified the problem, take corrective action (see chapter on ''Predators, Nuisance Animals, and Pests'').

Hawks can be a problem in late winter when their natural food is scarce. They have been known to attack ducks in flight. Hawks can also harass ducks on the sanctuary pond. All game-birds are nervous when any bird of prey is in their vicinity. Owls, especially the great horned owl, can raise havoc with ducks; however, once the problem is corrected, one can go for months and even years without an owl problem.

Raccoon hunting at night can be encouraged as a public relations gesture with local hunters and to reduce the population. Foxes, coyotes, and mink have to be controlled by trapping, either by the preserve operator or a local trapper.

Snapping turtles need special attention for they are capable of drowning adult ducks. If you find that the ducks are not using the entire body of water and are spending most of their time on the bank, check for snapping turtles. You can set 10–12 separate lines tied to tree limbs along the shoreline or to floating 1-gallon plastic jugs. The nylon line should be at least twice as long as the depth of the water and tied to a strong, sharp hook. Both the hook and the line should be able to withstand the pulling force of a man. The hooks are baited with chunks of tough neck beef from 1 to 2 inches square, and rebaited every day for a week. You will usually catch most of the turtles in a couple of nights.

Hoop nets provide another method of catching turtles. Such nets come in various sizes as to length, depth, and mesh. They should be stretched out and staked so that no more than 6–12 inches of the top of the hoop net is above water. The net should also have a stake set through the mesh near the rear hoop to keep the turtles from rolling the net. In Illinois the best bait is 1 or 2 fresh carp carcasses, minus their filets, suspended by a cord from the rear hoop about 6 inches from the top.

How does one handle a highly indignant snapping turtle in a hoop net or on a set line? Take a wooden club and hit the turtle squarely on its nostrils, knocking it out. You can then pick the turtle up by the tail and put it in a burlap bag, or in an empty garbage can with a tied-down lid.

Duck Blinds

Duck blinds should be on skids, sturdy, and large enough to hold 2 hunters. They should be camouflaged with corn stalks or brush to look like duck blinds.

For safety reasons the blind should be built to prevent shooting to the sides and behind the blind. All shooting should be restricted to the front and overhead. A shelf should be provided to hold ammunition boxes. If a bench is provided for the comfort of the hunters, only permit shooting from the standing position.

The blinds should be located so as to present various degrees of difficult shooting — beginner to expert. Locating blinds in timber and on the face of a hill as compared to the open will usually do the trick. Since the blinds are on skids, their location can and should be changed from time to time with the use of a tractor. If possible, the shooting should be toward the north or west so that the hunters will not be firing into the morning sun.

There should be a cleared area behind the blinds to assist in locating and retrieving dead and crippled ducks. The use of retrievers is mandatory. The dogs should be obedient, broken to mark fallen birds, and to make ''blind'' retrieves. Retrievers are part of the overall show. Duck hunters enjoy watching good retrievers work almost as much as they do the shooting. Besides, good retrievers keep the hunters in the ''bullpen'' entertained.

A Duck Shoot

Duck shoots should be conducted in the morning. Shotguns must be open and unloaded at all times except in the duck blinds. Hunters should not be permitted to leave the blinds to retrieve ducks — to do so is to invite an accident.

A minimum of 2 people is necessary to supervise a duck shoot, the manager of the hunt and

A Nilo duck blind for 2 hunters. Note the high sides to restrict shooting towards an adjoining blind (courtesy Winchester Group, Olin Corp.).

a dog handler. The manager of the hunt explains the shoot and the safety rules to the hunters, assigns them to blinds, rotates hunters among the blinds, checks on any malfunctions of shotguns, keeps track of the ducks killed from a given blind, and starts and terminates the shoot. The dog handler concentrates on marking all dead and crippled ducks and handles the retriever(s).

Mallards should be released in varying numbers and time intervals. The best signal between the release site and the manager of the shoot is none. If one must be used, why not a duck call? The individual at the release site can usually tell how many ducks were dropped by the hunters on a given flight and allow ample time for the birds to be retrieved by the Labradors. At Nilo it is customary for a group of 10–12 hunters to be busy for 60–90 minutes harvesting 4 ducks apiece, and they will expend 10–12 boxes of ammunition in the effort. Don't hurry a duck shoot — the hunters may get the impression that they are getting the rush treatment.

Hunters who are not in the blinds should be in the "bullpen" — a shelter open on 1 side with a gun rack, perhaps even a space heater. The rough shelter should be positioned so that the hunters can watch the shooting and the retrievers. Don't let hunters wander around the shoot while waiting for their turn in a duck blind. If they must have a reason for being confined to the vicinity of the "bullpen," their personal protection from falling, spent shot pellets should suffice.

Regardless of all precautions, an occasional walking duck will appear in the blind area. Un-

The "bullpen" where duck hunters view the shooting and wait for their turn in the duck blind (courtesy Winchester Group, Olin Corp.).

A Labrador retriever doing what comes naturally (courtesy Winchester Group, Olin Corp.).

doubtedly, it is a bird that has some physical disability from a previous shoot. Walking ducks are always a subject for laughter to the hunters but one of embarrassment to the preserve operator. The manager of the duck shoot and the dog handler need to be constantly on the alert for a walker. If one is spotted, send a retriever after the walker and treat the bird like an ordinary crippled duck.

It is always a nice gesture to lay out all dead ducks in limit groups with their breasts up and their head tucked under a wing. This act of respect will be appreciated by the discerning duck hunter. Dead ducks deserve a better fate than being thrown onto a pile.

For reasons of safety only the manager of the shoot or the dog handler should shoot any crippled ducks. All cripples should be dispatched as quickly as possible. After the shoot, the manager should check the sanctuary pond for any cripples. A .22 rifle can be a very effective tool to dispatch cripples around the pond.

Crippled Ducks

Charging the hunters for crippled ducks on a shoot is a problem, but charge you must. Crippled ducks don't recover to fly again. The best system is a flat surcharge — a minimum of 10% — of the total bill for shooting mallards.

Shotguns of gauges smaller than 20-gauge should not be used. The .410-bore and the 28-gauge shotguns in the hands of an average shooter simply cripple too many ducks. For those hunters who insist on shooting a .410-bore or a 28-gauge shotgun, 1 possible solution is to increase the surcharge for cripples.

Cold-weather Shoots

When the temperature falls below freezing, ducks are reluctant to leave the pond and usually squat on the ground in an effort to warm their feet. The problem becomes more acute when there is snow on the ground and the temperature sinks below the zero mark. Consequently, some preserve operators close their duck operation after freeze-up. But mallards can be flown throughout the preserve season, and one can have an outstanding shoot on clear, crisp mornings with an inch or more of new snow.

At Nilo we have spread straw over the snow to entice the ducks from the sanctuary pond. The problem is not as critical with a catch pen adjoining the sanctuary pond as compared to a holding pen 400–500 yards away. However, hunger will usually bring the reluctant birds to the holding pen by the second evening.

A couple of hundred ducks will usually keep a water hole open on a sanctuary pond by their activity. But you may want to consider an aerator. This is a small electric pump which supplies a constant stream of air bubbles through a plastic pipe at the bottom of the pond. As these bubbles rise to the surface, they carry a certain amount of warm water (39° F) to the surface, and this upward flow will maintain some open water in the sanctuary pond during subfreezing temperatures. Of course, one must have a pond deep enough so that it does not freeze solid.

Cold weather also calls for the judicious use of shelled corn as supplemental food. The weight of ducks must be monitored closely. During periods of extreme cold, ducks can lose weight rapidly; the amount of such high-energy feed as corn must be increased along with a balanced feed ration and vitamin supplements. The condition of ducks is easily checked by inspecting the condition of shot ducks and the carcasses of processed birds.

Mallards on the ice at the sanctuary pond. Note open water in lower right corner of photo (courtesy Winchester Group, Olin Corp.).

New Ducks

On a large-volume preserve the holding pen may not be large enough to hold all of the ducks needed throughout the preserve season. In such cases, an advance contract is made with a game breeder for delivery of adult flyers during the hunting season. The correct time to introduce new birds is when they will not comprise more than two-thirds of the total flock.

If the ducks are held on a sanctuary pond, new adult ducks can be introduced directly from the delivery truck to the pond. However, all shooting should be stopped for about a week to give the new recruits a chance to adjust to their surroundings. After a week, one should flight ducks with caution until assured that the new ducks are thoroughly integrated with the resident flock.

If a holding pen is used, the new ducks should be housed in an enclosed section of the pen with food and water for about 3 days. Then, 50–100 birds can be released into the resident flock every day a shoot is not scheduled. Avoid integrating or using new ducks on foggy days, and be sure that nothing (hawks, stray dogs, hunters, etc.) interferes with the new birds landing on the sanctuary pond for a few days.

It always helps to have some mallards at the sanctuary pond as decoys, regardless of whether integrating new ducks or conducting a shoot. It is 1 case when a "loud-mouthed" susie is a precious asset.

Guidelines for a Quality Shoot

Throughout the management of a hunting preserve one finds that attention to numerous details is the key to success, and so it is with a duck shoot.

Herewith, some general guidelines to a quality operation:

1. Assure yourself that the terrain, timber, and water supply on your preserve are conducive to a quality pass-shoot for ducks.

2. Buy a good strain of flying mallards from a reputable breeder.

3. Build portable duck blinds that look like duck blinds, complete with camouflage, and change the location of the blinds to offer repeat hunters a new challenge.

4. Don't let hunters visit the holding pen, release sites, or the sanctuary pond.

5. Establish a club limit of 4 or 5 ducks per hunter.

6. Use well-trained retrievers to pick up all crippled and dead ducks. They are part of the show.

7. Rotate the hunters into blinds of varying shooting difficulty. Call a break in the shooting to do so.

8. Don't speed up the shoot. Let hunters "sweat out" the next flight of ducks; and, above all, don't yell, "Here they come."

9. Vary the number and the time of ducks released.

10. Build a "bullpen," a shelter, for the hunters waiting for their turn in a duck blind. Don't let them wander around the shoot.

11. Permit shooting only from duck blinds.

12. Do everything possible to avoid walkers (crippled ducks from previous hunts) from coming through the blind area.

13. Pick up all expended shotshells at the end of every hunt.

14. Dispatch all crippled ducks as quickly as possible.

15. Lay out the dead ducks in limit groups, with their breasts upright.

16. Have a gun rack available near the "bullpen."

17. Avoid the use of any whistle, radio, or telephone to signal the next flight of ducks. If you must use some signal device, use a duck call.

18. Don't allow any vehicles in the immediate area of a duck shoot.

19. Make the shooting difficult; it's the only challenge on a duck shoot. One beginner's blind is sufficient.

20. Wear camouflage or neutral-color clothing. Blaze orange is appropriate for upland hunting, but not for a duck shoot.

21. Offer duck shooting only in the morning. Avoid afternoon hunts.

22. If possible, change the release sites and the location of the blinds on an annual basis.

References

1. Dickey, C. 1960. Shooting preserve management. Natl. Shooting Sports Foundation, Inc., 1075 Post Road, Riverside, CT.
2. Kozicky, E., and J. Madson. 1966. Shooting preserve management — the Nilo system. Winchester Group, Olin Corp., E. Alton, IL. 311pp.
3. Mullin, J. 1977. Portable duck release. Wildlife Harvest 8(3):4-5. Goose Lake, IA.
4. _____. 1981. Spring farm mallard shoots. Wildlife Harvest 12(9):6-8. Goose Lake, IA.
5. Schellinger, D. 1985. Personal communication. Spring Farm, Box 301, Sag Harbor, NY.
6. Smith, L. 1937. American game preserve shooting. Garden City Publ. Co., Inc., Garden City, NY. 175pp.
7. Whalen, B. 1985. Tank release of mallard ducks. North American Gamebird Assoc. Convention, Las Vegas, NV. (Contact Bill Whalen, Whistling Wings, Inc., Hanover, IL.)

Sanctuary Pond – Catch Pen

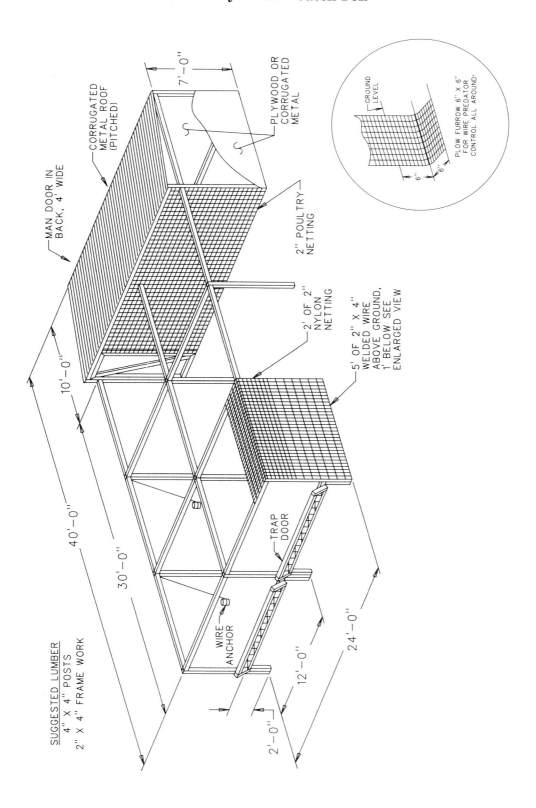

CORRUGATED METAL ROOF (PITCHED)

PLYWOOD OR CORRUGATED METAL

MAN DOOR IN BACK, 4' WIDE

7'–0"

2" POULTRY NETTING

2' OF 2" NYLON NETTING

5' OF 2" X 4" WELDED WIRE ABOVE GROUND, 1' BELOW SEE ENLARGED VIEW

10'–0"

40'–0"

30'–0"

SUGGESTED LUMBER
4" X 4" POSTS
2" X 4" FRAME WORK

WIRE ANCHOR

TRAP DOOR

2'–0"

12'–0"

24'–0"

GROUND LEVEL

PLOW FURROW 6" X 6" FOR WIRE PREDATOR CONTROL ALL AROUND·

6"

6"

APPENDIX B
Mallard Holding Pen

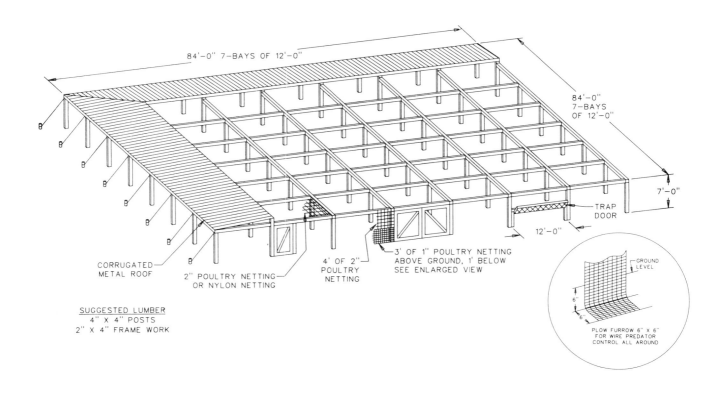

84'-0" 7-BAYS OF 12'-0"

84'-0" 7-BAYS OF 12'-0"

7'-0"

TRAP DOOR

12'-0"

CORRUGATED METAL ROOF

2" POULTRY NETTING OR NYLON NETTING

4' OF 2" POULTRY NETTING

3' OF 1" POULTRY NETTING ABOVE GROUND, 1' BELOW SEE ENLARGED VIEW

SUGGESTED LUMBER
4" X 4" POSTS
2" X 4" FRAME WORK

GROUND LEVEL

6"

6"

PLOW FURROW 6" X 6" FOR WIRE PREDATOR CONTROL ALL AROUND

APPENDIX C
Automatic Trap for Returning Mallards at the Holding Pen

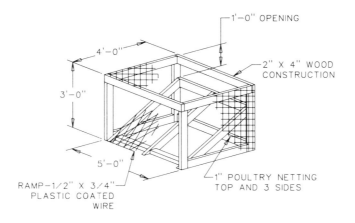

1'-0" OPENING

4'-0"

2" X 4" WOOD CONSTRUCTION

3'-0"

5'-0"

RAMP—1/2" X 3/4" PLASTIC COATED WIRE

1" POULTRY NETTING TOP AND 3 SIDES

Chapter 10

THE CHUKAR PARTRIDGE

In the United States the chukar partridge has adopted the rugged mountain country of the West — steep slopes, rock outcroppings, cliffs, and bluffs with abundant sage, cheatgrass, and bunchgrass, along with brushy creek bottoms and swales.

Western hunters can attest to the favorite maneuver of the wild chukar — run uphill and fly down. And, as with game-farm chukars, they will usually execute a graceful curve before alighting.

The first introduction of chukars occurred back in the early 1930s. The hope was to find a gamebird that could exist in dry, desolate highland habitat of little use to humans except as cattle-sheep range. Since cattle and chukars do not compete for most of their food, the two are compatible as long as the range is not abused.[3]

The Pen-reared Chukar

The chukar partridge is amenable to artificial propagation (see chapter on "Gamebird Be-

havior"), but for every gain there usually is a loss. The relative ease of artificial propagation[6] resulted from the bird's inclination to domesticate in captivity. Although the chukar is a larger bird than the bobwhite it can be propagated in captivity at a cost not much greater than the bobwhite. However, especially in the East, the game-farm chukar cannot acclimate to wild conditions. Chukars that are not recovered by hunters seem to gravitate to open areas and give the appearance of lost chickens, which does not endear them to hunters or to preserve operators.

On the other hand, the chukar can be an operator's salvation on wet days. They will remain where stocked for long periods, providing the cover is suitable, and good quality pen-reared chukars fly strongly and present a sporting challenge to any gunner.

Chukars can also be a preserve operator's salvation for late-season hunting (March and early April). With the approach of spring, gamebirds (especially pheasants) come into breeding condition; the hens become heavy with eggs and would rather hide, walk, or run rather than fly, and the cocks are more interested in establishing a breeding territory than in survival. Chukars, however, are not affected by the onset of spring to the same degree and continue to provide quality hunting.

The chukar partridge is unlikely to ever be the mainstay of a hunting preserve. But they have made an excellent supplemental bird. The most common technique for chukar hunting on preserves is to release some chukars along with the main attraction, ring-necked pheasants.

On the Game Farm

Twenty years ago there were few game farms raising chukar partridge, but the number has increased with the popularity of the bird on hunting preserves.[2] We now have a few breeders who produce chukars on a year-round basis. There is also considerable discussion on the virtues of crossing chukar partridge and red-legged partridge, with claims that the hybrid is a wilder and better flying bird. Maybe so, but after years of exposure to other wonder birds, such as the "Golden" mallard and coturnix quail, I have

reservations. On the other hand, the red-legged partridge may be a good addition to gamebirds offered by hunting preserves if they can be produced in numbers at reasonable costs and gain acceptance by American sportsmen. The red-leg is intermediate in size between the chukar and the gray (Hun) partridge and is supposed to be faster on the wing than a chukar. Only time will tell.

Year-round production makes good business sense, *if* the birds are being produced for table use and dog training. However, some of the mallards I have seen being produced on a year-round basis failed to have proper feathering and were not good flying birds. The birds were "out of sync" with Mother Nature. But, if good flying chukars can be produced throughout the year and there is a demand for 12-month hunting for pen-reared, non-native gamebirds, the chukar partridge has great possibilities in the eastern United States.

As far as hybridization of gamebirds is concerned, why bother? The chukar partridge, if reared in the right environment and hunted properly on a preserve, does a very creditable job of providing quality hunting. However, we should

The chukar partridge (courtesy Winchester Group, Olin Corp.).

always be thankful for innovators in any human endeavor and not be too critical of their efforts. Progress depends on such people.

Quality Chukars

More than 25 years ago, Paul M. Daniell,[2] Feathered Game Farms, Georgia, a pioneer in rearing chukars for hunting preserves, stressed the importance of rearing chukars in isolation and flight conditioning the birds. These important environmental points were again stressed by David Leyland.[5] David stated that — for a fast flying chukar — the birds should be reared in isolation from humans and other gamebirds, or they will domesticate easily. Game-farm personnel who attend the birds should wear clothing of the same color (neutral-colored coveralls), yet different from what the hunters will wear in the field. He strongly recommended automated watering and feeding to reduce contact with man.

Paul McDaniell[2] stated that the chukar — for satisfactory hunting — will always require flight conditioning. A chukar that has not been flight-conditioned will only make 1 good flight and will require about 30 minutes before being capable of making a second flight. He stressed that the holding pen for chukars on a preserve cannot be too big, and recommended a pen at least 23 feet wide, 150 feet long, and at least 6 feet high. At Nilo we did not encounter any difficulty with the flying ability of our adult chukars held in a pen 60 feet long, 12 feet wide, 10 feet high, and 2 feet off the ground (Appendix A), but we purchased good flyers.

As with other gamebirds, the hunting preserve operator should inspect his source of chukars and check for isolation, flight-conditioning pens, quality of the birds, and sanitation.

Rearing chukars for hunting preserves is a specialty best left to knowledgeable game breeders. It's another case where it is better for the preserve operator to buy rather than to rear.

Transportation

The less time chukars are in transit between a game farm and a hunting preserve, the better.

They are not as delicate as bobwhite quail or so quickly stressed, but the general opinion among game-farm operators is that chukars should be crated, delivered, and uncrated into a preserve holding pen in as little time as possible. Some game breeders recommend that the hunting preserve operator include terramycin in the drinking water for a few days after delivery.

Shipping crates are usually constructed to maximize the space within a delivery truck. One breeder uses plywood crates 30 inches long, 21 inches wide, and 9 inches high with 1/4-inch wire mesh across both ends of the crate to allow for adequate ventilation and will load no more than 25 birds in each crate.

Holding Pen

Holding pens for chukars on hunting preserves vary in size. The general rule is that each adult chukar should have a minimum of 2 1/2 square feet of space and a chance to exercise his wings by flying. One large preserve has a holding pen 16 feet wide, 100 feet long, and 10 feet high.

Above all, the holding pen must be isolated from disturbance by man and/or dogs. If necessary, the pen can be screened with corn stalks, burlap, or a picket fence.

Chukars can be held on the ground in some areas but, when in doubt, keep the birds on wire and reduce the prospects of losses from gapeworms, roundworms, and blackhead (see chapter on "Gamebird Diseases"). The floor of the pen should be plastic-coated wire with a 1/2- by 1-inch mesh. The sides of the pen for the first 3–4 feet can be 1-inch poultry netting and the remainder covered with 2-inch poultry netting. The top of the pen can be covered with 2-inch poultry or nylon netting. The holding pen should be at least 2 feet off the ground.

At 1 end of the holding pen there should be an enclosed area of sheet metal or plywood construction of the same width as the pen, high enough to accommodate the height of a man, and 10–12 feet in length. A trap door — usually a board of 10–12 inches in width, as long as the width of the pen, and controlled by a rope — needs to be installed.

When chukars are needed for stocking, a catch box (Appendix A) can be set up adjoining a sliding door on the enclosed shed. The size of the catch box is dictated by the average number of birds that will be needed for a hunt. The sides and the bottom of the box should be plywood, but 1 end of the box should be 1/4-inch-wire hardware cloth, and the other end should be a sliding panel. The top of the pen should be 2 strips of overlapping rubber. The box can be supported by a folding wooden stand that holds it securely to the shed and at the same level as the floor of the shed.

Feed, Water, and Dust Baths

Adult chukars on a hunting preserve should be fed the same rations (and the same brand if possible) as that used by the breeder. It's a good idea to harvest some of the food plots, and offer penned chukars the same grain they will find in the field when released. This will help the birds adjust to field conditions after release, and may keep them from losing so much weight that they fly weakly.

Water should be available on a free-choice basis. Automatic waterers and feeders help reduce disturbance to the birds, and should assure the availability of ample food and water. Enough feeders and waterers are needed to reduce competition for either water or food because competition among birds can trigger cannibalism.

Chukars need areas for dusting, especially when the birds are held on wire. Shallow trays (2 by 4 feet and 2–3 inches deep) should be placed in the sheltered area of the pen and filled with sand or dry soil. The trays should be emptied and cleaned at least twice a week and refilled. Do not let the dusting trays become water soaked. Some preserve operators will add an insecticide to help control external parasites.

Trapping and Releasing

Birds to be released on the next morning, or if rain is forecast, should be housed overnight in the sheltered part of the pen. They can be slowly driven from the open pen by 2 men walking down the sides, and trapped by quickly lowering the bottom board of the enclosed area into place.

In the morning, the catch box is placed next to a sliding door on the enclosed portion of the pen. The sliding panel on the catch box is removed, and the operator or a helper enters the shelter area through an access door on the opposite side. The birds will see the light coming through the wire mesh on 1 end of the catch box and will quickly enter. When enough birds are in the catch box, the 2 sliding panels can be dropped, separating the birds in the catch box from the enclosed or shelter area of the holding pen.

With the releasing crates in position, the operator reaches through the 2 overlapping rubber strips on top of the catch box and grasps a chukar

The chukar is released in the field by grasping it around the thighs and wingtips and flipping it into suitable cover on its back. A pair can be released by using both hands (courtesy Winchester Group, Olin Corp.).

90

over both wings. When the bird is removed from the catch box, the operator quickly inspects each bird by sight and feel. If a chukar does not appear to be of top quality, it should not be placed in the releasing crate.

Once chukars are in the releasing crate, they quickly become rather docile. The crates should be stored in a cool, shady area until about 30–60 minutes before a hunting party is scheduled.

Chukars are released as singles or as pairs, in desirable cover. The birds are grasped high on the legs, with the wings in the palm of the hand and are flipped on their backs into the proper holding cover. The operator should depart as quickly as possible or the chukars may flush. As a rule, the chukars will remain in the general area for an hour or longer.

The tendency for chukars to covey is very strong, and they will start calling soon after release, trying to get together. The tendency to call increases later in the day, but there is less calling when 2 chukars are released together than when singles are released.

In the early days at Nilo, we tried releasing 5 or 6 chukars together using a wire basket. It was a mistake. When the birds were encountered in the field, they were reluctant to fly. A single bird would run off to 1 side, but not take wing. A hunter is quickly disgusted by birds running around on the ground in front of him; all semblance of desired sport is lost. Such behavior results from a chukar's reluctance to leave the other members of the group, and it is easily overcome by releasing 2 birds at a time. Singles or doubles flush readily when released in proper cover.[4]

Rainy weather affects the field performance of chukars, but not to the degree that it does other gamebird species — and for good reason. Chukars are not likely to move around as much as other pen-reared upland gamebirds when released in the field. If the birds are dry when released, and hunted within an hour, they will give a respectable field performance unless the rain becomes a deluge.

Release Cover

If given a chance, chukars prefer to run. To prevent this, stock the chukars in cover that is easier to fly from than to run in. Such cover should be dense at ground level but relatively thin overhead, so that the bird can easily break into flight. If the cover is not dense at ground level, the chukar will run; if it is too dense overhead, the bird will have difficulty in taking flight, and may even be caught by the dog (see chapter on "Hunting Preserve Cover").

Hunting Dogs

The use of different hunting dogs in combination with the proper release cover for chukars can make the difference between a high- and a low-quality hunt. Chukars are curious by nature. When pointing dogs are being used in cover where chukars can run, the birds will often stand and calmly survey the dogs on point and the oncoming hunters. The guide then has to flush the birds by chasing them, which is disturbing to the hunters and not a safe practice for the guide. This action may stimulate laughter by the hunters, but it's not the sort of entertainment your hunters are paying for. It is a highly undesired distraction from quality hunting.

On the other hand, flushing dogs never give the chukars time to be curious. Their aggressive, unhesitating charge forces the birds to fly. The unexpected burst of a frightened chukar adds greatly to the sport of the hunt — even though it did not include a stylish dog on point.

If pointing dogs are used, chukars should be planted in dense ground cover, such as unmowed hayfields, which inhibits their walking or running. The dogs can be trained to flush the birds on command with either a verbal or hand signal.

Dogs used to hunt chukars must be trained not to catch a live chukar. If a hunting dog starts to catch chukars, it soon becomes addicted to the challenge, and highly proficient. This acquired trait in a hunting dog must be nipped in the bud.

Hunting Chukars

Chukars on a hunting preserve are usually hunted in the same manner as pheasants, and for this reason some preserve operators mix a few chukars into a pheasant hunt.

The guide is an important part of a chukar

Springer spaniels and chukars go together like apple pie and ice cream (courtesy John B. Madson).

hunt. He should never call the attention of his hunting party to a bird on the ground. Above all, he should never try to flush a chukar by kicking at it. If it is necessary to flush the bird, the guide should use a flushing whip to strike the cover in the vicinity of the bird. If his dog should catch a chukar, he can excuse the act as a crippled bird *and* be aware that he has a dog discipline problem.

Chukars have more predictable flight patterns than pheasants, but do not fly as erratically as quail. Chukars have a remarkable ability to rise quickly and gain air speed within a few seconds, rivaling a pheasant on sustained flights. The chukar isn't as rugged as the pheasant, but what he lacks in hardiness he makes up for in speed.[1]

Every effort should be made to pursue chukars that are missed by a hunting party. Chukars do not acclimate to wild conditions — not in the East, anyway. They become exceedingly tame and suffer weight loss after a few days in the wild.

The chukar is a covey bird that can be readily decoyed back to the holding pen. Since it is not native in the eastern United States, one should have several box traps with open ends around the perimeter of the holding pen to live-trap such birds. The Havahart is ideal (see section on ''Equipment Suppliers'' in the chapter on ''Short Subjects'').

The 12-gauge shotgun with modified bore appears to be an ideal combination for hunting

92

chukars, especially with a "low brass" load of #7 1/2 shot.

Dead chukars should be aired in a cool spot by the guide at the earliest opportunity. The chukar is a supreme table bird. He has some shortcomings in the field — which may be overcome with time, study, and experimentation — but has few rivals on the dinner table.

References

1. Crawley, M. 1962. Chukars can produce sporty hunting. Modern Game Breeding 32(11):16.
2. Daniell, P. 1959. Flighting the chukars on shooting preserves. Modern Game Breeding 29(12):6-8.
3. DuPertuis, L. 1980. The chukar is a tough old bird. Washington Wildlife 30(4):16-17. Washington Dept. of Game, 600 N. Capitol Way, Olympia, WA.
4. Gunn, C. 1962. The unusual nature of the chukar. Modern Game Breeding 32(1):11-13.
5. Leyland, D. 1973. The chukar partridge — the hunting preserve. Wildlife Harvest 4(8):4-5. Goose Lake, IA.
6. Reynolds, T. 1958. Propagation of chukars. Game Bird Breeders Gazette 7(2):15, 17-18. 1328 Allen Park Dr., Salt Lake City, UT.

APPENDIX A
Chukar Holding Pen and Catch Box at Nilo

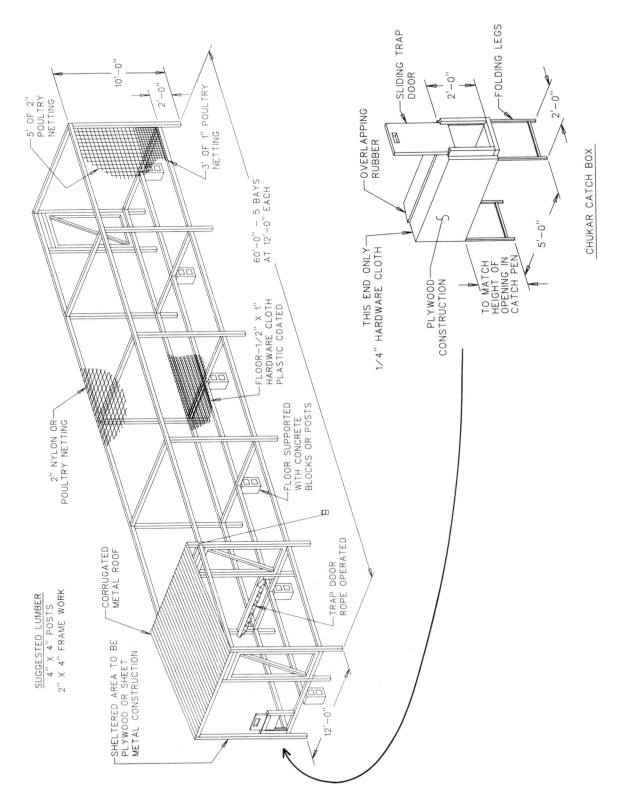

Chapter 11

THE GRAY (HUNGARIAN) PARTRIDGE

The gray partridge is native to central Europe, which probably gave rise to its more popular name both on and off hunting preserves throughout North America, Hungarian partridge or ''Hun.''

The most successful releases of this partridge occurred near Calgary, Alberta, Canada, from 1908 through 1911. The Hun continued to fan out across the agricultural lands of Canada, especially to the southeast and down into the United States, becoming a major gamebird in North Dakota and Montana. It became popular for state game commissions to import and release adult Hungarian partridges from Czechoslovakia and Hungary. Today, there are established wild populations in the grain-belts of Canada and in the northern United States. These populations wax and wane with weather conditions during the nesting season. A dry spring results in early nesting and above-average production of young. Conversely, above-average precipitation during the nesting season (and for about 3 weeks after

hatching) precludes chances for a high fall population of Huns.

Hungarian partridge are chunky birds, the adults weigh 14–16 ounces, with both sexes

The gray (Hungarian) partridge (courtesy Clark Ganshirt).

the same size. They are slate gray or bluish-brownish-gray, with stubby wings. Huns will chatter raucously when flushed as a covey and are known for their long, low-altitude flights. In flight, their rust-colored tail feathers are readily seen.

Males have rust-colored throat and cheek patches; those areas on a female are much lighter. Also, the females have buff-colored cross-barring on the "elbow" feathers of the wing, and more colored barring on their backs.[5]

Understanding the Hun

Like the ring-necked pheasant, the Hun is wild by nature. But, unlike the pheasant, they are difficult to rear in captivity — compatibility of breeding pairs, egg production, and fertility are the major problems. Whereas pheasants are polygamous (1 male with a harem of 2 or more females), Huns are monogamous and very selective of their mates and will only breed successfully as pairs. Field studies of Hungarian partridge suggest a lifetime pairing unless one of the birds dies. Both males and females guard their partner against intruders. Weigand[5] observed in Montana that the most furious battles between Huns occurred when a female guarded her male against other females.

On the negative side, Hungarian partridge are quarrelsome in groups, prone to disease, erratic in egg production, nervous, and difficult to handle and to rear in captivity. Mortality of chicks during the first week of brooding continues to be a major problem among breeders. On the positive side, the species is readily sexed, easy to hatch, and without any major dietary problems.[3]

In the last year or two, there has been considerable discussion about new blood lines from Europe — Hungarian partridge that will produce more eggs, with a higher rate of fertility. Maybe so, but an old axiom of life teaches that, for every gain, there is a loss. Will these so-called "new blood lines" still produce a wild bird, a gamebird that offers a challenge to the most discriminating sportsman? Or will "new blood lines" tend to relegate this regal gamebird to the status of a chukar partridge?

Huns on Hunting Preserves

John M. Olin always believed in the Hungarian partridge as a hunting preserve gamebird. He never liked the chukar partridge because of its domestication in captivity. Further, he knew that Huns could be raised successfully in captivity. This had been proven to him in the 1950s when Western Cartridge Company maintained a game farm. Mr. Olin's interest in the Hungarian partridge was rekindled by his friend, Joseph Nickerson of England, who reared large numbers of Huns on his shooting estate. Between 1968 and 1971, shipments of 200–500 gray partridge eggs were received from Nickerson and delivered to Orr Hill, Bison Hills Game Farm, Missouri, for hatching and propagation. Hill had little success, but in all fairness he just didn't have the time to devote to the project, since his main effort was the production of chukar partridge and bobwhite quail.

In 1972, Carl Patterson of Buffalo, Missouri, joined Orr Hill in the Hungarian partridge rearing effort, and by 1974 they were enjoying success — the hens averaged about 40 eggs each with a fertility level of 85%. This high success was accomplished by removing the "fear of man" from the adult breeders. The breeders were visited regularly by Carl Patterson. In a sense, he made the birds his pets. Once the fear-of-man syndrome had been broken, compatible Hungarian partridge breeders settled down to serious egg production and egg fertility. There was no attempt to make pets out of the chicks. The young birds were relatively isolated from man and, for the next 5 years, we were able to feature outstanding hunting for Huns at Nilo.[2]

Unfortunately, Mr. Patterson had some personal health problems and encountered disease problems (fowl pox) with his Hungarian partridge, so this magnificent gamebird was dropped at Nilo.

In captivity, the problem of compatibility of mating pairs — so important to egg production and fertility — has been met with 2 techniques. One is to observe birds that have paired together, and then to separate them from the rest of the wintering flock into breeding pens. The other technique is to hold male and female birds apart until they are physiologically ready to breed, and then "force-pair" the birds and watch the paired breeders to see if they are going to be compatible. Most breeders probably use a combination of both techniques.

A number of gamebird breeders today are engaged in rearing Hungarian partridge. One of the most devoted of the group is Clark Ganshirt, Game-farm Manager at the Max McGraw Wildlife Foundation, Dundee, Illinois.[1] Another is Jean Marc Ridel and his wife Nadine, Black River Game Farm, Ontario, Canada.[4]

The Management of Huns

Currently, the main problem is to find a game breeder who has Hungarian partridge and is willing to sell some of his birds. Huns are premium gamebirds and, as such, command a high price. If you do find a supplier, treat him as a business partner and consider yourself lucky.

Transporting the birds between the supplier and your hunting preserve should be done as expeditiously as possible. Like bobwhite quail, transport Huns in adequate sized, semi-darkened crates with good air circulation.

Holding Pen

At the McGraw Wildlife Foundation, Clark Ganshirt holds his Huns in a wire pen, 12 feet wide, 60 feet long, and 6 feet high. The birds are on 1/2- by 1/2-inch welded wire (hardware cloth) 3 feet aboveground. The top of the holding pen is covered with 1-inch galvanized wire netting. Evergreen boughs and sorghum heads are placed in the pen to keep the birds occupied. Huns need about 5 square feet of space each to keep cannibalism in check. Since they have strong social ties, it is best to keep birds from different sources or holding pens separate, if possible. One breeder used "flags" of surveyor's tape about 12 inches in length, suspended from the ceiling, to minimize the chance of birds flying into the netting on top of the pen.

At Nilo we had a shelter on 1 end of the pen; the shelter (a 12-foot section of the pen) had sheet-metal sides and top, and a trap door to admit the birds into the shelter. The shelter offered protection in severe weather, kept feed from getting wet, and helped in capturing the birds. The basic design of a chukar holding pen is applicable for Huns (see chapter on "Chukar Partridge").

At McGraw's, Ganshirt built a catch pen 6 feet long, 25 inches wide, and 18 inches high. The back has a screen about 6 inches wide across its entire length to admit light. There is a double top. The first roof, designed to protect the catch box from the rain, swings back and exposes 3 trap doors, each 12 inches by 12 inches. In addition, there are 2 guillotine panels that separate the birds in the catch pen and help to keep them from piling onto one another. On opening one of the trap doors, there are 2 pieces of overlapping rubber through which one inserts his hand and arm to catch a bird. The arrangement helps to minimize the feather damage to a Hun; yet gives the operator a chance to check the physical condition of each bird before being placed in a releasing crate.

Feed, Water, and Dust Baths

As with other gamebirds, use the same feed for holding the birds as the breeder, and follow his directions on watering and the use of dust baths. The general recommendation is that Huns should be maintained as adults on a ration of 20% protein — a pullet developer and grain mixture (equal parts milo, wheat, and corn fed in separate feeders).

Cover for Huns

Good releasing cover is about the same as required for bobwhite quail, especially if one wants to enjoy a covey rise. This is discussed in detail in the chapter, "Hunting Preserve Cover."

Releasing Huns

Hungarian partridge are special. Although some hunting preserves release them as singles and pairs, as with chukar partridge, the real sporting qualities of this gamebird are lost if this technique is used.

The most sporting way to hunt Huns is to release them by hand, with a slight disorientation, in groups of 4–6 birds. The bird will remain together, and if the overhead cover is not too dense, the partridges will rise as a covey. Unlike chukars, the Huns we enjoyed at Nilo remained hidden until flushed, and usually took flight as a covey.

Ganshirt uses the same releasing crate for chukars or Huns. It is 24 inches long, 12 inches wide, and 9 inches high with overlapping rubber strips on top. The crate has holes for air circulation.

Hunting Huns

The chance to hunt Huns on a preserve is a special treat, and a chance to maximize the sporting qualities of this grand gamebird. They should be hunted over a good pointing dog. Unlike chukars, Hungarian partridge will usually remain hidden until flushed. The direction of the flight is never certain and, as in bobwhite quail hunting, 2 hunters are sufficient. One can permit 3 experienced shooters, but beyond this number both safety and sport are compromised.

Even at the risk of sounding like a "broken record," I repeat that Huns are for the discriminating sportsman who appreciates pointing dogs, a covey rise, and difficult wing shooting. Don't offer them as just another gamebird. They are something special!

The Future of the Hun

We are still learning both how to rear Huns in large numbers at a reasonable cost and to manage this gamebird on hunting preserves. The preserve industry can be thankful that there are game breeders and preserve managers who continue to work with this grand gamebird. Like the ring-necked pheasant, the Hun has an innate wildness that does not seem to "cool down" in captivity.

The final decision on the role of the Hun on hunting preserves rests with the patrons and managers. The manager's role is to call attention to the unique sporting qualities of today's Huns, as compared to chukar partridge. To do so, he must stock and hunt the birds to maximize their wild characteristics. But it remains to be seen whether the preserve hunter will appreciate the sporting qualities of this unique bird and be willing to pay the additional cost. The most sensitive nerve in the human body is the one that runs between the heart and the billfold. Currently,

Huns are far more costly to rear in captivity than chukar partridge and the added expense, as with any other quality product, must be passed on to the consumer.

References

1. Ganshirt, C. 1982. Backyard huns. Game Bird Breeders Gazette 31(4):8-9. 1328 Allen Park Dr., Salt Lake City, UT.
2. Kozicky, E., and C. Patterson. 1977. Gray (Hungarian) partridge on shooting preserves. Ann. Meeting of North American Game Breeders and Shooting Preserve Operators Assoc., Las Vegas, NV.
3. Muller, H., D. Neil, and W. Werner. 1971. Reproducing, raising, and releasing gray partridge. Bulletin 548S, Colorado State Univ. Exp. Sta., Fort Collins, CO.
4. Ridel, N. 1984. European gray partridge. Wildlife Harvest 15(7):4-8. Goose Lake, IA.
5. Weigand, J. 1982. Montana's cosmopolitan game bird. Montana Outdoors, Sept./Oct., Montana Fish & Game, Helena, MT.

Chapter 12

THE WILD TURKEY

Few gamebirds can match the wild turkey for sport in the wild. It is a magnificent trophy that has even been regarded as big game at some times and places. Whereas most gamebirds are harvested in the fall, wild turkeys are also hunted in the spring of the year. There are few sounds of the wild that offer more of a thrill to a hunter in the spring than a gobbler announcing the break of day from some roosting site shortly before he flies down to gather his harem. The spring hunting of wild turkeys is a ''disease'' for which we must seek frequent treatments — always hoping we'll never be cured.

The restoration of the wild turkey to much of its original range in North America is a tribute to modern game management. The greatest strides in restocking occurred with the development of the cannon net and transplanting wild-trapped birds into good but unoccupied habitat. For example, it is estimated that the states of Illinois, Indiana, Michigan, Minnesota, Missouri, Nebraska, North Dakota, Ohio, South Dakota, and Wisconsin had 14,000 wild turkeys in 1958.

By 1983, the estimate was 265,000–342,000 in these same states (National Wild Turkey Federation report, 1986).

The Turkey on Hunting Preserves

There are 6 subspecies of wild turkeys: the Eastern, Florida, Rio Grande, Merriam's, Mexican, and Gould's. The domestic bronze turkey developed from the Mexican turkey.[3]

Wild turkeys found on hunting preserves vary from the Eastern subspecies to a mixture of several subspecies — and for good reasons. Hunters on preserves expect turkeys to react much the same as ring-necked pheasants. They want the bird to fly. To accommodate the wishes of the hunter, game breeders have favored a smaller turkey. For example, the current wild turkey at the McGraw Wildlife Foundation, Dundee, Illinois, is a cross among the Eastern, Rio Grande, and Merriam's subspecies. They average about 9 pounds in weight as yearlings and are good flyers.

As discussed in the chapter, ''Gamebird Behavior,'' wild turkeys will domesticate in captivity and lose their fear of man. Behavior of any animal is dictated by genetics and environment, and it is obvious that environment plays an important role in the behavior of pen-reared wild turkeys. As with bobwhite quail, wildness can be improved in captive flocks by backcrossing to wild birds (wild-mating of hens). This technique was used very successfully in the early days of the Pennsylvania wild turkey restocking efforts. Leon P. Keiser, Superintendent of the Pennsylvania Wild Turkey Farm in the early 1940s, told me that the first generation of a backcross between a wild gobbler and a game-farm hen was difficult to rear in captivity. The young birds were nervous and, in turn, stressed, which made them highly susceptible to disease and prone to physical injury within a holding pen. However, it was these birds that helped to restock a large portion of the current wild turkey range in Pennsylvania.

The superiority of a wild-mating system (backcrossing) of propagation for the production of birds for release to the wild was well-documented in many studies.[1, 4, 7] In brief, the technique consisted of a large (5–10 acres), open-top holding pen. Ten-20 game-farm hens, with the flight feathers clipped on 1 wing, were placed in the pen with food and water within primary wild turkey range in the state, during the spring of the year. Wild gobblers flew into the pen and mated with the hens. Eggs within the pen were gathered every day or two and stored in a cool cellar until collected by state game-farm personnel on a weekly basis. Later, someone within the Pennsylvania Game Commission made the decision to play the ''numbers game,'' and all production of wild turkeys was confined to the game farm. The emphasis was placed on quantity, rather than quality, of pen-reared wild turkeys. When the effective but expensive technique of wild-mating game-farm hens was terminated, the quality of the Pennsylvania pen-reared turkey suffered, and all too many state game agencies that imported wild turkeys for stocking from the State of Pennsylvania were disappointed in the results.

Early journals indicate that colonists and settlers had little difficulty approaching to within easy gunshot range of turkeys.[3] No one knows what happened to the original large wild turkey populations, but they were high-quality tablefare for a growing nation, and the range and abundance of wild turkeys shrank to an all-time low in the early 1900s.

In the 1940s, field evidence indicated that wild turkeys required about 10,000 acres of timberland and abandoned cultivated fields to sustain a population with a minimum of harassment by man.[2, 5] Today, it's a different story. Man befriended the wild turkey and became concerned about its welfare. Huntable populations of turkeys now exist in many rural woodlots in close proximity to man in such states as Illinois, Iowa, Minnesota, Michigan, and Wisconsin — states that were either devoid of or had only remnant flocks of turkeys in the 1940s.

However, contrary to survival in the wild, extreme wariness is not an essential attribute of wild turkeys on hunting preserves. Although attempts have been made by preserves to duplicate turkey hunting in the wild, the effort never gained in popularity with hunting preserve patrons. Such efforts have consisted of releasing birds near a blind and having the guide call the bird to within gunshot range, driving turkeys over guns, and even ''pitch shoots.'' Hunters on preserves apparently would rather shoot an occasional turkey as an incidental bird to a pheasant hunt (the great demand for turkeys on preserves usually coincides with Thanksgiving and Christmas). On hunting preserves the wild turkey adds to gross income and provides patrons with a further variety of gamebirds. I am not aware of any hunting preserves that feature pen-reared wild turkey as their primary gamebird.

The Pen-reared Wild Turkey Controversy

In recent years there has been considerable controversy on the release of wild turkey stock on hunting preserves. Purists contend that pen-reared stock will dilute the genetic strain of wild birds and/or introduce disease to wild stock.

Both of these allegations have been refuted by a geneticist and a pathologist as recently as 1982.[6] Dr. Bob Shoffner, Professor of Animal Science, University of Minnesota, pointed out that it is not possible to alter the genes, or other genetic balance, of a wild turkey by the introduction of pen-reared stock. Dr. Dave Halverson, D.V.M. from the University of Minnesota Avian Health Department, addressed the problem of disease transmission from pen-reared to wild turkeys. He indicated that most illnesses of turkeys in the wild tend to be of a parasitic nature, both internal and external. Such parasites include worms, blood-protozoa (spread by mosquitoes and black flies), lice, and mites. The nomadic feeding movement of wild turkey flocks minimizes the possibility of these birds developing diseases that require constant exposure to a pathogen. The purist seems to lose sight of a basic law of nature — survival of the fittest. If a "sick" game farm turkey was released to the wild, the bird would have difficulty keeping up with a flock of wild turkeys, and be a prime candidate for predation. In the chapter, "Gamebird Diseases," Drs. Vezey and Schwartz state that diseases of pen-reared birds are not usually a serious threat to native birds. In theory, one should consider the release of sick, pen-reared birds as a potential hazard; however, this probability does not warrant the undue amount of concern expressed by some wildlife biologists.

Management on a Preserve

The McGraw Wildlife Foundation has featured wild turkeys as supplemental gamebirds for over 30 years. They rear their own birds, and they sell excess stock to other hunting preserves.

Holding Pen

McGraw's holding pen for adult birds, isolated from human disturbance, is 40 feet in width, 140 feet in length, and 8 feet in height. The first 3 feet of the sides are 1-inch mesh, with the remaining 5 feet, 1 1/2-inch mesh chicken wire. The top is covered with 3-inch mesh chicken wire. With the exception of larger-mesh chicken wire for the top and sides, the general construction follows the specifications of a ring-necked pheasant holding pen. The catch pen consists of a section of the pen, 10 feet by 40 feet in size, on one end of the holding pen. McGraw provides a minimum of 40 square feet of space for each bird in their holding pen.

The birds are fed the same rations as ringnecks — 1/2 shelled corn and 1/2 a 14% protein holding ration. Fresh water is kept available in large, open pans.

The only disease of any significance that the McGraw Wildlife Foundation has encountered has been gapeworms, and they use thiabendozole to control this parasite.

Catching, Releasing, and Hunting Wild Turkeys

Early on the morning of an intended release, a small crew drives a group of turkeys into the holding pen. Individual birds are caught with the aid of a net or by hand. Two or 3 turkeys are placed in a large (2 feet in width, 3 feet in length, and about 2 1/2 feet in height), darkened crate with sufficient ventilation.

The birds are transported to a hunting area and released as individuals. The release technique is to slightly disorient the bird and place it in suitable cover — fencerows, small woodlots, or tree lines.

Wild turkeys on hunting preserves are best hunted with a flushing-type dog in conjunction with a pheasant hunt. The usual practice is for hunters to pay on the basis of birds killed instead of released.

Survival

Pen-reared wild turkeys do survive in the wild. There is an established free-ranging wild turkey population at the McGraw Wildlife Foundation. The McGraw Foundation is an oasis of wildlife habitat along the Fox River in northeastern Illinois, completely surrounded by a megalopolis of people and industry.

Dr. George V. Burger, Manager of the McGraw Wildlife Foundation, has observed that the birds that escape initial hunting pressure either go wild or become tame. If the birds are treated to a handout of food by well-meaning local citizens, they become completely domesticated and eventually constitute a nuisance. On the other hand, if the turkeys remain on the McGraw acreage and are subjected to harassment by hunters, they become wild and are most difficult to hunt even within a limited woodland acreage. Hence, one could easily deduce that hunting pressure is important to the development of wildness in pen-reared wild turkeys.

The future of the wild turkey on hunting preserves appears to be relegated to the role of a supplemental gamebird. However, with the ever-growing popularity of spring hunting for wild turkeys, the role of turkeys on hunting preserves could change. This would be especially true for preserves with birds and habitat capable of furnishing a truly "wild" hunting experience, and a clientele willing to take the time *and* pay a premium price for the experience.

References

1. Gerstell, R., and W. Long. 1939. Physiological variations in wild turkeys and their significance in management. Pennsylvania Game Comm. Bull. 2, Harrisburg, PA. 60pp.
2. Kozicky, E. 1948. Life history and management of the wild turkey *(Meleagris gallopavo silvestris)* in Pennsylvania. Unpublished Ph.D. Thesis, Pennsylvania State College, University Park, PA. 307pp.
3. Lewis, J. 1973. The world of the wild turkey. J. B. Lippincott Co., Philadelphia, PA. 158pp.
4. Luttringer, L. 1936. Breeding refuges for wild turkeys. Pennsylvania Game News 7(7):5-7. Harrisburg, PA.
5. Mosby, H., and C. Handley. 1943. The wild turkey in Virginia: its status, life history and management. Virginia Comm. of Game and Inland Fisheries, Richmond, VA. 281pp.
6. Mullin, J. 1982. Pen-reared wild turkeys. Wildlife Harvest 13(6):50-52. Goose Lake, IA.
7. Wessel, C. 1937. The wild turkey propagating areas. Pennsylvania Game News 8(4):8-9. Harrisburg, PA.

Chapter 13

EXOTIC BIG GAME RANCHING

Charles Schreiner, IV; Harvey Goff;
and Hal Swiggett
Y.O. Ranch, Mountain Home, TX

(Editorial Note: Exotic big game ranching has become a successful operation in Texas and has provided quality trophy hunting for a number of sportsmen. But it takes authorizing legislation, a sizeable acreage and financial investment, and good management; otherwise, such hunting can degenerate into a ''pasture shoot,'' which is neither beneficial to the success of the rancher nor to the concept of exotic big game ranching. And the sportsman who participated in such a shoot will not be a repeat client or a convert to exotic big game trophy hunting.

The singular most successful exotic big game ranch in the United States is the Y.O. Ranch, Mountain Home, Texas, owned and operated by the Schreiner family. Charles Schreiner, IV, Manager, has been gracious enough to write this chapter on the basic guidelines for exotic big game ranching with the help of Harvey Goff, Y.O.

Ranch Biologist, and Hal Swiggett, who has worked with the Y.O. Ranch hunting program for 20 years.)

Exotic big game hunting started in the late 1930s in Texas. Following World War II it became recognized as a viable sport by a few hunters and as a profitable venture for the careful landowner.

Exotic big game ranching is here to stay. Although it came to life in Texas, there are exotic big game ranchers in many other states. Species might be more limited because of climatic conditions. And, contrary to what some might think, each good, seriously run ranch helps the other. If a hunter has a good experience on an exotic big game hunt, *HE WILL* go on another. It is addictive. Who knows, he might visit your exotic big game ranch next. And, *HE WILL* return to the ranch of his first experience every so often.

What It Takes

A common question is "What's all this going to cost?" It isn't cheap. Deer-sized animals will run about $200 per head for "stockers." Super exotics, meaning larger animals, will deplete a check book by $1,000–$10,000 per head. A 2-male-to-5-female ratio is recommended to start your herd. When making that first purchase, specify that 1 male be a yearling and the other a breeder. The different ages will build more inter-activity with better breeding results. Large trophy males will cost up to 6 times more than stockers.

Want to grow your own trophies? Plan on 3,000–4,000 acres as a minimum. Here, if properly managed, a good trophy hunting program could be developed with 5–7 species. To be fair, "properly managed" should have been underlined. Management is the key to any successful business, whether it be wildlife, groceries, or clothing. It's just that wildlife, exotics, if you will, are blessed with the same problems confronting any livestock producer, plus their own individual peculiarities. In other words, do everything right and even then something may happen to turn a sure profit into a banking disaster — Murphy's Law is alive and well. These estimates on acreage are assuming a stocking rate of 1 exotic big game animal per 12 acres. Numbers should be shifted to fit your particular area.

One rancher raised a bull elk up to 7 points on each side with massive antlers worthy of any trophy room. The elk was sold. Two days before his hunter was to arrive he found the bull dead. Some poacher apparently just wanted to see if he could kill that huge animal as it had been shot with no effort whatever to take any portion of it — meat or antlers. A good many years of time and expense down the drain, with nothing to show for it except the antlers.

Now that you have the animals and a place to put them, how are you going to keep them there? With an 8-foot, game-proof fence and, at the going price today, that 8-foot fence is going to cost about $8,000–$20,000 per mile. In case that sounds high, think for a moment on the cost of what goes inside that fence. It's a cheap investment. Fencing is a capital investment and should be amortized over a number of years. In most areas a high fence should last at least 20 years.

Sheep and goat net wire will make a good game-proof, 8-foot fence. That 8-foot fence needs to be built with 10-foot line posts and 12-foot corner/gate posts. The wire does not have to be buried. Heart cedar or steel posts every 30 feet with 3 cedar stays in each panel assure the sturdiness of your fence. A 10-foot fence with V-mesh, heavy wire as the bottom 3 feet around 5 acres will handle a pen-raising program.

Electric fences are not desirable for wildlife; however, there are several experimental high fences of this kind in place, and as of this date, the verdict is still out. The maker is Snell Fencing in San Antonio, Texas.

Working/holding pens are very important. These need to be solid-walled so that animals can't see out and panic. The loading chute also needs to be solid-sided, with cell-block sliding doors. Twenty- by 30-foot pens are adequate for 4 or 5 days, but long-term holding, such as all winter, calls for pens 50 by 150 feet. The Caesar Kleberg Wildlife Research Institute at Texas A&I University, Kingsville, has an excellent example of a state-of-the-art set of working pens.

Trapping animals can be done in several ways. Eight-foot, prop-wing nets are good. Animals can be hazed into the net. Drop nets (nets hung on poles and left up so animals learn to feed underneath) are also good. Rifle nets, a 19-foot, 3-cornered net shot over an animal with a .308 caliber blank, are good — particularly for taking selected animals. Solid wood trap pens can be efficient by feeding animals into them; the animals trap themselves.

Then there are drugs. Capture guns are extremely efficient, particularly when taking a specific animal. Once the amount of drug to body weight is established, individual animals can be drugged, handled, and released in a matter of several minutes. This is by far the easiest on manpower. Netted animals can be a problem — even hurting themselves to the point of death — when they become entangled in the net. Establishing the amount of drug to body weight can be extremely tricky, and only experts in this field should be allowed to perform this task. On the Y.O. Ranch we use wing nets and capture guns primarily.

Exotic Big Game

Most exotic big game species have done well on the Edwards Plateau of Texas because of the variety of browse, grasses, and forbs, as well as the relatively mild climate, including a low average rainfall that leads to only moderate to light parasite infestations. Even though their native environment might differ, exotics adapt readily to what is available in most instances. They differ a bit by species but — put in a pasture of suitable acreage — they will find the terrain most suited to their liking. If a given species prefers more open cover, they will end up in that section of the pasture. Should rocky canyons be their "thing" then the game manager should put them in the pasture nearest to that condition. Some species prefer dense thickets. They will survive in more open pasture but, to get the real sport of hunting, the terrain must fit the species.

Probably the most important species (should we limit it to five) would be axis deer, fallow deer, blackbuck antelope, sika deer, and aoudad sheep, not necessarily in that order, but more than likely close. Axis deer are native to India, are medium-sized, standing 35–38 inches high at the shoulders, and weighing, usually, 120–200 pounds live weight. Their color is rufous brown, profusely dappled with white spots that persist throughout the life of the animal.

Fallow deer, from the Mediterranean region of southern Europe and Asia Minor, stand about 39 inches high at the shoulder, weigh from 85 to 175 pounds, and have flattened and palmated antlers with numerous points. There are 3 colors of fallow deer: white, chocolate, and spotted.

Blackbuck antelope are native to India and Pakistan. Small animals, blackbuck stand 29–33 inches high at the shoulder, and weigh from 75 to 100 pounds. The buck is dark brown above, on the sides, and on the outside of the legs. The doe is yellowish. Both sexes are white on the underparts, inside the legs, and sport a white circle around the eyes. Males gradually assume a shade close to black as they age.

Sika deer (a redundancy, as we understand that "sika" means deer) are from Japan and Formosa. Standing 33–35 inches high at the shoulder and weighing up to 150 pounds, sika

The axis deer (courtesy Hal Swiggett).

The white fallow deer (courtesy Hal Swiggett).

look like miniature elk, at least as to their antlers. Their coat is rather long, with coarse hair turning from light brown during the summer to dark in winter. Normally, white spots, plainly visible during the summer, are at least partially discernible on the darker winter pelage.

Aoudad sheep are native to northern Africa. Largest of the animals listed, they can stand from 37 to 39 inches high at the shoulder, and have been recorded at 320 pounds. They are tawny brown in color. Mature animals have a fringe of hair, called the mane, which begins under the throat and extends down the front of the neck to the brisket, then on down the forelegs to the knees, where it is called the ''leggings'' or ''chaps.'' This is more developed on males.

Supplemental Feeding

Use supplemental feeding only when needed. Allow the animals to survive on their own whenever possible. It is best for the animal and definitely best for sport hunting. An animal coming to a pickup on the run doesn't do much for sport hunting. However, during a drouth when there is no grass or browse, supplemental feeding becomes a necessity. Ice storms, or snow-covered ground, demand the same procedure but, whenever possible, let the animals make it on their own.

Not always, on big ranches, are supplemental feeding programs successful where animals not indigenous to the area are pastured. Though all have come from zoo stock or from ranch-raised surplus, they are still instinctively wild and shy away from man-made food. We have spent hours, days, and weeks in pastures trying to teach some of the more skittish exotics to eat. Even then we aren't always successful, as can be attested to a few days after an ice storm.

A good supplemental feed during periods of stress is a 16–20% protein range pellet made for wild game. One-half-inch sheep pellets do fine; these will be 20% protein.

Disease

Problems are more apt to come from injuries and parasites, rather than from disease. Few problems are caused by disease if the animals are well nourished. Parasite-free and well-fed is the secret, if there is one, as most species are relatively disease free. Let them become undernourished and it is a whole new ball game. That's where supplemental feeding comes in. Skill in management is probably the best way to put it. Ivermectin, a horse wormer, can be used as a soluble and spread over supplemental feed. It is a very good control for internal and external parasites.

Trophy Animals

Concerning sporting qualities of exotics, healthy, mature animals offer the most sport. The more that an animal has lived on his own, the harder he will be to put on a wall.

Price-wise, it will be the size of horns or antlers that will determine dollar value. In most instances, some of the rarer species will naturally bring a higher price but, even then, they must be of trophy quality in size and not just rare.

Horn/antler size, so long as the animal is in good health (meaning properly nourished), is

The blackbuck antelope (courtesy Hal Swiggett).

controlled by age, nutrition, and genetics. True, a healthy young animal can grow a horn/antler of impressive dimensions, but always bear in mind that however good he looks at 2, 3, or even 4 years of age, he will be much better at 5 or 6 years. It does, and always will, take age to grow massive, well-constructed horns or antlers. Individual animals will show different genetic propensities for horn/antler growth.

Surplus Exotics

Whenever males and females are put together, nature soon expands the population so that hunting or live capture of surplus animals becomes a matter of self-preservation. An overstocked pasture makes reducing those numbers mandatory, whether the rancher wanted to have an exotic big game hunting pasture or not. The surplus can be trapped and sold should the rancher desire, but 1 way or the other animals have to removed.

Axis deer can now be sold commercially as meat. If a rancher decides on these beautiful spotted deer from India, he can utilize his surplus by calling a wild game processor who will come to his ranch, harvest the surplus, process the meat, and sell it over the counter just like any other meat. Blackbuck antelope are gaining in popularity for meat as well.

Poaching

Poaching is a problem. Today, in Texas, exotics belong to the landowner, just as any other livestock. Poaching an exotic brings the same penalty as rustling a cow or horse. Proving the offense is all that is needed for the animal to be paid for and, in some cases, poaching even becomes a penitentiary offense.

Hunting Exotics

Always keep in mind that your guide is representing you. When he says something, or does something, it is the same as if you said or did it. Your guide will be the determining factor in whether or not the client comes back for another hunt. The hunter may get a fine trophy;

The aoudad (Barbary) sheep (courtesy Hal Swiggett).

but if the guide wasn't knowledgeable, friendly, courteous, and helpful in every way possible, chances are it will make little difference what happens back at headquarters. The theme for the client's thinking has already been established.

When it comes time for the hunt, be sure that your guide knows the pasture and has a good, dependable vehicle. The guide must know what makes a trophy in each of the species. He must learn to judge horn length and basal diameter. In the case of deer (sometimes it is profitable to combine whitetail hunts with exotics) the rancher should establish a minimum and see that his guide sticks to it. Age, more than anything else, grows big antlers, so the guide must know an immature animal when he sees it. Sometimes a young buck can look mighty impressive — especially to a hunter who has never seen one before. Often, hunters will demand to shoot a specific animal, using as their authority the fact that they are paying for the hunt. The guide must stay in control. If he lets a hunter shoot an immature animal, even though he is gloriously happy at the moment, and that hunter takes his trophy home, has it mounted, and hangs it on his wall, it is there for all to see. And, usually, it will have the name of the ranch where it was killed. This is, without a doubt, the worst thing that can happen so far as public relations are concerned. Sooner or later, someone who knows about the species will see it and point out its shortcomings. At that moment the rancher lost any chance of a repeat hunt because that hunter knows then that he wasn't given the best of care, even though he did it to himself. The guide has to be in command and make the decision as to what is or is not a trophy.

The best record book for exotics is the *Burkett Trophy Game Records Of The World,* San Antonio, Texas. It is the most accurate and repeatedly fair system in existence.

In the case of blackbuck antelope, color is the big thing (after the length of the horns). They can be shot year-round, since they have horns rather than antlers, but only during cooler months will they be black and beautiful. Often a hunter will want 2 blackbucks — 1 in the lighter summer coloration and the other black.

Sheep can give a guide a hassle. Most any ram near full-curl will excite a beginning hunter. If the guide doesn't know a mature ram when he

The mouflon sheep (courtesy Hal Swiggett).

sees it, trouble is on the way to that hunter's city. Spindly horns with a tight curl are not considered a trophy, so don't let a client take such a head home and hang it on his wall.

If you are into sheep, it's best to cull every year and ship to a stockyard. Less money, for the moment, but a lot better reputation, which means more money later.

Depending on the size of the ranch, radios can come in mighty handy. If a hunting pasture is several miles from headquarters and the vehicle breaks down, it can be a decided inconvenience. If it is near dark, it can be worse than that. Not every exotic hunter is an experienced outdoorsman. Chances are he won't take kindly to staying alone in the dark while your guide goes for help. Chances are, too, he won't be in physical condition to walk "home."

A radio also can be handy in the event of a crippled animal. Many ranchers keep dogs trained to trail blood, so a cripple can usually be found. With a radio the guide can get help in a matter of minutes.

Speaking of crippled animals, do not be afraid to over-gun your hunters; in the hands of an experienced shooter a .222 and the like will kill most of our exotics, but a lot of game has been lost with 6mm rifles. A proper hit means no problem. Most hunters after exotics have little actual experience shooting big game. They are excitable, and seldom know where a heart or lung is located; and, if they did, they couldn't hit them. Bigger calibers are not a cure-all, but a .270 Winchester, .308 Winchester, or .30-06 Springfield provides insurance in dropping badly hit animals. Magnums are never needed in exotic big game hunting, except in the case of some of the larger species.

It is also good to have a range where hunters can check the sights on their rifles. One hundred yards is standard — with a good solid bench and sand bags. A spotting scope helps and is well worth the investment. A range performs 2 purposes. It allows the hunter to reassure himself that his rifle is ready. If not, the rifle can be resighted. It is a good policy to insist that each hunter try his rifle since scopes can be knocked out of alignment in aircraft baggage compartments and associated handling. Even more important, using the range allows the guide to determine if the hunter does in fact know how to handle his rifle. This also provides a time for gun handling suggestions should they be needed — and time for prayer should those suggestions not be heeded.

Care of Hunters

If providing lodging, sleeping quarters must be dry, clean, and warm (or cool, as the case might be). If the client wanted to rough it, chances are he would have booked a pack-in mule deer or elk hunt. Lodging facilities needn't be Hilton or Holiday Inn class, but just clean, comfortable, and warm. It is essential to provide good solid food — everyday type — and lots of it. A man might be a light eater at home, but put him on a ranch, in a Jeep or pickup all day, and he will eat his way through most of a cow and never look back.

Repeat Business

Repeat business is the lifeblood of an exotic big game hunting ranch. Sometimes a hunter will get hooked on a particular species and keep coming back to improve his trophies. Others might eventually want one of everything you offer for a complete collection from your ranch. It doesn't hurt to put high standards on your trophy selection because no real sportsman expects to get his trophy every trip — even with exotics.

If a client sees game and has a good guide who explains that a particular animal isn't trophy quality, rest assured that hunter will be back if he does not score. Chances are he will bring a friend, because he knows trophies are the most important thing in your operation. You have already proven trophy quality comes ahead of money. He knows that because your guide could have let him shoot a lesser animal on the first trip.

Obviously, the above procedure can be undertaken only if the guide knows for sure what the ranch has to offer and holds out only for that. A real honest-to-goodness trophy from 1 ranch might not be so spectacular on another, but make sure that your hunter gets a trophy for which he doesn't have to apologize for at home at a later date.

An exotic big game hunting ranch has only its reputation to survive by. A flash in the pan operation — ''shoot what comes first'' — might have a good year or two; but, in the long run, it will be quality trophies that win out with good company, good food, and a warm, dry bed.

The above applies only to game ranches that want to develop a clientele of repeaters who often get in the habit of making an annual trek and then spend the next 11 1/2 months planning the next trip. Again, repeat business is the lifeblood of every successful exotic big game ranch.

Supplemental Income

Selling surplus animals to zoos and other ranches is always a possibility, but you will find that most zoos are selling, too, rather than buying. Marketing stockers is highly competitive. Animals are sold, but there are lots of them for sale. Probably the most certain source of income from surplus animals is the marketing of axis deer for meat. Blackbucks are getting a foothold here, too.

Should you be thinking of mixing livestock and wildlife, bear in mind that properly managed wildlife will make more money than livestock. Deer hunting combines well with exotic big game hunting if the deer herd is large enough to sustain such a program.

Photographic safaris are another possibility. These are more time consuming and will, normally, require 1 guide for each photographer. An accomplished wildlife cameraman might spend several hours trying for a photograph of 1 particular animal. Your hunting guides occasionally will prove to be too impatient for photo safaris.

May We Suggest?

If you are seriously interested in exotics, please seek professional advice. The Exotic Wildlife Association (E.W.A.), 1811-A Junction Highway, Kerrville, TX 78028, has recently adopted a good code of ethics and screens its members accordingly. Being a member of E.W.A. will afford practical information and contacts for animals, as well as timely legal and legislative updates.

Supplemental Reading

Atterbury, J. T., J. C. Kroll, and M. H. Legg. 1977. Operational characteristics of commercial big game hunting ranches. Wildlife Soc. Bull. 5(4):179-184. 5410 Grosvenor Lane, Bethesda, MD.

White R. J. 1987. Big game ranching in the United States. Wild Sheep and Goat International, Box 244, Mesilla, NM. 355pp.

Chapter 14

HUNTING PRESERVE COVER

There are no pat formulas or set techniques for good hunting preserve cover. Each preserve is unique. We can discuss the basics of good hunting preserve cover and the effect that one needs to achieve, but the final cover crop will depend on soil, climate, and the individual preserve operator's needs and ingenuity.

A combination of natural and planted cover is ideal, with the 2 types blended together to offer the ultimate in release and holding cover for gamebirds, attractiveness to the hunter, and possible returns in crops, timber, and Christmas trees.

Good cover throughout the 5–6-month hunting preserve season can mean the difference between profit and loss. It also prolongs the time birds will stay on the preserve and can have a marked effect on the ratio of birds released to birds harvested.

Release cover should provide a given gamebird with sufficient security so it will remain in such cover for several hours. The cover should also be of such density and height as to enhance the sporting attributes of the bird, and should duplicate as closely as possible the vegetative cover in which wild gamebirds of the same species would normally be found.

The purpose of holding cover is to attract and hold pen-reared gamebirds for an extended period of time. Good holding cover usually is not conducive to maximizing the sporting attributes of a given gamebird. The successful hunting of holding cover may require special hunting techniques and/or cover management efforts.

The requirements for suitable release and holding cover vary to some degree with different species of gamebirds, and may be difficult, if not impossible, to develop in some geographical areas of the United States. The critical time of the year for cover on a hunting preserve is January through March.

Selecting a Preserve Acreage

Good cover on a hunting preserve starts with the selection of the proper acreage. After one has decided on the primary gamebird to be flighted on the preserve, he or she should look for an acreage that has a good natural population of wild birds of that species from September through March. If the acreage is attractive to wild gamebirds of a given species, it will also be attractive to their pen-reared counterparts, and the costs of developing proper vegetative cover on the preserve will be greatly reduced. The availability of agricultural land that can be plowed and cultivated for cover is important. Bulldozing, root plowing, chaining brush, clearing timber, and removal of the debris are expensive and time consuming.

The lay of the land is important. The best terrain is rolling, with a good interspersion of cultivated areas (10 or more acres in size) and timber. Flatland can be monotonous to the hunter, and does not lend itself to the isolation of hunting parties on small acreages. Hunting is a personal sport, and the best hunting areas on preserves are those isolated from others and from human activity, or even buildings. It may be impossible to eliminate all such distractions, but the fewer the better. The main purpose of timber on a hunting preserve is to separate the individual hunting areas.

Developing an Acreage

One of the first tasks after determining the location of the clubhouse, dog kennels, and holding pens for gamebirds is to make a cover plan for the entire hunting preserve. It should be a long-range plan, since pine plantings and shrubs take a number of years to develop and become useful holding cover.

A recent, large-scale (16 inches to the mile) aerial photo of the preserve acreage is essential. It will reveal the best tracts of land to develop into hunting areas. Natural boundaries, such as timber, gullies, and lakes, can easily be seen. An aerial photo is also an asset in determining necessary access roads. A preserve needs a good system of all-weather roads to facilitate the release of gamebirds on hunting areas and to transport hunters.

The land-use history of the property should be obtained for reference. With the help of a local U.S. Soil Conservation Service agent, soil types

and the fertility level of each type can be determined. This information is essential on hunting areas prior to planting annual and perennial vegetative cover.

Seeking Help

Once the operator decides on the types of cover he needs for his hunting preserve, he should seek the help of experts in selecting the species and varieties of plants best suited for the soil and climate on his preserve.

You can obtain help through the local soil conservation district if you are a soil conservation district cooperator — and if you aren't, you should be. The U.S. Soil Conservation Service has assigned personnel to soil conservation districts to aid landowners in planning suitable crop rotation, controlling erosion, and establishing and maintaining soil conservation practices.

The farm crops or agronomy department of your local land grant college may be of assistance through the local county agricultural agent. He will have information on both annual and perennial plants for the different soil types on your hunting preserve.

You may even be able to obtain financial help for cropland retirement under the cropland conversion program, or cost-sharing aid on conservation-practice installations under the agricultural conservation program. Check with your local committee of the Agricultural Stabilization and Conservation Service.

Other hunting preserves are also good sources of information. Remember, however, that a few hundred miles can make a big difference in the type of vegetation that can be grown on a given acreage. Each area's soil capabilities and limitations are linked to the local climate and must be understood and respected.

Hunting Areas

A hunting area is a basic land unit, a subdivision of the preserve, wherein a party of 2−4 hunters can hunt for 2 or 3 hours without backtracking into the same hunting cover. Most hunting preserves have 4 or more such hunting areas to accommodate their daily guests. Each hunting area is a mixture of planted and natural cover for releasing and holding gamebirds, with boundaries such as roads, gullies, lakes, or woods separating each area. The size of each hunting area is largely determined by easily discernible boundaries.

A few hunting preserves do not divide their acreage into hunting areas. Each hunting party is permitted to hunt the whole preserve. But such permissiveness is predicated on special hunting-safety features, such as the mandatory use of blaze-orange hunting jackets and caps. For safety reasons, the hunting parties are prone to separate on their own. As each new hunting party goes into the field, the preserve manager will alert the group as to how many hunting parties are in the field and the general area in which they are hunting. Then he will suggest where the new party should hunt. Also, the manager will drive through the hunting preserve to check on the hunting parties, pick up shot birds, and release additional pheasants out of the sight of any hunting parties.

Release Coverts

Release cover on a hunting preserve is usually subdivided into "release coverts," small units of cover designed to retain given gamebirds for several hours or longer. The vegetation within these coverts should be rather short (30–40 inches high) and dense enough to cover the backs of the birds and provide them with a sense of security.

Dense cover at ground level impedes the walking or running of gamebirds and forces them to fly to escape an approaching hunting party. Also, the cover must be low enough to provide safe and sport shooting and not hinder the take-off of a flushed gamebird. Proper release cover can be achieved through either natural or planted cover, and the suitability of given release cover will change with the time of year and the species of gamebird.

The release coverts should vary in size. Avoid uniformity. Variety in preserve cover is the spice of hunting.

Each release covert may or may not be surrounded by a "stopping strip" (20 or more feet

Leo George, Nilo Manager, standing in ideal release cover — hybrid sorghum — for ring-necked pheasants.

in width). The purpose of a stopping strip is to help hold gamebirds, especially pheasants, in a release covert. As the hunting party approaches a release covert, pheasants will start to move or squat and try to hide. If they do move, they will come to the edge of the release covert and see an open area (stopping strip), and retreat back into the release covert and try to hide from the approaching hunting party.

A few hunting preserves do not mow stopping strips around their release coverts, in order to add to the overall naturalness of the hunting area. However, their release coverts (sorghum) are islands in a sea of very dense hayfields, so the best escape route for a pheasant from the sorghum patch is by air.

Release coverts can be planted in long, winding strips (20 or more feet in width) on a contour. Before the hunting season, stopping strips are mowed beside and through the release cover at varying intervals, creating coverts for the release of gamebirds.

On large acreages of tillable land, the preserve operator may alternate rows of field corn with sorghum plantings. Prior to the hunting season, the corn is harvested for feed and the harvested areas serve as stopping strips. Another preserve operator may plant the entire field into some types of suitable sorghum and mow a portion of the field for mourning dove hunting. Strips can then be mowed through the remainder of the sorghum field for preserve hunting.

Holding Cover

Holding cover is vegetation that will attract and hold released gamebirds, especially pheasants, on a hunting area for an extended period of time during the late fall and winter months. Birds that are missed by 1 hunting party may be found by the next group of hunters. Such holding cover is always enhanced by the proximity of feed, such as corn or milo. During periods of snow, it may even be advisable to scatter milo and/or corn in holding cover. Examples of hold-

A hedgerow of bush honeysuckle, excellent holding cover for gamebirds throughout the year.

ing cover are brushy areas; clumps of pine trees; plum tickets; tall grasses; hedgerows; marshy sites with cattails, sedges, grasses, and forbs; and/or woodlots.[12]

Holding cover, either natural or planted, should be large enough not to fill up with drifting snow, and yet not so large the cover cannot be surrounded by hunters. Otherwise, the pheasants will circle away from the hunters by running. One technique used at the McGraw Wildlife Foundation for large brushy areas (winter holding cover) is to mow paths with a tractor "brush hog" every 40–50 yards, and have the hunters break up into drivers and blockers, with a hunter assigned to walk the open paths on either side of the brushy cover. The same technique can be employed on a large marsh, once the water and the ground have frozen hard enough to support mowing equipment.

Scenic Cover

As much as possible, the hunting areas should look "birdy" — the sort of place where one would expect to find quail and pheasants in the wild. One hunting preserve even features cornfield hunting of pheasants with the hunters alternating as drivers and blockers. Such cornfields are 10 acres or more in size and as weedy as possible — with only 1 cultivation versus the usual 3.

Old trees standing in cultivated fields can be cut down and permitted to become overgrown with vines and brush. This adds to the huntable landscape and helps break the monotony of a large field.

Small ponds for water storage are useful for watering dogs while on a hunt, and usually provide cover in the form of cattails or planted reed canary grass. They can be constructed high on a watershed with a tractor and blade, and may be shallow basins only 15–20 feet wide. They are islands of a different type of cover, adding variety.

Eroded gulleys can be converted into beautiful lakes. Lakes add immeasurably to the beauty of a hunting area, and provide picturesque locales for fishing, camping, or picnicking.

Trees and shrubs such as sassafras, persimmon, and bittersweet should be left in clumps wherever possible. Their annual burst of fall color adds greatly to the attractiveness of a hunting area.

Gamebird Cover

Both release and holding cover vary to some degree with each gamebird species. The species of plants, both planted and natural, to develop such cover vary in different regions of the United States. Consequently, it is important for a preserve operator to decide on the primary gamebird he wants to hunt. Other species, if flighted, can be given secondary consideration. Or, the operator can develop various hunting areas with specific gamebirds in mind.

If a preserve operator understands the cover requirements for releasing and holding a given gamebird, he can use his own ingenuity to provide such cover. Unfortunately, at this time, with the exception of the ring-necked pheasant north of the Mason-Dixon Line, we do not thoroughly understand the mechanics of good holding cover for all pen-reared gamebirds on hunting preserves. But one can quickly grasp the concept of good holding cover for different species of gamebirds on the preserve by studying where the unshot birds tend to congregate. You learn as you go.

We do understand enough about good release cover for various gamebirds to establish such cover that will: (1) provide each bird with a sense of security for a few hours; (2) provide safe and sporty shooting; and (3) resemble natural cover for wild birds, with the exception of the chukar partridge.

Ring-necked Pheasant

The ring-necked pheasant likes vegetative cover that provides overhead protection and freedom of movement at ground level. A pheasant is also strong enough to burst through a canopy of overhead cover on takeoff if he must, but he prefers to run. Hence, he prefers holding cover such as plum thickets, woodlots, brushy areas, and fencerows. A pheasant can be a difficult bird to pin down in such cover with a dog. He is going to keep running ahead or circling within the cover. If he does take wing, he may not offer the hunters a shot. So the preserve operator provides holding cover that can be hunted successfully, either by limiting the area of the holding cover or by cutting paths through the brushy cover. Good release cover for pheasants provides sufficient overhead cover to give the bird a sense of security but has vegetative roadblocks in the form of dense ground cover to discourage the pheasant from running. When I speak of "overhead cover," of course, it's in terms of pheasants, not hunters.

Excellent release and holding cover for ring-necked pheasants — 6 rows of harvested corn for access by hunters, 6 rows of weedy, standing corn, and a strip of tall, open-pollinated sorghums, Richmond Hunt Club, Richmond, Illinois.

Pen-reared pheasants soon adapt to hunting pressure, and the survivors on a hunting area are quick to band together. At Nilo it was common to observe gun-wise pheasants flying off the hunting areas into the surrounding woods at the first few shots being fired by hunters on the other end of the area. Such birds require special hunting techniques.

Large, open fields with appropriate release cover for pheasants are both good and bad. When ring-necked pheasants are flushed, they usually head for woody cover. You will get long flights if the birds are missed in large, open fields, but such fields also lower chances of a second flush. Some thought should be given to dividing large fields into smaller units by planting rows of brushy cover, such as bush honeysuckle, shrub dogwoods, or autumn olive.

All vegetative planting should be done on the contour rather than a straight line, for 3 reasons: (1) running pheasants are less likely to be seen by the hunters, (2) soil erosion is better controlled, and (3) walking is easier for the hunters.

Bobwhite Quail

The field performance of bobwhite quail is influenced by the type of release cover. Good flying birds can exhibit sub-quality field behavior unless released in the right kind of cover.

Bobwhite quail are not rugged "brush busters" as are good-flying ring-necked pheasants, nor are they as likely to run. The sporty hunting of bobwhites requires cover with dense ground vegetation that provides light overhead cover. The purpose of dense, low ground cover is to inhibit the birds from walking away from each other as the hunting party approaches. If the overhead cover (3–4 feet above ground) is dense and the ground cover (4–6 inches above ground) is non-existent or sparse, you will seldom get a covey rise for the hunting party. The birds will walk or run around in the vegetation and be reluctant to take wing. If a bird does flush, it may quickly settle back to the ground. It isn't a problem of the bird not being able to fly — it apparently just doesn't want to leave the other birds. Also, even though the released birds have come from the same game farm and were held in the same holding pen on a hunting preserve,

Ron DeBruin, Oak View Hunting Club, Prairie City, Iowa, in a brome grass field, excellent release cover for chukars, quail, and "Huns."

the birds lack the strong social bond of a wild covey. Wild coveys of bobwhites have a leader, and act as a unit.[3] Newly released bobwhites are bewildered and haven't had the time to unite into a social unit. If you are trying to feature a covey rise with pen-reared quail for your hunters, dense ground vegetation with light overhead cover is a necessity. The light overhead cover induces the quail to escape an advancing hunting party by flight instead of on foot.

Natural cover should be employed, wherever possible, to enhance the attractiveness of a hunting area. For instance, to a soils expert broomsedge is an indicator of acid soil of low fertility. But to hunters it means quail, and patches of this wild cover, with appropriate ground cover, should be maintained for releasing quail.

Daisy fleabane is natural roosting cover for bobwhite quail. Most quail hunters know this; when they flush a covey of pen-reared quail from a patch of daisy fleabane, they are pleased to find quail where they feel quail should be.

Many southern hunting preserves do little or no planting of vegetative cover for bobwhite quail hunting, especially those preserves blessed with a ground cover of wire grass and stately longleaf pines for an overstory. It is a combination of happy circumstances. The pines are thinned to maximize their annual growth which, in turn, permits enough sunlight to reach the ground for the growth of wire grass. Morever, the thinning of middle-aged and mature pine trees makes the shooting of quail interesting but not too difficult. Such hunting areas may be 200 acres or more in size.

Farther north, wheat and oat stubble fields underplanted with red clover or Korean lespedeza are ideal release sites early in the hunting season. Later in the hunting season, sorghum patches (with the overhead cover broken down by the weather), brome grass, alfalfa, or timothy hayfields left uncut after the first mowing, or idle fields with a goldenrod overstory are good sites for the release of bobwhite quail.

The importance of holding cover for bobwhite quail may not be as important as getting them to eat and maintain their vigor. Bobwhites are delicate creatures compared to pheasants. The stress of release into the wild is great, and good flyers can become poor flyers within a couple of days. Released pen-reared quail need time to adjust to their new environment with its strange food and surroundings. They do not have the physical reserve of larger gamebirds. Lehmann[3] states that wild blue quail quickly adjusted to confinement and within a few hours were eating milo, wheat, and cracked corn, whereas wild bobwhite quail were slow to eat in confinement and lost weight rapidly. If bobwhites were held for more than 3 days, their vigor and flight were noticeably impaired.

One helpful management effort is to provide sorghum seeds or cracked corn to pen-reared bobwhite quail while still in the holding pens. Some southern hunting preserves scatter cracked corn and milo on roads and trails within a hunting area. Other hunting preserves use feeders as a central point for releasing and holding quail.

Most hunting preserves have sufficient holding cover, such as plum thickets, shrub honeysuckle, sorghum patches, brushy fencerows, and briar patches. It appears that the main problem with holding unshot bobwhite quail in good condition on a hunting preserve is getting the birds to feed, rather than a lack of holding cover.

Chukar Partridge

Since chukar partridge are secondary gamebirds on hunting preserves, they are released into cover designed for ring-necked pheasants or bobwhite quail. The proper release cover depends on the type of dogs that are used to hunt chukars.

If a flushing dog is used, chukars can be released into the same cover one would use for pheasants. If a pointing dog is used, the release sites should be very dense grass cover (brome, timothy, orchard, prairie, or fescue grasses). Such cover makes it difficult for the birds to walk or run in front of the hunting party and forces them to fly. The overhead cover should be light. Chukars are not as capable as pheasants of breaking out of overhead cover.

Even though the chukar partridge has more physical reserve than a bobwhite quail, little has been done to develop suitable holding cover for this species, and for good reason. Chukars do not survive long on a hunting preserve. They have a propensity to wander into open areas where they are prime targets for predators. They do have a strong inclination to drift back to the chukar holding pen if they can hear the calling of birds within the pen.

Gray (Hungarian) Partridge

Gray partridge are still a new gamebird on hunting preserves. The field behavior of gray partridge that can be produced in large numbers at a reasonable price is still an unknown entity.

Good quality, pen-reared gray partridge can be released in small coveys, much the same as quail. And, like quail, they require about the same type of release cover. Dense hayfields have proven to be ideal release sites, where the birds have difficulty moving about on foot. Otherwise, gray partridge will flush as singles or pairs instead of as a covey for the same reasons as bobwhite quail.

Not enough is known about appropriate holding cover for gray partridge. But, at Nilo, where the cover is primarily tailored for pheasants, gray partridge were found in the field by hunters a week or more after the last release. However, this was back in the 1960s, with experimental gray partridge reared from the eggs of good wild stock from England.

Wild Turkey

Currently, wild turkeys on preserves have been hunted as incidental gamebirds. They are usually released on an individual basis in everything from hedgerows to small woodlots. Long-term survival of unharvested birds is low, except for the occasional turkey. Pen-reared wild turkeys are capable of reverting to the wild; when they do, the chances of a hunting party with dog encountering one is slim to none. On the other hand, if you have some woodlots on your hunting preserve, you may have the start of a resident wild flock.

Sorghums

Sorghums are the main annual crop planted for the release of gamebirds on hunting preserves throughout the eastern two-thirds of the United States. However, sorghums do not do well in the southeastern part of the country unless insect damage is controlled. There are 4 reasons for the popularity of sorghums as release cover on hunting preserves: (1) they are hardy, drought-resistant plants; (2) most hunting preserves are not located on good farmland with fertile soils, and sorghums grow well on a variety of soils; (3) sorghums provide excellent release cover for most gamebirds, especially in late fall and winter; and (4) cultivation normally is not necessary.

The most commonly used sorghums are the hybrids or combine sorghums, which offer good protection (up to 30 or more inches above the ground) for gamebirds but aren't difficult to fly out of. Tall (open-pollinated or "forage") sorghums may grow to 8 or more feet in height, but after snow and ice has broken down this rank cover it makes good release cover, especially for pheasants. Some of the most popular tall sorghums are black amber cane, atlas sorgo, broomcorn, sudangrass, shatter cane, and sorghum almum.

All hunting preserves north of the Mason-

Tall or open-pollinated sorghums provide excellent pheasant release cover late in the hunting season after the weather has broken down the cover.

Dixon Line should have a variety of sorghums, especially combine and tall sorghums. The combine sorghums are ideal for early hunting, whereas tall sorghums are needed for late in the preserve season. Further, a variety of release coverts is more pleasing to the hunter's eye and is good insurance for some cover in dry growing seasons. Corn may be planted early in 40-inch rows in a release patch, and a mixture of tall sorghums broadcast between the rows after the first cultivation of the corn. With a little rain after broadcasting the sorghums, such release patches are excellent for the release of pheasants in late winter. The cornstalks both support the sorghum from going flat, and provide protection from wind damage to the release patch.

In deciding what varieties of sorghum to plant, contact both the U.S. Soil Conservation Service agent in your area and your county Agricultural Extension Specialist for advice. Make sure they understand that you are interested in good stands of game cover rather than maximizing grain production. Also, be sure that the sorghum seed they recommend is not repellent to birds. Seek out varieties that are high in starch and low in tannin. Sorghums can vary in protein from 8.3 to 13.1%; in starch, from 44.5 to 68.3%; and in tannins, from 0.4 to 3.7%.[11]

All sorghum seed should be treated with a fungicide. Good germination depends on a well-prepared seed bed and drilling versus broadcasting the seed. However, if you drill your sorghum patches in 7- or 14-inch rows, go back over the plot several times in a serpentine fashion with the drill to break up the row effect. Or, broadcast some tall sorghums in both ends of each plot for the last 10–20 feet.

The rate of planting is important. The McGraw Wildlife Foundation, Dundee, Illinois, plants at the rate of 12–15 pounds per acre. At Nilo, Brighton, Illinois, the rate is 20–25 pounds per acre. The reason for this high rate of planting as compared to commercial fields is to maximize the number of plant stalks and to lighten the heads of mature grain. If one carried the planting rate to extremes, the sorghum stand would be too weak to remain erect and the growth of the individual plants would be stunted. McGraw and Nilo both check the fertility of the soil on a regular basis and fertilize accordingly. At Nilo the application of liquid nitrogen has been essential for strong stalk growth.

Every preserve operator needs to experiment with different varieties of sorghums and rates of planting. Keep records of what you do and any changes that you make. And, last but not least, don't put all of your faith in 1 variety of combine sorghum. If you do, you are inviting disaster in an abnormal growing season.

The basic sorghum release patch should vary in size and direction, and be wide enough to keep from drifting full of snow. The length of individual patches can be controlled with a "brush hog" tractor mower. The McGraw Wildlife Foundation likes 40-foot clearings between release coverts.

Growing sorghums for effective release patches require different techniques and varieties in various regions. For instance, in Texas — where the climate is semi-arid — one may have to plant large fields of sorghum for pheasant and chukar hunting. The natural ground vegetation is too sparse to hold released birds. Row cropping of sorghum may be a necessity for moisture conservation, along with cultivation. One thought is to plant a suitable combine sorghum early and, on the last cultivation, broadcast a panicum grass, such as Kleingrass.

The Duck Creek Hunt Club, Spur, Texas, plants several large fields (30–40 acres) of hegari. When the hegari matures and if the stand is too dense and tall for hunting, cattle are permitted to forage on the crop until they open up the field.

Irrigation of sorghum fields may be necessary.[4] If so, large tracts of sorghum are necessary. They can be opened up with cattle and/or mowing. Or, a portion of the sorghum crop can be harvested and developed into a mourning dove hunting site by flattening the stalk residue with a "brush hog" tractor mower.

Shatter cane or sorghum almum have proven to be a good cover crops in south Texas. They are less susceptible to bird damage, and will volunteer a new crop the second year if the soil is disced early enough in the year to take advantage of late winter rains. In Illinois, the planting date for sorghum may be early June. In south Texas, it may be February.

Perennial Cover

Planting annual crops of vegetative cover is both costly and time consuming. Perennial cover may be slow to develop, but it should be an essential part of cover management on a hunting preserve.

Dr. George Burger[2] summarized an excellent article on perennial and native cover on hunting preserves: "While perennial cover should be used along with annuals for a variety of cover and food, and not considered as replacing all annual crops, they do have certain great advantages over annual plantings. They save the preserve operator time and money each year; are not seriously affected by weather changes that can ruin annual crops; can withstand trampling by hunters and weathering better than most annuals; and add variety to the sought-after 'natural' look to a preserve."

119

Pine Trees

Clumps of pine trees can be the salvation of hunting on a preserve when the ground is covered with a foot or more of snow, especially for releasing and holding pheasants. The clumps should be big enough not to drift full of snow, yet small enough to be hunted successfully by a party of 4 hunters.[5]

It takes a number of years (7 – 10) before pine trees become important holding cover, when they are planted as seedlings. As the seedlings mature into small trees, they should be thinned. Some preserve operators sell thinned pines as Christmas trees. If you are interested in the Christmas tree business, contact your State Forester and obtain information on the proper species to plant, the time and method of pruning, and a source of seedlings. A little time with the pruning shears in the spring will increase the quality and marketability of the trees.

The operator should watch the height of his pine trees. Since the most important holding cover for pheasants is up to 30 inches above ground, pine trees, unless wanted for scenic reasons, should be topped out when they reach the height of about 8 feet. The trees can be cut about 30 inches above ground, leaving the lower 2 or 3 whorls of limbs. These limbs will continue to grow and provide cover. In time, one of the limbs will form another tree. Check with your State Forester on the advisability of using this technique in your geographical location.

At the McGraw Wildlife Foundation, where they pioneered the management of pine trees to provide holding cover for pheasants, they either top the pine tree by cutting the leader or cut the trunk of the tree part way, just enough to bend the tree to the ground — a living brushpile.[9] With larger pine trees, the lower whorls of branches are cut half-through and bent to the ground.[1] The middle whorls of limbs are removed for hunter visibility and to permit the penetration of sunlight necessary for better ground cover.[10]

Shrubs and Brush Piles

Clumps of natural or planted shrubs on a hunting area are extremely valuable in late fall and winter as holding cover. Or you can plant a row of shrubs to divide large hunting areas. If snow is a problem, you will have to increase the width of the row accordingly, with additional plantings. Some of the shrub plantings used on hunting preserves are autumn olive, spreading junipers (Pfitzer, Andorra), arbor vitae, bush honeysuckle, wild plum, hawthorn, and caragana.[6, 7] It depends on the suitability of a given shrub for your area, availability, and price.

Brush piles have popular appeal and are useful to rabbits in late fall and winter. Some

A clump of pine trees provides excellent holding cover for all gamebirds.

preserve operators will use small brush piles for stocking pheasants, especially when snowfall has obliterated all other vegetative cover.[8] On the other hand, large brush piles can be a nuisance. Neither man nor dog can retrieve crippled birds that escape into the depth of the brush pile. Bobwhite quail may be difficult, if not impossible, to flush from a brush pile. It is for this very reason that most southern quail preserves do not allow any brush piles on their hunting areas.

Native Grasses and Hayfields

Arrowhead Hunting and Conservation Club, Goose Lake, Iowa, has made tremendous use of native prairie grasses on their hunting preserve. Besides providing excellent late winter cover for releasing and holding gamebirds and adding to the scenic beauty of the preserve, Arrowhead attracts many visitors as a prairie-grass demonstration area.[7, 8, 10] The use of native grasses (warm-season grasses) holds potential as perennial release cover for all gamebirds, and should be considered by preserve managers in the prairie grass region of the United States.[13]

Hayfields next to sorghum patches make good release cover; however, the hay should be mowed at the first signs of invasion by brush. Mowing should be early in the growing season so the grass has sufficient time to grow a second crop prior to the hunting season. Some of the grasses that provide good hayfields for stocking gamebirds on a hunting preserve are brome, orchard grass, timothy, and fescue. Again, depending on the geographical location of the preserve, one wants to seek the most adaptable grass for his area, and may want to consider a mixture of 2 or more grasses.

Succession

Succession is defined as the natural replacement of 1 type of vegetative cover by another. For instance, hayfields left unattended will be invaded by brush and eventually by trees in many regions of the United States. Hence, perennial vegetative cover requires husbandry. Succession of plant cover can be set back by grazing with livestock, cutting or mowing the vegetation, and/or plowing the ground. Without such treatment, ideal perennial cover for either releasing or holding gamebirds on a hunting preserve can become of little value in a few years.

Fire may also have to be used, especially for native grasses. One of the problems on southern preserves is that the ideal time to burn the ground cover coincides with the hunting season. However, if southern operators don't burn the ground cover, there will be an invasion of hardwood saplings and pine tree seedlings plus the nemesis of southern hunting — briars. The answer on southern hunting preserves may be to only burn half of their hunting areas in a given year. In the Midwest, a hot burn may result in an invasion of blackberry briars. If you decide to use fire to control succession, seek professional advice on the time of year and the proper atmospheric conditions — wind, humidity, and ground moisture — for the ground cover you want to burn.

A good discussion on plant succession and making use of natural cover on hunting preserves was written by Dr. George Burger.[1] He recommended the following 4 steps:

1. Find out what native plants you can expect to appear on your land by getting a general picture of local succession stages.

2. Decide *which stage* will give the cover needed, and *where* it is needed.

3. Work forward (by fallowing) or backward (by burning, cutting, plowing, or disking) through the successional stages to reach the desired natural cover.

4. Plan a long-range rotation program of annual crop plantings and natural cover.

References

1. Burger, G. V. 1960. Making use of natural cover on shooting preserves. Modern Game Breeding 30(2):12-15. (Reprints available at Max McGraw Wildlife Foundation, P.O. Box 9, Dundee, IL.)
2. _____. 1961. Perennial and native cover for shooting preserves. Game Breeders Gazette, 1328 Allen Park Dr., Salt Lake City, UT. (Reprints available at Max McGraw Wildlife Foundation, P.O. Box 9, Dundee, IL.)

3. Lehmann, V. 1984. Bobwhites in the Rio Grande Plain of Texas. Texas A&M Univ. Press, College Station, TX. 371pp.

4. Mullin, J. 1973. Preserve hunting in the desert. Wildlife Harvest 4(11):14-15. Goose Lake, IA.

5. _____. 1973. Better cover from pines. Wildlife Harvest 4(11):28-29. Goose Lake, IA.

6. _____. 1977. Game bird cover. Wildlife Harvest 8(6):44-45. Goose Lake, IA.

7. _____. 1977. Cover for preserves. Wildlife Harvest 8(11):6-8. Goose Lake, IA.

8. _____. 1978. Winter cover. Wildlife Harvest 9(2):16-18. Goose Lake, IA.

9. _____. 1978. Living brushpiles. Wildlife Harvest 9(11):35. Goose Lake, IA.

10. _____. 1979. Pruning shrubs. Wildlife Harvest 10(5):26-27. Goose Lake, IA.

11. _____. 1981. Milo varieties. Wildlife Harvest 12(7):33. Goose Lake, IA.

12. _____. 1983. Holding cover for hunting resorts. Wildlife Harvest 14(5)8-9. Goose Lake, IA.

13. Toney, T. 1979. Native grasses for wildlife. Wildlife Harvest 10(6):38-42. Goose Lake, IA.

Chapter 15

HUNTING GUIDES AND DOGS

Good hunting guides and dogs represent 50% or more of a quality hunt. Too often, their importance is underrated by preserve operators. Guide and dog must be a smooth team, and their sole objective is to provide a hunting party with an enjoyable, successful, and memorable hunt.

Hunting Guides

A good guide can make or break the day for a hunting party. When you hire a guide, look for a man with whom you would trust your business — because that is exactly what you are doing. He is the director of your field show, and the fortune of your hunting preserve rides on the quality of his performance.

Some hunting preserves are fortunate to be able to retain guides on a full-time basis. During the non-hunting season, they perform other duties from dog training to rearing gamebirds. Such employees lend continuity to a staff. Other hunting preserves hire part-time employees on an ''as needed'' basis. They also can and do per-

form very well for a preserve operator, if selected with care and instructed on how to manage a hunting party in the field.

For starters, the guide should be dressed as a hunter, and not as a farm hand. He should be courteous, well-groomed, and in good physical condition. He should have a positive mental attitude towards the prospects of the hunt and have all of the tools of the dog-handling trade — whistle, leash, and flushing whip. His clothes should be appropriate for the weather conditions. The hunting vehicle should be clean, litter-free, and have comfortable quarters for the hunting dogs, with an ample supply of water and drinking bowls, and sufficient room for transporting hunters and their shotguns.

The preserve operator should introduce the hunting party to their guide. If the preserve operator has not given any instructions on hunting safety, the guide should do so prior to the hunt. The guide also checks to make sure that the hunters have the proper ammunition for the hunt and, if needed, reviews the safety features on a

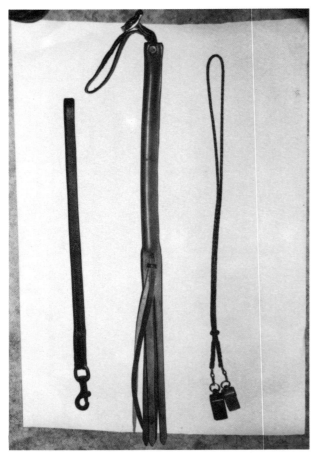

Necessary tools of the trade for each guide — leash, whistle, and flushing whip.

shotgun. It is advisable for the guide to carry extra shotshells of the right gauges and a spare shotgun.[2]

The ideal guide is also an expert shooter who can give gun-handling tips to the hunters when — and *only* when — they ask. He should praise a good shot, *and* have a stock of excuses for a missed bird — strange gun, poor light, long range, difficult angle, bird in the sun, etc. — and have the good judgment when to use such excuses and when to remain silent.

The guide should *never* divulge preserve management techniques. Guests hesitate to discuss management with the operator, but they will ask the guide. The most common question is, ''When were the birds released?'' Such prying questions deserve either no response or an evasive answer.

The guide should structure the hunt so as to have the dogs working into the wind. Wind in the

dog's face helps the dogs to scent birds and work a closer pattern.

The guide positions the hunters on either side of him. Left-handed shooters should be on the right of the guide. If the guide feels uneasy about the gun handling ability of a guest, he should position the hunter next to him. Good guides can quickly judge the gun handling ability of each guest. Careless shooters should be watched closely and, if necessary, cautioned about any breach of shotgun etiquette. The first such caution can be the ''silent treatment'' — pushing the safety on or lifting the shotgun barrel to the proper angle. A verbal reprimand can be a source of great embarrassment to a member of a hunting party and should be reserved for repeat offenders.

If a bird flushes, and the guide is in the line of fire, the guide should drop out of the way. It's the safe thing to do and it's appreciated. He can explain that it is a breach of club rules for him to remain standing and block a shot.

The guide should never kick at or flush a gamebird with the end of his toe; it just isn't done on a quality hunting preserve, regardless of the circumstances. He should use a flushing whip.

The guide's personal problems should be left at home or at the clubhouse. The amount of conversation depends on the personality of the hunting party. Some hunting parties like to exchange small talk, jokes, and personal experiences. Other groups may be quiet. The guide must judge the temperament of each hunting party, with the help of the preserve operator, and act accordingly.

All commands to the hunting dog should be given in a low voice with a minimum use of the whistle. Under no circumstances should a dog be

A guide hunting chukars, with his springer spaniel and 2 hunters.

punished or subjected to abusive language while guests look on. The training and discipline of hunting dogs should be confined to those times when guests are not scheduled.

The welfare of the hunting dog(s) should be uppermost in the guide's mind. If it is a hot day, the guide should stop the hunt and provide the dog(s) with water. If a dog is tired, it should be kenneled in the hunting vehicle and allowed to rest while another dog is used.

Likewise, it is important to watch for physical fatigue in the hunting guests. One can always stop the hunt to water or rest the dog. Don't let an enjoyable hunt turn into a physical endurance contest. The pace of the hunt should be geared to the physical limitations of the hunters.

The guide can set a good example by not being too proud to pick up such litter as shotshell cases, books of matches, and/or cigarette butts. Litter doesn't belong in the clean landscape of good game range.

Guides should not carry a shotgun unless requested to do so by a hunting party. Hunters did not pay for a shooting exhibition. The birds are theirs to hit or miss. Besides, the guide should be giving his full attention to the behavior of the hunting dog and the safe handling of shotguns by the hunters.

As a bit of showmanship with good pointing dogs, it may be advisable, especially with plantation-style hunting, to hunt with 2 dogs. There are few things that will raise the blood pressure of a hunter more than watching a dog on point with the second dog honoring.

"Pres" Mann, Hunters Creek Club, Michigan, insists that all of his guides are hunters themselves and enjoy the handling of bird dogs. There are many good reasons for Mann's requirements. It doesn't take many questions for a hunter to evaluate another hunter. Also, a guide who is a hunter understands the gung ho hunting party that wants to pursue a missed bird, work difficult cover, or just talk about hunting. In the final analysis, the guide and his hunting party are enjoying one of our great American traditions together, and companionship between the guide and the hunters can blossom into a lifelong friendship.

All retrieved crippled birds should be dispatched as quickly as possible and without fanfare. Dead gamebirds should be treated with respect by the guide. Above all, he should not throw the birds into a pile or carry too many in a hunting jacket. Take time to return to the hunting vehicle and handle the gamebirds with an appropriate degree of reverence.

At the end of the hunt the guide should accompany the hunting party back to the clubhouse and provide them with an official tally of the hunt. If he is invited to join the hunting party for a meal and/or refreshments and has the spare time, he should do so; but only after he has kenneled the hunting dogs and initiated the processing of any gamebirds bagged by the hunting party.

Some successful hunting preserves hold seminars on guiding for their employees each year. One hunting preserve supplies their guides with a manual of instructions.

Guides on an "as needed" basis usually have their own bird dogs or retrievers; however, all guides and dogs should be checked for competence by the preserve operator. If necessary, the preserve operator may hold training sessions for both dogs and guides.

All compliments and complaints by a hunting party should be discussed by the preserve operator with the guide after the departure of the hunting party. At times there are personality differences that will clash — 1 hunting party will thoroughly enjoy a given guide and his dog, whereas the next party will not. The good preserve operator tries to match the personality of the hunting party with a given guide.

Hunting Dogs

Good dog handlers make good hunting-preserve operators. The difference between poor- and high-quality hunting dogs on a hunting preserve is just as striking to a hunting guest as the difference between poor- and high-quality gamebirds. It takes a professional approach to train hunting dogs for preserve use. Hence, it is no surprise that more than two-thirds of the successful preserves I visited were managed by men who trained and handled hunting dogs for a livelihood at some time in their careers.

Breed Selection

There is no such animal as an all-around hunting dog. Every breed has its specialty.

Since successful hunting preserves sell a certain amount of "atmosphere," one should feature the dog breeds that are traditional in a given geographic area for hunting a given gamebird. For instance, in the South, English pointers and setters are the traditional bobwhite quail dogs. If you are operating a preserve with plantation-style hunting for bobwhite and hunting from vehicles, wide-ranging English pointers and setters are a natural choice. On the other hand, if you are operating a hunting preserve north of the Mason-Dixon Line, with smaller hunting areas and heavier cover, you either have to train your English pointers and setters to hunt closer to the guns or use closer-ranging dogs, such as Brittany spaniels or German shorthaired pointers.[1]

Basically, there are 3 groups of hunting dogs used on hunting preserves — pointers, flushers, and retrievers.

Pointing dogs are a must for bobwhite quail and gray partridge. Both of these gamebirds hold well for pointing dogs. The most common pointing breeds on hunting preserves are English setters and pointers, German shorthaired pointers, and Brittany spaniels.

English setters and pointers are wide-ranging dogs, and they are a pleasure to watch but, unless they are broken to work within shotgun range, they can be a problem. It is distracting to guests to hear a handler constantly "hacking" a dog by whistle and voice commands — trying to keep the dog close-in while the dog's breeding dictates wide ranging.

The German shorthaired pointer and Brittany spaniel are close-working pointers that seem to fill the needs of a hunting preserve better than English pointers or setters, except on plantation-style hunting preserves. A hunting preserve in Iowa features vizslas for pheasant hunting. This Hungarian import is cautious by nature and works both body and foot scent of gamebirds. Ron DeBruin, Oakview Hunting Club and Kennel, Iowa, believes vizslas have great potential on hunting preserves for ring-necked pheasants.

The pointing-dog breeds should be trained to find and hold birds. They must be staunch on point and steady to wing and shot, seemingly oblivious to flushing birds and to shotgun shooting. These traits in a dog are especially important if bobwhite quail or gray partridge are flushing as singles or pairs, rather than as coveys. All pointers should be force-broken to retrieve all downed game on command and to hunt for cripples or dead birds.

Flushing dogs are exemplified by the English springer spaniel. They work in front of the guns, seeking out and flushing gamebirds. They make excellent dogs for chukars and pheasants.[3] Springers must be broken to respond to both whistle and hand commands and to be steady to wing and shot. Retrievers — Labradors, Goldens, and Chesapeakes — can easily be trained to flush pheasants and chukars and have the stamina to "bust" through heavy cover early in the hunting season.

The most popular retriever on hunting preserves is the Labrador. It is an amiable breed, rather easy to train, and hard working. The lab's specialty is to deliver dead and crippled birds to the handler, but they also make excellent close-ranging, flushing dogs for pheasants and/or chukar hunting. Retrievers are bred to retrieve waterfowl under all conditions. Their usual role is to walk or sit quietly by the hunter's side, mark fallen birds, and to retrieve them on command. They should be trained to obey whistle and hand signals in retrieving birds they did not see fall. This is called a "blind" retrieve, and it is an impressive and useful piece of dog work.

One of the problems with hunting dogs and pen-reared gamebirds is a tendency for some dogs to catch rather than flush or point gamebirds in the field, and they soon become quite proficient in this act. The judicious use of an electric collar may be the best cure. Also, before placing all of the blame on the dog for such behavior, one should check the quality of the pen-reared gamebirds, the type of cover into which the birds were released, the amount of "disorientation" applied to released birds, the period of time between the release of the birds and the hunt, and the time of the year. For example, in the spring of the year, hen pheasants are heavy with developing eggs and are more prone to remain "hidden" than to take wing when approached by a hunting party.

How to Start a Kennel

Once the decision is made as to the breed of dogs for your hunting preserve, the best approach is to seek out the best bloodlines that you can find. As Falk[5] says, "The criteria normally involved in deciding are reliability and integrity of the supplier, specific bloodlines desired, availability, and price." Make sure that the supplier specializes in hunting dogs and not in bench show stock. Be prepared to pay the price for good dogs. Remember that it costs as much to feed a "palooka" as it does a good hunting dog. Only invest your money in registered dogs. Registered dogs assure you of the lineage of the dog, and you can command a higher price for the offspring. About 6 mature and trained dogs should be the minimum number for a new hunting preserve.

The mature dog should be broken to your requirements and ready for field work. By all means, do not buy a dog shown at the end of the chain, or in a kennel run. Insist on a field demonstration with gamebirds. A good dog trainer can work wonders with a dog, but there are 2 things over which he has no control — the desire of the dog to hunt and the quality of his nose. Both traits come through inheritance.

Hunting dogs are advertised in the principal hunting and fishing magazines, *Wildlife Harvest*, and dog periodicals (Appendix A). You can also make contacts for reliable dog suppliers through other hunting preserve operators.

A number of successful hunting preserves either started or became commercial hunting-dog kennels. Dogs do age and replacements must be found. What better source than your own kennel? Surplus dogs can be sold, and operating a boarding and training kennel is a natural source of supplemental income to your preserve operation.

"Pres" Mann, Hunters Creek Club, Michigan, sells surplus hunting-dog puppies to his members. He doesn't hide a new litter of pups; on nice days shortly after weaning, he places the pups within a small wire enclosure near the clubhouse in full view of the dining room. While the hunting guests are taking a luncheon break, "Pres" will release the pups from the enclosure and play with them by using a bird wing on the end of a 5 — 6-foot string, which, in turn, is tied to the end of a long bamboo pole. Naturally, his members are attracted to the sideshow. Not only will "Pres" sell the puppies, but he will probably gross several thousand dollars worth of income for each pup for boarding and training fees. Further, as the pup matures, he will use the dog on his hunting preserve as part of the training routine. "Pres" thus proves that one can have his cake and eat it too.

Training

It is beyond the scope of this book to delve into training hunting dogs. There are a number of good books on the market (Appendix A). One of the most enjoyable books is Bill Tarrant's *The Best Way To Train Your Gun Dog — The Delmar Smith Method.*[7] Once in a blue moon one finds a unique combination — a colorful and gifted dog handler working with a gifted writer — which produces a classic "how-to" book. Bill Tarrant's book is such a classic. It is very enjoyable reading, easy to understand, and loaded with common (dog) sense — a good dog trainer thinks like a dog to train like a pro. The basis of Smith's dog training technique is "point of contact, repetition, and association."

The book also has excellent information on the physical characteristics of good hunting dogs as well as kennel and doghouse construction and the feeding and care of hunting dogs. Whether or not all aspiring dog trainers can achieve success with the Delmar Smith Method remains to be seen. If not, there are other books and training methods.

Another good dog training book is *Hunting Dog Know-How*, by David M. Duffey.[4] Dave Duffey has operated both a commercial dog kennel and a hunting preserve and has written feature columns on dog training for outdoor magazines. The book is well written. Duffey has taken many time-honored, dog-training techniques and made them understandable for the novice trainer. He also has some sage observations on hunting dogs and handlers. Duffey says, "At one time or another many dog owners will have to face up to the question of whether a dog is worth spending more time and money to develop. . . . Just as not every dog is a good dog, neither is every man a good trainer. There are humans who have a sixth sense when it comes to handling animals. They seldom have problem dogs, while another man never has a good one."

Every dog does not respond the same to a given training technique. Dogs are individuals, just as people are. What works for 1 dog may not work for another. Therefore, dog training is more of an art than a science.

Another book that should be in your library is John Falk's *The Complete Guide to Bird Dog Training.*[5] John Falk is a professional writer, but his avocation is training bird dogs. As he says, "No single book on bird dogs and the various methods of training can say it all. But where one book may lack sufficient detail on some aspects [of training], another one may shine."

Appendix A provides sources of dog training equipment, breed periodicals, dog registries, kennel supplies, and sources of information on the care and feeding of dogs.

Dog Kennels

The importance of good dog kennels comes second only to a good clubhouse on successful hunting preserves. A number of years ago, the trend was to combine a game farm with a hunting preserve, but the trend is now changing to a combination of a commercial kennel and a hunting preserve. It's a natural "marriage." Both a commercial dog kennel and a hunting preserve are forms of the outdoor recreation business. One can buy good-quality gamebirds for a hunting preserve, but the quality of the hunting dog is the sole responsibility of the hunting preserve

An attractive, durable, and efficient dog kennel at Nilo.

operator. Very few men have the ability and the time to master: (1) hunting preserve management, (2) the training of hunting dogs, and (3) the rearing of quality gamebirds. One of the three is going to suffer from lack of attention and, more often than not, it does.

Dog kennels come in every size and description — from heated kennels to strictly outdoor living, with adequate doghouses for the climate. But the better kennels have a number of things in common.

Chain-link fencing is standard. Cement floors with a broom finish throughout the kennel are necessary for cleaning purposes. Cement floors should be designed with a good drainage (1 inch to a linear foot). The drainage should lead to a trough on the outside of the chain-link fence. The trough should be wide enough to accommodate a square-nosed shovel and deep enough to prevent overflow. A good septic tank with adequate tile fields is essential. The other recourse is a sewage lagoon. Check local ordinances on sewage disposal.

The individual dog runs may vary from 4 to 6 feet in width, 15 to 24 feet in length, and a minimum of 6 feet in height. If you cannot arrange for compatible dogs in adjoining kennel runs, you may have to attach sheet metal to the fence separating the 2 kennel runs. If you have hunting dogs that are fence climbers, you may have to install a wire roof on the kennel run.

A clean, effective, and pleasant kennel, Elkhorn Lake Shooting Park, Bucyrus, Ohio.

Doghouses come in various sizes and descriptions. The design of doghouses depends on the climate where the hunting preserve is located. Basically, in a cold climate they should be waterproof and draft free. The draft-free area within the doghouse is achieved with an interior baffle or tunnel for the entrance. A baffle is usually a plywood board that extends from the floor to the

129

roof, for about three-fourths of the length of the doghouse. Tarrant[7] recommends that a tunnel entrance be 11 inches wide, 18 inches long, and 18 inches high. The exact size of the tunnel will vary somewhat with the size of the dog.

Good bedding, such as cedar shavings, or marsh or prairie hay, is essential in cold weather. The doghouse should be elevated for ease of cleaning, exercise for the dog, and to avoid dampness seeping into the bedding. The other alternative is to provide an elevated box inside a heated kennel.

You will need to build a storage area for feed, a whelping area, and a working room to mix feed, and to administer and store medicine. A source of hot water is essential for cleaning feeding bowls and water buckets. Some kennels have installed self-feeders, but there are no fool-proof automatic watering devices for outdoor kennels in areas with extended periods of below-freezing weather.

If your kennels are in the open, shade is important. A number of southern kennels are open to the weather on all 4 sides, but have an elevated metal or fiberglass roof that provides shade, and a dry working area through the center of the kennel.

A southern kennel with artificial shade, Quailridge, Norman Park, Georgia.

The whole kennel area should be surrounded by a security fence at least 6 feet in height. Such a fence keeps stray dogs away and provides a yard for training and exercising dogs.

It is difficult to make solid recommendations for dog kennels on any given hunting preserve. Each geographical area and preserve operator will have different requirements for satisfactory kennels. But, if you have quality hunting dogs, you will find it almost impossible not to be selling, boarding, and training hunting dogs to supplement your income. Hence, when you draw up your plans for dog kennels, ask yourself whether you are as proud of your kennel facilities as you are of your clubhouse. If so, you are on target; if not, go back to the drawing board.

Feeding and Care of Dogs

Again, the best guidelines the author has seen in print on the feeding and care of hunting dogs are in Bill Tarrant's *Best Way to Train Your Gun Dog — The Delmar Smith Method*.[7] It has the basics, but there are a few additional thoughts on the subject that have appeared in the literature or from my interviews of preserve operators.

Mullin[6] discusses keeping your hunting dogs from becoming victims of heat stroke. Dogs dissipate body heat by panting, and through the pads of their feet. Hence, it is important for a dog to have good air circulation because when a dog pants it heats the air it rebreathes.

Dogs should not be confined in a sunny or unventilated area. Dog crates can be death traps if the dog is confined in a crate in the hot sun without air circulation.

Many hunting preserves install small ponds to entrap surface runoff on their hunting courses. Such areas provide a spot for the dog to cool-off and get a drink of water. Other preserves, especially in the South, will have 30- or 50-gallon drums cut in half lengthwise and buried in the ground to the lip of the drum to provide water for hunting dogs.

The other alternative is to carry an abundance of water on the hunting vehicle and give the dog a frequent drink. When the dog is finished drinking, roll the dog over and pour the remainder of the water in the drinking bowl over the dog's chest and stomach. When a dog becomes overheated, his hunting efficiency drops.

The other extreme, cold weather, also requires special consideration for hunting dogs. Rudy Wendt, McGraw Wildlife Foundation, Illinois, is a firm believer that the hunting dog must have a warm place to sleep. Otherwise, the dog will not have sufficient energy to hunt every day. His dogs have a heated sleeping area and swinging doors to an outside run. He also feeds his dogs 30% protein with a minimum of 16% fat during the winter months.

Dogs soaked with snow and icy water should be towelled and brushed dry before outdoor kenneling.[6]

The feet of dogs require special attention in crusty snow and/or in icy weather. Check the tracks of your hunting dog. If one or more of the pads are cut, you will note blood spots.

Establish a working relationship with a good dog veterinarian. Dogs should be checked for worms at least twice a year. Heartworms in dogs have become a universal problem. One or more of the new prophylactic drugs for heartworm only require treatment on a monthly basis; ask your veterinarian. Dogs have to be treated with a preventive vaccine for distemper, parvovirus, rabies, and hepatitis on a routine basis. A good veterinarian will help you to remember. Dogs should also be checked for external parasites, such as ear mites, fleas, and ticks. On a daily basis, dogs should be checked for lameness, cuts, and sores.

Kennels have to be disinfected on a regular basis. In warm months the kennels should be washed down twice a day. Few things are more repulsive than a dirty kennel. If the kennel is constructed for ease of cleaning, the chore is neither time consuming nor menial.

Summary

A good hunting dog is a valuable asset, and will cost the hunting preserve operator between $400 and $500 a year to maintain without any allowance for kennel depreciation. A good dog will bring back more repeat customers, when handled by a good guide, than will all of your genial hospitality and stories at the clubhouse. He will also help to maintain a high rate of recovery on released gamebirds. Directly and indirectly, a good hunting dog is an indispensable money maker on a hunting preserve, and every precaution should be taken to safeguard it.

Cader Cox, Riverview Plantation, Camilla, Georgia, pointing out the water spigot on a hunting vehicle. Note the high seat for the hunters, the dog crates, and shotgun boxes on the side of the crates.

References

1. Bachman, A. R. 1971. Bird dog handling. Game Bird Bull. 4(5):163,165-166. RD2, Hegins, PA.
2. Correll, T. 1978. Suggestions for guiding the hunt. Game Bird Bull. 11(6):3. RD 2, Hegins, PA.
3. Crawford, T. 1978. English springer spaniels at Hillendale game farm. Game Bird Bull. 11(6):1,14. RD2, Hegins, PA.
4. Duffey, D. M. 1983. Hunting dog know-how. (Rev.) Winchester Press, 220 Old New Brunswick Rd., Piscataway, NJ.
5. Falk, J. R. 1986. The complete guide to bird dog training. (Rev.) Winchester Press, 220 Old New Brunswick Rd., Piscataway, NJ.
6. Mullin, J. 1979. Winter dog care. Wildlife Harvest 10(1):43-44. Goose Lake, IA.
7. Tarrant, B. 1977. Best way to train your gun dog — the Delmar Smith method. David McKay Co., Inc., New York, NY. 186pp.

APPENDIX A

Information on the Care and Training of Dogs

This list of suggested reading on training, care, and feeding of dogs, dog periodicals, breed registries, and equipment is not complete; however, it will help a preserve operator with the basics of operating a dog kennel. (But, no endorsement of any product, distributor of supplies and equipment, or publication is implied.)

Publications on Training

Duffey, D. M. 1983. *Hunting dog know-how.* (Rev.) Winchester Press, 220 Old New Brunswick Rd., Piscataway. NJ 08854.

Falk, J. R. 1986. *The complete guide to bird dog training.* (Rev.) Winchester Press, 220 Old New Brunswick Rd., Piscataway, NJ 08854.

Tarrant, B. 1977. *Best way to train your dog — The Delmar Smith Method.* David McKay Co., Inc., New York. NY.

Wolters, R. A. 1964. *Water dog.* E. P. Dutton, New York, NY.

Care and Feeding of Dogs

Allied Mills
Wayne Dog Food
110 Wacker Drive
Chicago, IL 60606

Borden Chemical Co.
Pet Products
Box 419
Norfolk, VA 23501

Ralston Purina Co.
Checkerboard Square
St. Louis, MO 63199

Carnation Co.
Friskie's Pet Food Div.
Carnation Bldg.
5045 Wilshire Blvd.
Los Angeles, CA 90036

Gaines Dog Research Center
250 North St.
White Plains, NY 10605

Dog Periodicals

The American Brittany, 4124 Birchman, Fort Worth, TX 76107.

The American Field, 222 W. Adams St., Chicago, IL 60606.

The German Shorthaired Pointer, Box 395, Saint Paris, OH 43072.

Hunting Dog, 215 S. Washington St., Greenfield, OH 45123.

Retriever Field Trial News, 1836 E. Saint Francis Ave., Milwaukee, WI 53207.

Gun Dog, P.O. Box 343, Mount Morris, IL 61054.

Breed Registries

American Kennel Club, 51 Madison Ave., New York, NY 10038. (Registers all purebred dogs.)

The Field Dog Stud Book, American Field Publishing Co., 222 W. Adams St., Chicago, IL 60606. Registers all purebred dogs, but specializes in the pointing breeds.

Equipment

Bill Boatman and Co., 220 Maple St., Bainbridge, OH 45612. (Training equipment.)

Bob Long Kennel Runs, Route 3 North, Gambrills, MD 21054. (Kennel fencing.)

Brinkman Mfg. and Fence Co., Route 8, Huntoon & Auburn Rd., Topeka, KS 66615. (Kennel fencing.)

Canine Pal Sales Co., 421 E. 39th Ave., Gary, IN 46409. (Doghouses.)

Canvasback Dog Training Equipment, Box 3556, Postal Station B, Winnipeg, Manitoba, Canada R3H OW9. (Training equipment.)

Dogaloo Co., 6817 North 22nd Place, Phoenix, AZ 85016. (Doghouses.)

Dunn's Supply Store, Grand Junction, TN 38039. (Training equipment.)

Hallmark Supplies, Main St., Menomonee Falls, WI 53051. (Training equipment.)

Hulme Sporting Goods and Mfg. Co., Box 670, Paris, TN 38242. (Training equipment.)

K. D. Kennel Products, 1741 N. Broadway, Wichita, KS 67214. (Dog crates.)

Kennel-Aire Mfg. Co., 725 N. Snelling Ave., St. Paul, MN 55104. (Dog crates.)

Mason Fence Co., Box 711B, Leesburg, OH 45135. (Kennel fencing.)

Sporting Dog Specialities, Inc., Box 68, Spencerport, NY 14559. (Training equipment.)

Chapter 16

PREDATORS,
NUISANCE ANIMALS,
AND PESTS

In the book entitled, *Practical Game-Preserving*,[2] written in 1906 by William Carnegie, an Englishman, more than 100 of 400 pages are devoted to ground-dwelling and winged predators. Obviously, the problems of predation, nuisance animals, and pests have confronted gamekeepers and preserve operators throughout the years.

Predators, nuisance animals, and pests are a fact of life in managing a hunting preserve, and a preserve operator has to be constantly aware of both potential and ongoing problems. He must know when and how to take action, and be able to employ control techniques that are reasonable, selective, and humane.

A predator is an animal that lives by preying on other animals, or any critter that beats you to one that you want yourself. Predators are important to an ecosystem, and a few can even be tolerated on a hunting preserve. They help clean up the landscape of weak or crippled gamebirds.

On the other hand, a sudden influx of predators can pose a real problem to all gamebirds on your preserve, including penned birds. When it happens, you must be in position to alleviate the problem as quickly as possible.

Nuisance animals are feral cats and dogs, muskrats, starlings, and English sparrows. Pests are considered to be animals detrimental to man — rats and mice.

Laws and Regulations

In recent years, most birds have been protected by state and federal laws. The current exceptions are starlings, house sparrows, and common pigeons (rock doves). All wild mammals are protected by state law with the exception of rats and mice. However, these regulations recognize that various species of wildlife may require control in some circumstances, and the law provides for the alleviation of damages by the appeal process to state and federal wildlife agencies. But control *cannot* be instigated by the person sustaining the damage until he contacts the agency and receives authorization,[4] and therein lies a problem. How does one obtain speedy authorization when a predator problem arises?

The only recourse that an operator has is to maintain a close working relationship with the state wildlife agency, which, in turn, is in the best position to help with federal clearance if necessary. The preserve operator needs to know how to expedite the approval of control techniques *prior* to a need.

Currently, poisons may not be legally used to control predatory mammals, birds, or reptiles. However, they *can* be used to control rats and mice.

Predators

It is essential that the preserve operator acquire some basic knowledge of predator control. He must be able to identify the animals causing losses or damage, and take appropriate measures to relieve the problem. Or, perhaps he can call on the expertise of some local trapper. In a sense, a hunting preserve is a banquet table set almost daily for various predators that not only kill gamebirds but, through harassment, can be a contributing factor in gamebirds leaving a hunting area.

My experience at Nilo indicates that one need only control specific, individual predators or respond to a sudden influx of predators. The numbers and types of predators will vary with the time of the year, the availability of other prey, and the weather. One winter at Nilo, 14 red foxes were trapped in about 4 weeks near our mallard holding pen. They were both killing and harassing the ducks returning to the pen in the evening. However, there was no necessity to conduct an ongoing predator-control program after the problem was alleviated; the returns would not have justified the expenditure of the time and effort involved.

One should acquire the necessary equipment to control predators within his area before the opening of the hunting preserve season. It is not always possible to obtain traps, scents, and baits on short notice. Some suppliers of trapping

material can be reached only by mail; the wait can be expensive.

Your equipment should include steel and live traps of the proper size and type for predators in your geographical area, necessary baits and scents, and a trapping manual or book, such as Chansler's, *Successful Trapping Methods.*[3] Good advice on proper equipment and methods can be obtained from the animal damage control personnel within your state wildlife agency.

Mammals

Within this group are mink, weasels, foxes, coyotes, raccoons, opossums, and skunks. Weasels and mink are very neat killers and do deadly work in a bird pen. They bite birds through the skull, the back of the neck, or under the wing. They apparently kill for the joy of killing and have a tendency to stack their victims in a neat pile. "Hot" wires on the sides of holding pens will all but eliminate weasels and mink. One winter at Nilo we lost about 40 pheasants to a male mink before he electrocuted himself on one of the hot wires. He had found a hole not more than 3 inches in diameter where the 1-inch wire was hog-ringed to the 2-inch poultry netting.

Foxes and coyotes seldom invade a properly constructed holding pen for gamebirds. They will, however, patrol your hunting areas and kill or harass gamebirds. They usually carry off their victim. One should look for tracks and scats of these animals as an indicator to their abundance.

Steel traps are essential in the control of coyotes and foxes. Seldom will they enter a live trap. However, to prevent unnecessary damage to the legs of non-target species, one should use traps with offset jaws and/or a new trap on the market, "Soft-catch," manufactured by Woodstream Corporation, Lititz, Pennsylvania. Both bait and dirt-hole sets are effective, but such sets will also attract dogs. They should be checked at least twice daily. A non-target animal can be released by using either an old coat or a "hog-catcher," a steel wire noose at the end of a hollow steel pole. In either case, it is advisable to have someone to help you.

Raccoons, opossums, and skunks are seldom a serious threat to adult gamebirds on a hunting preserve, but they can cause serious losses of penned birds. These predators can be controlled by either live or steel traps. Skunks and opossums usually only kill 1 victim in a clumsy, mauling manner; raccoons like to eat the heads of as many birds as possible.

Birds

In the United States and Canada there are about 52 species of hawks and owls. Of these, only 4 are frequent problems on hunting preserves: Cooper's hawk, goshawk, red-tailed hawk, and great horned owl.[8] Only the great horned owl and red-tailed hawk were serious predators at Nilo, and then only in late winter — when natural prey was scarce.

All avian predators are protected by state and federal law. Any control program requires both federal and state permits. Hence, a preserve operator should check with his state wildlife agency on the procedure to expedite the necessary permits when the control of hawks and owls becomes a necessity. Live trapping is an acceptable alternative to shooting problem hawks and owls. The live traps most commonly used are the pole trap, bal-chatri trap, Swedish goshawk trap, and noose-carpet trap.

A pole trap is usually 10 or more feet in height and should be large enough to support a muskrat trap at the top and not sway in the wind. Hawks or owls like to perch above the surrounding vegetation to get a good view of the ground area. The ring at the end of the trap chain is inserted through a wire (baling wire) that runs from the top of the pole to the ground. The jaws of the trap should be padded to prevent serious injury to the legs of the trapped bird. It is not necessary to bait the trap; however, pole traps are not selective for hawks and owls, and some songbirds will be caught. Pole traps should be located at the area where predation is a problem, and only long enough to alleviate the problem.

Pole traps should be tended 3 – 4 times a day. Wear heavy leather gloves that extend well above the wrists when working with hawks or owls. Hawks and owls are capable of inflicting painful injury with either their talons or beaks. When a hawk or owl is caught, offer the bird a stick, which it will promptly grab with its beak. Tape the bird's legs with masking or adhesive tape and restrain the bird's wings with velcro strips.

The McGraw Wildlife Foundation, Illinois, disposes of live-trapped hawks and owls by releasing them 5 – 10 miles off the property. In the fall (October through November) they take the birds south, and in the spring (February through March) they go north — working with the migrating tendency of the birds. Using this technique, they have had only 6 of 100 red-tailed hawks return to Foundation grounds; great horned owls seldom returned.[8]

The Swedish goshawk trap[6] has been used successfully on some preserves. Jeff Hughes, Wild Wings of Oneka, Minnesota, enlisted the help of the Minnesota Falconry Club, which assumed the responsibility of getting the permits and doing all of the work. In 1 season they caught and removed 153 raptorial predators. Only 1 banded bird ever returned. The Swedish goshawk trap is costly to build, and because of its size, not easy to transport.

The bal-chatri live trap[1] has been used at the McGraw Wildlife Foundation, Illinois, for over 10 years. The trap is a quonset-shaped wire cage, the tops and sides are 1-inch chicken wire, and the floor consists of 1-inch welded wire, which also has a 4- by 5-inch trap door to insert a live decoy; pigeons and starlings work the best. The trap is 10 inches wide, 18 inches long, and 7 inches high. The top of the trap is covered with about 80 40-lb. test monofilament nylon nooses about 3 inches in diameter, in which the raptors are caught by their feet when they strike the top of the trap (see Appendix A). The trap is not staked down, so that the raptor in his struggle may drag the trap but not break the monofilament nooses holding him.[1]

The advantages of the bal-chatri trap are that it is easy to transport from 1 spot to another, it is raptor specific, and it can be used to catch a specific problem individual. Building the trap is easy but time consuming. Size and shape of the trap and strength of the monofilament may be modified for the target raptor.[8]

The noose-carpet trap[5] is a modification of the bal-chatri. Rather than a live bird, bait is supplied in the form of a dead bird. A piece of hardware cloth is covered with nooses and the dead bird is tied on top or under the hardware cloth. Red-tailed hawks, in particular, will decoy to dead birds or previous kills and are caught when they become entangled in the nooses.

Nuisance Animals

Feral cats and dogs, muskrats, starlings, and English ("house") sparrows fall within this category. Feral cats can easily be caught with live traps baited with sardines. Stray dogs can be a problem — mainly by harassing gamebirds in a pen, on a duck pond, or in the field. If you can identify the owner of the dogs(s), a heart-to-heart talk will usually suffice. If that doesn't do it, you can appeal to the local authorities — or take direct action.

Muskrats can be a problem at lakes and ponds, sometimes causing severe damage to dams. Local trappers are usually more than willing to trap such animals during the regular fur-harvest season. If you permit a trapper to harvest your muskrats on a yearly basis, your problem with muskrats should be few, if any. Properly conducted, muskrat trapping should not pose any hazard to your hunting dogs.

Starlings and English sparrows can create problems on a hunting preserve by eating and damaging gamebird feed and by spreading avian diseases. One of the most effective means of controlling these birds is by live trapping.

The trap is large (8 feet long, 6 feet wide, and 6 feet high) and uses live decoys (6 – 8 starlings or English sparrows) for bait (Appendix B). The efficiency of the trap increases with the number of birds in the trap. In addition to the live birds, bait in the form of cracked corn, milo, stale bread, or wheat is used to attract the birds. A pan of water is necessary for the decoys and trapped birds, plus a Christmas tree to serve as a shelter for the birds.[7]

The trap should be set in an open area near your gamebird pens, and works best when natural food is scarce in the winter months. The most humane method of killing the trapped birds is to gas them with carbon monoxide from your car or truck exhaust. Catch all of the birds (with the exception of the necessary decoys) and place them in a large plastic bag. Connect a flexible steel hose from your car exhaust to the bag and seal tightly for 5 – 10 minutes. Dispose of carcasses by burying, incineration, or garbage pickup.

Pests

Predators and nuisance animals will come and go on a hunting preserve, but rats and mice need constant control. Every preserve operator holding birds in pens has a rat and mouse problem or the potential for one. Rodents not only consume food, but will contaminate twice as much as they eat.

Good housekeeping is a large factor in rodent control. Too often one sees trash, unnecessary equipment, clutter, and containers near gamebird holding pens that provide excellent shelter and breeding areas for rodents. Keep the area around your gamebird pens clean.

Poisons are permitted in the control of rats and mice; however, before poisons are used, be sure to read all instructions and warnings on the container and *follow them carefully!* Control can be difficult with poison baits because of the competition offered by an abundance of attractive gamebird feeds. Also, rats and mice require different control techniques, and even different poisons. Don't try to solve a rat and mouse problem with a single control method. Check your state's regulations on the use of poisons for controlling rodents. Mice and rats can also be controlled with traps.

The anticoagulant poisons — Warfarin, Pival, Prolin, PMP, Diphacinone, and Chlorphacinone — all cause death by preventing normal clotting of blood. All are available as ready-made baits and some may be purchased as concentrates for preparing special mixtures.

A single dose of anticoagulant ordinarily does not kill unless a massive dose is consumed. Anticoagulants are most effective when taken in small amounts during several (5 or more) feedings. Ample quantities of bait should be made available as long as rat sign remains. If the bait is being accepted, a marked reduction in bait consumption and rat activity will be noted in 3 – 4 days.

Anticoagulant poisons are capable of killing cats, dogs, and other warm-blooded animals; however, the potential hazard is reduced because multiple feedings usually are required. Poultry species appear more tolerant, but the bait should be placed in protected feed stations. Ready-prepared baits are best for continued use. Bait placement should be wherever rats are accustomed to feed, or along their travel routes. However, such baits should be tied or tacked down if used in buildings. In some indoor situations water-soluble baits should also be offered. Paraffin bait-blocks are useful outdoors, in wet locations, and under buildings if repeated baitings with cereal is impractical. Other rodents, such as field mice and ground squirrels, can be controlled with the anticoagulant poisons in protected feed stations.

Mice are more resistant than rats to anticoagulants and, because of their dainty feeding at any 1 time, are more difficult to control. If food and cover are available, mice may be restricted to an activity area of 10 feet or less; hence, bait stations must be closer. Mice do not rely as much on water as do rats; they can exist for long periods of time on dehydrated foods and without free water.

If other poisons can be safely exposed, they may be necessary to reduce rat and mouse populations. Strychnine-treated small grains, such as millet or oat groats, make excellent mouse baits but are almost worthless for rats. Red squill is an effective poison for controlling rats but not mice. Zinc phosphide on oat groats is good bait for rats and mice, but not inside your gamebird pens.

It may also be necessary to rotate the use of various rodenticides to avoid bait shyness, especially in the same locations. And always follow directions and use caution!

References

1. Berger, D., and F. Hamerstrom. 1962. Protecting a trapping station from raptor predation. Jour. Wildlife Management 26(2):203-206. The Wildlife Society, 5410 Grosvenor Lane, Bethesda, MD.
2. Carnegie, W. 1906. Practical game-preserving. 3rd ed. Charles Scribner's Sons, New York, NY. 424pp.
3. Chansler, W. 1955. Successful trapping methods. D. Van Nostrand Co., Inc., Princeton, NJ. 151pp.
4. Cummings, M. 1974. Predator control. Wildlife Harvest 5(6):35-39. Goose Lake, IA.
5. Collister, A. 1967. Simple noose trap. Western Bird Bander 42(1):4. Western Bird Bander Assoc., 2003 Ida St., Napa, CA.
6. Meng, H. 1977. The Swedish goshawk trap. Wildlife Harvest 8(8):10-13. Goose Lake, IA.
7. Montgomery, R. 1980. Starlings with live traps. Wildlife Harvest 11(7):52-53. Goose Lake, IA.
8. _____. 1983. Controlling raptors on shooting preserves and game farms. Wildlife Harvest 14(1):16-21. Goose Lake, IA.

APPENDIX A
Bal-chatri Raptor Trap

How to Tie the Nooses

Quantity production is the quickest way to make nooses for the bal-chatri trap. Double the end of a length of nylon and tie an overhand knot, making a small eye. Slip the eye over a No. 3 knitting needle and pull the knot tight so that the knitting needle determines the final size of the eye. About 21 inches from the first knot, double the nylon making a second eye, slip it over the knitting needle and tighten it. Make a third eye 3 inches from the second. Continue in this pattern of long, short, long, short about 40 times; then, leaving the knotted nylon on the needle, pull on the wad of long loops to give tension, and immerse the knots in boiling water for 4 seconds to set them. Cut all the short loops. One by one,

remove the long loops which will have an eye, the future noose eye, at either end. Run 1 eye through the other to make a noose; pull the first noose shut and force it through the other eye. Fasten these 2 nooses to the chicken-wire top of the bal-chatri with 2 overhand knots. After having covered the top of the trap with about 40 pairs of nooses, open all the nooses and arrange them so that they stand upright in catching position.

Ordinarily, after a catch has been made, all closed nooses are opened, and the trap is again ready for use. However, after a trap has had considerable use, some nooses become twisted or broken and should be replaced.[1]

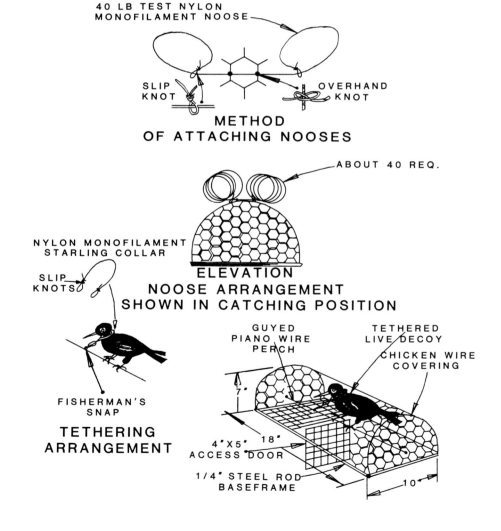

40 LB TEST NYLON
MONOFILAMENT NOOSE

SLIP KNOT   OVERHAND KNOT

**METHOD
OF ATTACHING NOOSES**

ABOUT 40 REQ.

**ELEVATION
NOOSE ARRANGEMENT
SHOWN IN CATCHING POSITION**

NYLON MONOFILAMENT
STARLING COLLAR

SLIP KNOTS

FISHERMAN'S SNAP

**TETHERING
ARRANGEMENT**

GUYED
PIANO WIRE
PERCH

TETHERED
LIVE DECOY

CHICKEN WIRE
COVERING

7"

18"

4" X 5"
ACCESS DOOR

1/4" STEEL ROD
BASEFRAME

10"

APPENDIX B
Starling and Sparrow Trap

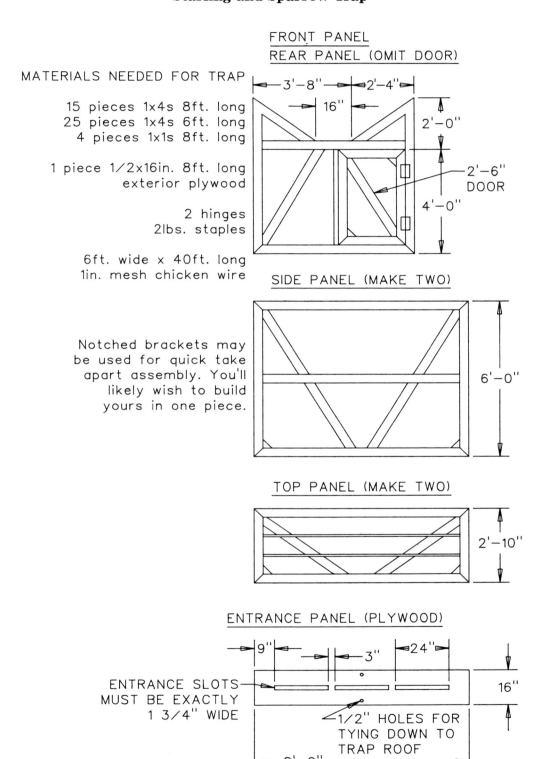

FRONT PANEL
REAR PANEL (OMIT DOOR)

MATERIALS NEEDED FOR TRAP

15 pieces 1x4s 8ft. long
25 pieces 1x4s 6ft. long
4 pieces 1x1s 8ft. long

1 piece 1/2x16in. 8ft. long
exterior plywood

2 hinges
2lbs. staples

6ft. wide x 40ft. long
1in. mesh chicken wire

3'-8"   2'-4"
16"
2'-0"
2'-6" DOOR
4'-0"

Notched brackets may
be used for quick take
apart assembly. You'll
likely wish to build
yours in one piece.

SIDE PANEL (MAKE TWO)

6'-0"

TOP PANEL (MAKE TWO)

2'-10"

ENTRANCE PANEL (PLYWOOD)

9"   3"   24"

ENTRANCE SLOTS
MUST BE EXACTLY
1 3/4" WIDE

1/2" HOLES FOR
TYING DOWN TO
TRAP ROOF

16"

8'-0"

Chapter 17

PROFITABILITY

The thought of operating a hunting preserve appeals to many hunters who relish the idea of the outdoor life and being afield with dog and gun. The management appears simple — just release the birds for the hunters and collect the fees. But such prospective operators are in for a rude and expensive awakening unless they do some groundwork and investigate and study the hunting preserve industry, serve an apprenticeship on a hunting preserve, and/or seek professional guidance.

To the best of my knowledge, no commercial hunting preserves (daily-fee or private) can earn

enough income from hunting alone during 5 or 6 months to show an annual profit. There must be supplemental income from other commercial or recreational activities. To be profitable, each commercial operator must decide on the proper mix of activities, based on his skills, location, and facilities.

Within the chapter, "Types of Hunting Preserves," there is detailed discussion on commercial hunting preserves, with decision-making guidelines for a choice. The purpose of this chapter is to present guidelines to manage a commercial hunting preserve at a profit. It is a formidable task. One cannot reduce the drive, personality, initiative, perseverance, and imagination of a given preserve operator to cold numbers. At best, one can only offer suggestions and guidelines from successful commercial hunting preserves (see Appendix A).

Metropolitan versus Rural Preserves

Two types of hunting preserves are emerging

in the industry. One is what may be termed a "metropolitan preserve," which is usually located less than an hour's drive from a city of 500,000 or more people. The other is a "rural preserve" located at a greater distance or near cities of smaller populations.

Metropolitan Preserves

The basis of profitability for metropolitan preserves is to become an outdoor recreational complex, and the best ones are designed for family-oriented recreation. The primary income of metropolitan hunting preserves derives from hunting, meals, and lodging. Secondary sources of income are derived from boarding, selling, and training dogs; fishing; clay target shooting; picnicking; field-dog trials; rifle, pistol, and archery ranges; and perhaps sales of Christmas trees and firewood.

The center of activities is a comfortable and clean clubhouse, which may or may not feature lodging, depending on the availability of modern motels nearby. Good food is served on a reservation basis, and special efforts are made to cater to business and club meetings, weddings, receptions, celebrations, etc. with specialty meals throughout the year. Kitchen and dining room help are hired on an "as-needed" basis, with the possible exception of the chef.

A city dweller usually becomes a member of a hunting preserve for the purpose of hunting. If the hunting is of the proper quality, chances are that you will attract other members of his family for summer activities. Bill Fortino[3] said,

"A preserve which does not measure up during the fall and winter hunting seasons will be unlikely to attract a customer and his family during a time when there are many other summer activities competing for their attention. A man who doesn't feel he got his money's worth during the hunting season is going to go away mad, and the summer heat is not going to cool him off. Any preserve with summer ambitions must establish a good rapport with its members during the hunting season." Fortino points out that summer activities not only provide off-season cash flow but offer the members economical family recreation as an attractive dividend on their membership dollar. The member likes the concept that you are working for him not only during the hunting season but year-round. And a member who feels that way is apt to begin hunting earlier in the season — where the real profits are — with the blessings of his family.

Managers of metropolitan preserves must create special events to ensure business volume. If a manager is not sure as to the type of special event to feature, he can check with the wishes of the membership. Special events can range from clay target tournaments, seasonal picnics, fishing derbys, and field trials to educational activities. Educational activities can include hunter education, fly-tying, dog handling, nature hikes, fishing seminars, bird watching, collection of maple syrup, archery, etc. One can charge reasonable fees for educational activities. The important thing is to try and involve not only the member but his family.

An attractive and efficient clubhouse and dining room, Hunters Creek Club, Metamora, Michigan.

142

There are other family-oriented activities, such as ice skating, cross-country skiing, and snowmobiling. Such activities can be scheduled at the end of the hunting day or when the snow is too deep for hunting.

All activities should be planned and conducted with the same care as your hunting program. They must be promoted and the participants offered a quality experience.

Rural Preserves

Rural preserves must feature quality hunting at a reasonable fee to attract patrons. However, they seldom are year-round recreational complexes. The travel distance is too great for their clients, and the operator cannot earn a fair return on the investment necessary for a large and comfortable clubhouse, food service, and lodging facilities.

As with metropolitan preserves, quality hunting is the main attraction and major source of income. However, other primary sources of income can be rearing gamebirds; boarding, training, and selling bird dogs; and/or livestock production. Secondary sources of income may be leasing land for agricultural purposes, field-dog trials, picnics, fishing, and/or outside employment.

Record Keeping

Herb Jordan[5] states that records should be kept only by those who wish to change their management for the better. Each activity on a preserve (hunting, dog kennels, food, pro shop, etc.) should be analyzed for profitability each year. Sometimes, it may not be easy to separate a given activity from another, such as the operation of a dog kennel and hunting revenues. Jordan listed 10 items of importance in financial management:

1. Purchase a business ledger, a cash ledger, and a record ledger from an office supply store.

2. Start a checking account and write checks for all of your expenses.

3. Paying bills with cash should be kept to a minimum.

4. Always get a receipt, whether you pay by cash or check.

5. Use free 30-day credit and record keeping whenever possible.

6. Add 3 – 5% to the price of products you sell for bookkeeping, record keeping, and business analysis.

7. Analyze all your expenses by running a total and dividing it by the units to get your unit cost per item.

8. Keep costs at a minimum but not at the expense of quality.

9. Margin of profit per item times volume of items sold equals gross profits.

10. If all record keeping fails, go back to your check book and the number of birds, dogs, clients, meals, etc. involved each year. You cannot guess about your business; you must know each phase of it. Keep records, analyze, and make necessary changes for profits.

The wave of the future for record keeping is the computer. Kathy Reiland, Gypsy Glen Farms, Illinois, states that the recent addition of a computer on their hunting preserve enables them to print out the membership, compute the sales tax, calculate the bird units (multiplies and subtracts), print out the billing invoices, and inventory gamebirds, dog food, shotshells, clay targets, and supplies. And, according to Kathy Reiland, their accountant can call and obtain a yearly printout sheet for income tax purposes.

The Value of Land

Back in the 1950s a number of preserve owners were able to purchase land at reasonable prices, especially submarginal agricultural land near metropolitan areas. They were able to earn a yearly living from their operations. When all land escalated in price during the 1960s and 70s, they made a handsome, long-term profit.

Today, land of any type is priced beyond its capability to provide an economic return from agriculture or as a hunting preserve, and there are fewer preserves today than 20 years ago. The price of land, especially submarginal agricultural land, may decline in the years ahead. In the meantime, some new preserve operators are leasing land for preserve operations from land-holding companies and investors.

It is possible to have a very respectable mobile

clubhouse, complete with modern kitchen facilities and, if needed, separate mobile units for lodging. For more information on such facilities, one should contact mobile-home sales outlets. The technique of using mobile facilities is quite widespread in Texas on lands leased by corporations for the purpose of hunting wild game.

Portable dog kennels have been developed, and the manufacturers of such equipment advertise widely in the various sporting dog magazines. Holding pens for gamebirds are not a major source of expense and only have a life expectancy of about 10 years.

So, the concept of leasing land to operate a hunting preserve is a viable one, but the operator should seek a lease of not less than 10 years with the option for renewal. One of the most successful hunting preserves in the nation, Hunters Creek Club, Michigan, operates on leased land.

Business Volume

Annual profits are keyed to the volume of business, and the volume of business is related to the promotion of quality hunting at a fair fee. Any business has to be promoted — even a good product must be brought to the attention of the public through advertising, publicity, and good public relations (see chapter on ''Promotion''). It is a never-ending task; learn all you can about it. There are certain fixed expenses involved in managing a hunting preserve, whether it operates at capacity or not. The greater the volume of your business, the lower the percentage of fixed expenses to be charged against every bird released.

Whereas 25 years ago a family-operated hunting preserve could earn a living on a volume of 5,000 birds per year, the necessary volume has now increased to at least 10,000. However, quality should never be sacrificed for volume. If it is, volume will disappear into the night like an Arab and his tent. One builds volume through quality hunting, repeat business, and word-of-mouth advertisement, in addition to constant promotion. You don't process hunters on your preserve — you entertain them. You are selling recreation — not dead birds. Recreation cannot be handled on a production-line basis, and it is a mistake to try.

The best criterion as to whether or not you are providing quality hunting at a reasonable fee is the percentage of your hunters who are repeat customers. If you are hitting in the vicinity of 70% or better and making a profit, you are doing well; if not, it is time to take stock and correct your shortcomings. As John Mullin, Arrowhead Hunting & Conservation Club, Iowa, once stated, ''The only person who doesn't need repeat business is the undertaker.''

The hardest step in any selling job is to get the customer in the door. Once you have him there, you should do everything you can to make him want to come back again.

Pricing

There are no hard and fast rules for pricing on hunting preserves — just trends. But, it is essential that pricing on your preserve be thoroughly understood by your members. To avoid any misunderstandings, it is advisable to print and distribute an annual price list for services and gamebirds.

Metropolitan Preserves

Any preserve operating a recreational complex for its members throughout the year should have an annual membership fee. After all, the preserve operator is maintaining and staffing an outdoor recreational area for the enjoyment of his members on a reservation basis. Some such preserves have a higher initiation fee than the annual membership and have different rates for businesses, groups, and families. The tendency is for such fees not to include any gamebirds. Rather, the members are asked in March to place an order by April 1 for a desired number of gamebirds for fall hunting. As an incentive, such gamebirds are discounted, as compared to prices within season. Additional birds are available throughout the hunting season but at a higher price.

Prices for gamebirds depend on the extra services offered at a preserve, but the current guideline is at least twice the cost of each gamebird to the operator at the time of release. However, rather than increasing the price on a monthly basis, the operator should determine his average cost for the season. The prices for all other services, such as meals, guides, processing gamebirds, fishing fees, clay target shooting, etc., are set early in the year.

Rural Preserves

Rural preserves will have an annual fee for their membership, but at a lower rate, and it will usually include a given number of gamebirds for the coming preserve season. Another technique is to include a number of "bird units" within the membership for fall hunting (pheasants = 2 units, chukars = 1 1/2 units, and quail = 1 unit). However, there are no refunds on birds or "bird units" not used by the members. Rural preserves will also have introductory hunts for non-members and daily-fee hunts. Their investment in facilities and services is less than a metropolitan preserve, especially in the clubhouse and food services.

Trends in Pricing

The most common pricing practice is charging for gamebirds released. The old philosophy of "guaranteed hunting" is no longer in vogue. Why should the preserve operator be responsible for the shooter's inability to hit a gamebird or, in some cases, for the wild field behavior of a hunter's dog?

Another method of charging is a flat fee for a half-day hunt, especially with guided hunts. The operator and the guide have a good estimate of the number of gamebirds that remain on a given hunting area within the preserve, and all they have to do is to stock a few additional birds to make a flat fee profitable. But, such hunts require hunters who are willing and able to hunt gun-shy gamebirds. Flat-fee hunts usually have a time limit, and the guide regulates the number of birds shot by where the party hunts and/or with an extra charge for more than a given number of birds. As the old saying goes, "It takes different strokes for different folks." The operator must decide on a system that is fair to him and to his guests. But always, the emphasis must be on recreation and not on birds bagged.

You should set a minimum fee per party of hunters. A preserve operator cannot afford to devote a half-day to a shooter who only wants to kill 1 or 2 pheasants. There are just so many days of good hunting weather and conditions in any preserve season. You may also want to consider a pricing differential between weekends and weekdays and/or the fall and winter months.

In-season Incentives

Preserves usually operate at full capacity on weekends, especially in the fall. But, you may have to offer some attractive incentives for weekdays and hunts during the winter months.

A family home converted into a clubhouse, Nilo.

Continental Shoots

Some preserves with the proper cover and layout hold continental shoots (see chapter on "Ring-necked Pheasant") with ring-necked pheasants and/or mallard ducks.

Pheasant Hunting Competitions

In the early years, this concept started as a statewide or regional pheasant hunting championship, but such hunts can only be held once a year. Hence, the popularity of this activity has forced a change from "championship" to "competition."

The rules for such an event differ among hunting preserves. At the Arrowhead Hunting & Conservation Club,[6] Iowa, entries for the competition are based on 2-man teams, and the entry fee is at least the cost of 6 released pheasants plus prize money. Depending on the number of entries, different hunting areas can be used, and a drawing is held before the hunt to determine the hunting area and the order of hunting for each team. The competitors are only allowed 6 shotshells per man and are limited to 30 minutes of hunting. They can use either a pointing or a flushing dog, but not one of the preserve dogs. Scoring is as follows: 10 points for each bird bagged, 3 points for each of the shotshells not used; and 2 points for each minute left of the 30-minute time limit after 6 pheasants are bagged. A field judge is assigned to each hunting area.

Miscellaneous Incentives

"Clean-up" or "Scratch" hunts are used at Wild Wings of Oneka, Minnesota, to stimulate weekday hunts during the winter months.[4] No birds are released for the hunt and, as an incentive, the price of birds bagged is reduced. Hughes also features special hunts — a "Club Shoot." He will liberate 400 quail on a given day and limit the group of club members to the first 40 that sign up, and he charges a flat fee per individual. Such hunts are publicized well in advance of the occasion.

Beuchert[2] used "Father-son Days" during the holiday season with a discount on pheasants to dads who brought youngsters. They also had "Banded-bird Hunts," with a free bird to the lucky hunter who bagged the banded bird.

The Pro Shop

Most hunting preserves with a respectable volume are missing profits by not having a pro shop, especially for hunting clothing, rainwear, and footgear. Sportsmen, both guests and members, are constantly forgetting to bring the right clothing. The secret of a successful pro shop is not to compete with the mass merchandisers; sell quality.

Bob Allen[1] gave some excellent pointers on a hunting preserve pro shop at the Sacramento meeting of the NAGA in 1974. He stated, "Clothing must be hung up to be displayed and sold properly. A simple clothing rack is about all that is required. It is helpful to have a lockable glass display case in which you keep more valuable objects such as shooting glasses and gun accessories. A peg board wall display is an excellent way to display items such as gun cases, shell bags, dog whistles and collars, shooting gloves, caps, etc.

"Clothing is of number one importance because of the profit margin it gives and because of the popularity of clothing items among shooters. Displays of gifts and novelties have a high margin of profit, such as Swiss embroidery emblems and highball glasses with your preserve logo. Footgear, both leather and rubber, in various sizes is important."

Shotshells of different gauges and shot sizes are a must item on a preserve. Shotguns can be handled on special order through a local gun shop.

Bob Allen recommends that all clothing and items be priced so there is no confusion in the customer's mind. A large, wall-mounted mirror and a place for a customer to sit down and try on boots or snake leggings is essential. Make arrangements for alterations at a local dry cleaner or alteration shop. Toward the end of the hunting season one may want to hold a sale. The key to success is to offer complete customer service and a complete guarantee for everything that you sell. Work with manufacturers who will back up their products and you, in turn, back it up to the customer.

If possible, the operator and his guides should wear the clothing and footgear sold in the pro shop. It not only improves the appearance of the preserve's personnel but also stimulates the interest of your hunters in the clothing.

Bob Allen is anxious to work with hunting preserves who have a pro shop. His address is Box 477, Des Moines, Iowa 50302.

Shoot-to-retrieve Field Trials

Shoot-to-retrieve Field Trials are gaining in popularity[6] and offer the preserve operator an excellent source of additional revenue, especially during the off-season. The preserve operator can either sponsor the trial himself, or lease the grounds (about 35 acres) and sell the birds to be stocked, as well as meals and refreshments.

The usual technique is to stock the field with 5–6 quail for a brace of dogs, and 3-wheelers are used to speed the stocking process. The dog handlers walk, and either can do their own gunning or have a gunner assigned. The judges (2 or 3) ride horseback and score the work of the dogs. Each "bird find" rates a score of 0–100 points. Steady to wing and shot is not required, but the dog must remain staunch until the bird is flushed by the gunner. The "find" is rated on intensity, style, and composure. A "stop-to-flush" (1 only) rates a score of 0–75 points. An honor or "back" rates from 0–75 points, and the dog must back on sight without command. Each brace of dogs is only allowed 30 minutes. Judges do take the traits of various pointing breeds into consideration when scoring.

All Shoot-to-retrieve Field Trials are sanctioned. There are regional championships which, in turn, lead to competition for National Dog-of-the-year. For more information on these trials write to National Shoot-to-retrieve Association, 9714 Montgomery Road, Cincinnati, OH 45242.

Shooting-dog Trials

Shooting-dog trials are a natural for a preserve owner, and the only limitation on possibilities lies in one's imagination. Any preserve owner who sells, buys, boards, and trains hunting dogs should conduct trials for his preserve members and hunting dog owners in his area. Such trials should simulate hunting situations, be appealing

A 3-wheeler is used on a number of preserves for releasing small numbers of gamebirds.

to dog owners, and can feature retrieving, pointing, or flushing breeds.

Anything that a preserve owner can do to stimulate the private ownership of hunting dogs is to his advantage. Hunting dogs are more responsible for taking their owners hunting than vice versa. In a sense they are the preserve operator's "silent" salesman.

Off-season Activities

Metropolitan preserves that are outdoor recreational complexes usually feature picnicking; fishing; clay target shooting; and ranges for rifle, pistol, and archery.

Picnicking

Most outdoor-minded families love picnics. Since hunting preserves are usually a "green oasis" near metropolitan areas, picnics are a natural off-season activity, both for the families of the members and for local businesses and social clubs. The availability of a good picnic area with a shelter or two for inclement weather can be promoted and is a good source of supplemental income, especially when the food is catered by the preserve. A few preserves have a specialty in barbecuing a pig or a lamb. Depending on the terrain and the natural features of a picnic area, one may be able to offer baseball fields, horseshoe pits, volleyball, boating, swimming, etc.

Fishing

Fishing is a good off-season income producer if a preserve has the necessary water facilities. Trout fishing has the greatest appeal, and a sizeable number of trout fishermen can be accommodated on a trout pond or a spring run, such as the one at the Max McGraw Wildlife Foundation, Dundee, Illinois. It all depends on whether a trout fishery can be developed in your geographic area with your water resources. Even in the South, ponds will be stocked with trout during the cooler fall and winter months solely for the entertainment of hunting guests. It gives the early arrival for the next day's hunt something appealing to do in the outdoors.

Warm-water fisheries (bass, bluegills, and/or catfish) also have possibilities. The successful

management of any warm-water fisheries operation takes management expertise and more than 1 or 2 man-made ponds. Fishing in small ponds has a tendency to go "sour" in a few years. When this happens, the pond has to be rejuvenated, and the process may take 2 – 3 years. Any hunting preserve with a large lake (25 or more acres in size), especially a natural lake, has the next best thing to a producing oil well on the property.

A large, natural lake with good fishing is a valuable asset on any preserve, especially if the clubhouse overlooks the lake — Hunters Creek Club, Metamora, Michigan.

Clay Target Facilities

Clay target facilities can vary from a practice trap mounted on a car wheel to a regulation trap and/or skeet field. The latter represents a sizeable investment, but there are a number of metropolitan preserves that have made such facilities profitable. It may require promotion beyond the membership of the preserve, including the organization of league shooting. On a membership preserve, automatic trap and skeet ranges can and are managed on a self-service basis. The preserve member with a friend or two operates the facility and pays for the clay targets that he uses. He or she may bring their own shotshells or purchase them at the preserve.

Perhaps the best clay target layout for competition shooting with a small financial investment on the part of the preserve operator is a "crazy quail" field, which is discussed in the chapter on "Short Subjects."

Pistol, Rifle, and Archery Ranges

Pistol, rifle, and archery ranges should be self-service with a flat fee for their use. Many city dwellers need a range to sharpen their shooting or archery skills. Plans for shooting ranges can be obtained from the National Rifle Association of America, Hunter Services Division, 1600 Rhode Island Ave., Washington, D.C. 20036. Local ordinances on shooting ranges should be checked.

Dog Kennels

Good hunting dogs on a preserve are developed. As explained in the chapter, "Hunting Guides and Dogs," one can contract for quality gamebirds, but every preserve is responsible for the quality of its hunting dogs. It takes time, training, and patience to produce a quality hunting dog. Whether a preserve operator realizes it or not, he is going to be in the dog business for the following reasons: (1) hunting dogs are only at their peak for 5 or 6 years until replacements must be found, and (2) guest hunters become particularly fond of a given dog and would like to purchase the animal.

A dog kennel makes it easier to hold Shooting-dog and Shoot-to-retrieve Trials and provides a ready market for gamebirds for dog training. In addition, dogs do need housing and food throughout the year, so dogs owned by preserve members can produce income on a monthly basis.

Personnel

Good personnel on a hunting preserve are difficult to attract and hold on a seasonal basis. Consequently, the preserve operator's family has been, and will continue to be, an important part of his work force. Preserves, with few exceptions, are family-operated businesses.

Some hunting preserves are fortunate enough to offer off-season employment to their personnel, such as rearing gamebirds or training dogs. However, the bulk of the personnel has to be on an "as-needed" basis. Hence, all activities on a hunting preserve should be by reservation only, with a minimum of 24 hours notice. Also, such activities as shooting ranges, picnics, fishing, etc., should be self-service until the volume of business justifies the assignment of personnel.

References

1. Allen, B. 1975. The hunting preserve "Pro Shop." Wildlife Harvest 6(6):20-22. Goose Lake, IA.
2. Beuchert, K. 1976. Preserve ideas. Wildlife Harvest 7(10):12. Goose Lake, IA.
3. Fortino, B. 1979. Summer activities for the hunting preserve. Wildlife Harvest 10(5):46-49. Goose Lake, IA.
4. Hughes, J. 1984. Wild Wings of Oneka. Wildlife Harvest 15(8):12-13. Goose Lake, IA.
5. Jordan, H. 1975. Record keeping on a game farm or hunting resort. Wildlife Harvest 6(2):12-14. Goose Lake, IA.
6. Mullin, J. 1976. Preserve ideas. Wildlife Harvest 7(10):12. Goose Lake, IA.

APPENDIX A

Questions and Answers on Profitability

During the last 10 years, as time and circumstances permitted, 10 successful hunting preserve operators were contacted for information on the preserve industry. They were asked 25 questions, and their answers were summarized as follows:

1. *How does one obtain the necessary acreage for a hunting preserve?*
> A. Buy the land, preferably submarginal farmland, within 1 hour's drive from a center of high human population (500,000 or more).
> B. Lease the land for 10 or more years from land speculators, land-holding companies, timber companies, etc. within 1 hour's drive from a center of high human population.

2. *Do you consider the support and help of your family important?*
All respondents agree on the necessity of family help and support, especially in the early years of a preserve operation.

3. *What personal attributes do you consider important in the manager of a hunting preserve?*
> A. Likes people
> B. Good businessman
> C. Promoter
> D. Avid hunter
> E. Enjoys his work

4. *How important is it to have sufficient capital to operate in the "red" for the first few years?*
The general conclusion is that a well-managed preserve needs 3 years to become a profitable operation. The lack of sufficient capital to operate for 3 years is the primary reason many hunting preserves fail.

5. *Is it necessary to integrate other seasonal activities to supplement your income?*
Additional sources of income are essential. Such sources are selling, boarding, and training dogs; recreational activities, such as fishing, picnicking, clay target shooting, field trials for dogs, archery and rifle ranges, youth camps, etc.; restaurant trade; and/or outside seasonal employment. Farming and game breeding are also involved. However, income from farming is usually from leasing the tillable excess acreage to a neighboring farmer. Intensive farming and hunting preserves are not compatible. Rearing gamebirds is a viable source of income for some rural hunting preserves.

6. *How important to total profits are extra services, such as providing meals, lodging, clay target shooting, training and boarding dogs, fishing, picnicking, processing shot birds, etc.?*
There is no unanimity of opinion on the relative importance of extra services as contributors to total profits, and for good reason. Each hunting preserve will develop a mix of extra services depending on its location, outside availability of such services, the needs and demands of its members, the physical assets of the preserve, and the availability of personnel.

7. *How important is business volume to the success of a hunting preserve?*
The general consensus among the respondents is that a commercial hunting preserve should be handling 10,000 gamebirds or more per season. Volume on a preserve is generated by quality hunting, good publicity and promotion, and by word-of-mouth advertising by its patrons.

8. *Do you need to establish a reasonable fee per hunter or party?*
"Absolutely" is the consensus of the respondents. Most preserves set a minimum fee for a party (2 or more hunters) for a half-day hunt.
As "Pres" Mann, Hunters Creek Club, Michigan, states, "Your first consideration is to attract people, and then set as high a minimum fee as your services will command."

9. *How should a preserve operator charge for hunting?*
The method of charging varies among preserves; however, the general tendency is to charge for birds released, instead of birds harvested per hunter.
"A Sporting Opportunity" has been tried with some success, but the drawback is that the definition of "A Sporting Opportunity" is sub-

ject to personal judgement. A flat rate for a half-day hunt is gaining in popularity.

10. *Does weather influence your income from hunting?*

The respondents varied in their response to this question. Operators with a positive mental attitude make inclement weather an asset instead of a liability. Their motto is, "It's always a good day to hunt." Then, they will structure a hunt to make the most of the situation. All that hunters need is a leader and a reasonable chance of having a good hunt. Other preserve operators consider inclement weather lost business and will try to reschedule a hunt.

We are also learning more about weather-conditioning gamebirds and how to handle such birds so as to provide quality hunting during periods of inclement weather.

11. *What percentage of gross income should be net profit?*

The general consensus is that 20–30% of gross income should be net profit, pre-tax.

12. *How do you handle investments in the clubhouse, bird pens, equipment, and dog kennels?*

The unanimous advice is to amortize as quickly as possible. Some differences of opinion exist among respondents on the necessary quality of the clubhouse and the dog kennels. They will not substitute for quality hunting, but they are important features of a successful hunting preserve.

13. *How important is repeat business?*

It is essential that 70–80% of your hunters come to your preserve at least once a season. In-season repeat business is created by special events — "clean-up" hunts, continental shoots, children's days, etc.

14. *How important is quality hunting (good birds, cover, guides, and dogs) to the success of a hunting preserve?*

The answer was best summarized in behalf of all of the respondents by Ron DeBruin, Oakview Hunt Club, Iowa, "Without quality hunting you have nothing."

15. *Do you hire guides on a daily or seasonal basis?*

The respondents differed in their replies. The large-volume preserves like permanent or seasonal employees as guides, since it gives them more complete control over their behavior, dress, and performance. However, there are many preserves that hire guides on an "as-needed" basis and have been well pleased with the results. Most guides working on a daily basis have their own dogs, and the operator has thoroughly checked the guide and the dog(s) in the field.

16. *Are there advantages to a private as compared to a public hunting preserve?*

All respondents agree that a private hunting preserve has many advantages over a public operation. However, it is necessary to attract new members and expand patronage. Hence, a number of new preserves operate both on a daily-fee and membership basis. When they reach a desired volume of business, they become a private club. Undesirable members can be handled by a membership committee.

17. *What percentage of released birds can one expect to recover on a hunting preserve?*

If the vegetative cover for releasing and holding gamebirds is of the proper type and there is daily hunting pressure, one should approach the 75% level or better at the end of the preserve season. But, the emphasis should be on sporty hunting rather than the recovery rate.

18. *How do you manage your dog kennels?*

All hunting preserves own some bird dogs. Preserve operators who are good dog handlers will train, sell, and board dogs. A few operators of private clubs are able to have their members own most of the dogs and allow the preserve to use the dogs.

If dogs are needed, the recommendation is to buy started dogs — dogs not quite good enough for the field trial circuit. The general consensus is that it is a mistake to rent dogs to members. Let the hunting party hire a guide and dog.

19. *How do you dispose of surplus gamebirds at the end of the hunting season?*

Schedule your supply of gamebirds to minimize any surplus at the end of the season. If you do have some birds left, advertise their availability for stocking or field trials. If necessary, hold a shooting-dog field trial on your preserve. A few operators will slaughter excess birds, smoke them, and market them as gourmet products.

20. *How does one decide on the proper game-birds for a hunting preserve?*

Depends on the local hunting tradition — ring-necked pheasants in the northern states and bobwhite quail in the South. Options for other gamebirds, especially mallard ducks and chukar partridge, provide hunter satisfaction and added income.

21. *How do you keep in contact with your hunters throughout the year?*

All respondents use a newsletter to maintain contact with their hunters on a monthly, bi-monthly, or quarterly basis. The newsletter should contain a "Schedule of Events." Some preserve operators use postcards or phone calls. All agree that it is important to keep the line of communication open, and to listen to the desires and the needs of their hunters.

22. *Do you consider a good brochure on the features of your hunting preserve essential?*

The respondents agreed that a good-quality brochure on the features of their preserve, including a map of its location, address, and phone number is essential in the beginning to establish the business. However, since prices are subject to yearly change, they should only be included as an insert.

23. *How much money should a preserve spend annually on promotion — advertising, public relations, and publicity?*

The respondents varied in their answers, depending on their location and business volume. Some depended solely on public relations and "free" publicity, such as the outdoor columnist for a nearby metropolitan newspaper. Others budgeted 2 – 5% of their gross volume for advertising, including *The Wall Street Journal*. Booths at sport shows have also been helpful, but require giveaways in the form of brochures and/or directories of hunting preserves.

24. *Have memberships in trade organizations been helpful to you?*

The respondents agreed that trade organizations have not only been very helpful in the exchange of information but essential to the future of the preserve industry. They all support the North American Gamebird Association and their state association, if one is available.

25. *Has the state wildlife agency been of help to you?*

The respondents gave the highest compliments to state wildlife agencies where an individual is assigned to encourage and help the hunting preserve industry, such as the State of Illinois.

Chapter 18

PROMOTION

"Promote or perish" is an old adage in the business world and for good reason; it has stood the test of time as a basic business principle. You can build a better mousetrap, but before the world will beat a path to your door, you will have to tell the world about it.

One informs the public through promotion of a product or service, and promotion consists of 3 phases: advertising, publicity, and public relations. Advertising is paid notice in newspapers, TV, radio, and magazines as well as brochures, signs, and other printed matter. Publicity is free notice in the media. Public relations is creating a favorable "image" and getting people to like what you have to offer.

Promotion is necessary on both the local and national levels. The future of the hunting preserve industry depends on public acceptance, which requires positive TV programs, movies, magazine stories, national directories, etc. Such effort requires the assistance of cooperating organizations on a national level.

The Home Front

As Howard J. Miller[5] indicated, planning a promotional campaign is the key to success. You must determine what you want to accomplish and who you want to reach with advertising and publicity, Part of the planning is setting a budget. A good rule of thumb is about 5% of your annual sales. However, the beginning preserve operator will have to consider the costs of promotion as part of his initial expenses.

Advertising

A good brochure is the most important single promotional item of any hunting preserve (Figure 1). It should tell the prospective hunter exactly what he can expect to find on your preserve and whet his hunting appetite. Elliott[2] points out that a brochure is a salesman, product catalog, rule book, and mobile outdoor show all wrapped up into 1 package. Advertising, publicity, and public relations all lead up to just 1 thing — people asking for your brochure. He further states that the brochure should reflect the ''KISS'' marketing philosophy — ''Keep It Simple, Stupid.'' The copy should be light, with good photographs and art; leave plenty of space, and yet tell your story. Don't confuse the reader with a history of the preserve, various membership plans, pricing structure, a biography of the owner, special events, and/or a rationale for hunting preserves. Basically, a preserve brochure is a descriptive folder that outlines the physical layout, hunting features, facilities, services, location, and the mail and phone contact. It should be a first-class, quality job that answers questions about the preserve.

Preserve brochures can vary from a standard 8 1/2- by 11-inch sheet of paper to a handsome full-colored booklet. It all depends on the clientele you are trying to reach and the amount of money you have to spend.

For most hunting preserves the basic 6-column folder from an 8 1/2- by 11-inch sheet of paper will suffice.

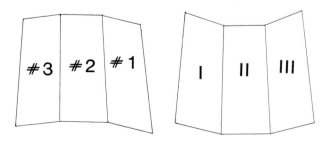

FIGURE 1: Layout for a brochure with an 8 1/2- by 11-inch sheet of paper.

Number the columns from left to right I - II - III, as shown. Column #1, your outside front cover, will back-up inside column I; column #2 will back-up II; and #3 will back-up III.

Column #1 needs to make an impression. Three elements are important on the front cover — the name of the preserve, the mailing address and phone number, and a good, action photograph that tells of the fine sport (hunters, dogs, flying birds, and habitat) on your preserve.

Column #2, the outside rear cover, should have a sketch map of how to reach your preserve. Repeat the name of the preserve and the phone number.

Column #3 is ideal for pictures, action photographs of hunting, or gamebirds in the wild but *not* in the pen. It should also contain some key phrases in large type, such as:

HUNTING UNLIMITED
SPORTY HUNTING IN NATURAL COVER
SIX MONTHS OF HUNTING (or your preserve season)
A SPORTSMAN'S PARADISE
TOP-QUALITY HUNTING DOGS

The inside columns (I, II, and III) are used to ''sell'' information that will make the prospect want to hunt on your preserve. Keep the paragraphs short — not more than 10 lines of type. Sentences should not be more than 10–12 words.[1] Study the brochures of other hunting preserves, but don't copy the material. Be original. Each hunting preserve is unique; stress sporty hunting. Break up the copy with good action photographs or wildlife art.

When you have developed a layout of your brochure, seek professional help. There are a number of 1- and 2-man advertising agencies that are eager to work with clients whose budgets are limited.

Four-colored printing is great but expensive. Consider colored stock paper and colored inks. Special effects are possible through the use of graphic art screens.

Check with your printer on paper stock, colored inks, spots of artwork, size and style of type, and have a firm understanding of production costs and delivery schedule for proofs and final copy. You should seek two or more printing bids.

When you have the galley proof from the printer, read it very carefully. Check for typos. Double check all dates, addresses, phone numbers, and figures. Send a corrected copy back to the printer and retain one for your files. Request a second proof and go through the same procedure. It may seem like a lot of work, but a brochure represents you and your preserve to a potential cash customer.

The number of brochures to order depends on the use — general or select distribution, direct mail campaigns, distribution at sport shows, etc. A good ballpark figure is 5,000.

Price List and Fees: Price lists and fees should *not* be an integral part of a brochure. They should be printed separately and included with the brochure when appropriate. The separate price list has flexibility and can be changed from year to year.

Most preserves avoid setting individual fees for each and every service provided. Instead, they have a flat charge for a day (or 1/2-day) hunt. The charge will provide a stated number of birds per hunter released in the hunting fields and services of dog and guide. Dressing and freezing of game, clay target shooting, transportation, hunting license, shotgun rental, and ammunition are additional charges and should be so indicated. Overnight lodging and meals are also separate charges.

A price list can also carry information, such as different rates for weekdays as compared to weekends, and/or special rates for father-son or father-daughter hunts. You may also wish to establish a minimum age for hunters and should so indicate. The price list is a good place to include the statement, "All hunting done in strict compliance with state game regulations."

Envelopes and Letterheads: Besides the usual name, address, and phone number of your preserve on your envelopes and letterheads consider some line artwork. Your printer can be of immense help with artwork, or you can use artwork from this book. Other sources are ammunition companies, sales catalogs, mail-order houses, brochures of other preserves, etc. However, don't clutter up your business stationary with illustrative art. Remember the "KISS" approach.

Don't use form letters for correspondence. It is necessary to develop a friend-to-friend relationship with your hunters, and correspondence is a good place to start.

Medallion or Symbol: Consider developing a distinctive symbol for your hunting preserve to use on brochures, letterheads, and envelopes as a "trademark." Above all, it should be original, and it may take a year or two for the right symbol to develop in your mind. When it does, you also have the opportunity of using the symbol as a medallion for your preserve.

The Nilo medallion.

Signs: Roadside billboards for Hunting preserves are an advertising concept that "died aborning." None of the successful hunting preserves I visited used highway billboards. On the other hand, *roadside directional* signs are not only useful but necessary. As Charley Dickey said years ago, "The propensity for hunters coming to a hunting preserve to get lost is only exceeded by the ability of most preserve operators in keeping their location a secret."

Roadside signs need not be elaborate, but they must be at every turn and intersection on all approaches off the main highway. They should be professionally prepared, freshly painted, and not hidden behind vegetative growth. The best preserves have a landscaped entrance with the name of the preserve. There should be directional signs to the parking lot at the clubhouse, arrows to the dog kennels, and arrows to the clay target facilities. Signs make an impression on everyone that sees them. They mirror the hunting preserve that they advertise. So, they should be of professional quality, freshly painted, and well maintained.

Paid Advertising: Paid advertising in the media varies with different hunting preserves. Successful preserves use paid advertising until they develop a desired volume of business. Once a preserve goes private, there is a feeling that paid advertising destroys the illusion of privacy for the members. Some metropolitan preserves advertise on a national basis — *Wall Street Journal* and/or hunting magazines. Rural preserves have more of a tendency to appeal to hunters within a couple of hours of driving time.

There are some guidelines for both types. One cannot depend on 1 insertion of paid advertising. Successful advertising requires repetition. One needs to plan on a minimum of 5 or 6 ads. A single ad is a waste of money.

When possible, a preserve operator should try to tie-in paid advertising with free publicity with radio, TV, or newspapers. If you are buying ads, make sure that they are inserted near the "Outdoor" or "Hunting and Fishing" column of the newspaper.

Yellow Pages: The old jingle, "Let your fingers do the walking," is helping to promote the "yellow pages" of the phone book. It's a good place to advertise — not only in the local phone directory but in the phone directories of surrounding metropolitan areas. Costs are reasonable, and one can evaluate the expense by asking new customers on how they learned about your preserve.

Publicity

Good publicity constitutes free promotion, and it's available if the preserve operator will plan and work to obtain it. A few hunting preserves have been successful operations in areas where a market survey would have predicted failure. Why? The operators were "experts" in obtaining good publicity through the media, and/or made a "sales pitch" on their preserve before every civic group within their area that was looking for a speaker. Like all good things in life, good publicity just doesn't happen — it has to be fetched.

Hunting preserves are unique in that they are a new form of private enterprise, offering hunting to an ever-increasing number of landless sportsmen. Preserves are oases of wildlife habitat. They have gamebirds and hunting dogs and, in contrast to many landowners, they welcome hunters.

Some publicity leads: Are you the first hunting preserve in the area? Are you playing host to any celebrities? What type of exotic gamebirds do you feature? Are you hosting a league trap shoot, fishing derby, National Hunting and Fishing Day, Boy Scout Jamboree, hunting-dog field trial, "Mountain Man" rendezvous, birdwatchers group, conservation club, or an archery or muzzle-loader's group? There are innumerable feature stories and events at every hunting preserve if you will look for and develop them. Such events are double-barreled; they not only provide free advertising for your preserve, but create good public relations. And, the "icing on the cake" is that they can provide a source of revenue — food, refreshments, birds, shotshells, etc.

Watch the local papers and TV stations, and listen to the radio, for the personalities who frequently handle outdoor material or cover the field sports. When you have thought up some story angles, take them personally to the newsroom or the studio. Introduce yourself to the receptionist and tell her who you would like to see. When you get in to see the outdoor columnist, sports editor, or whomever, remember that he's probably working on a deadline and doesn't have much time to visit.

Be prepared to introduce yourself and explain your visit in less than 60 seconds. Be brief and business-like. For instance, "My name is Jim Jones. I operate a hunting preserve 10 miles north of town, and I think that I have some story and picture material that may interest you and your readers. May I talk to you for a few minutes?"

When you have made your pitch — whether you have sold him on the idea or not — take your leave courteously and promptly. Never be long-winded or tedious when you visit a newspaper office or a broadcasting station. Time is money in such places.

Your first job is to interest a writer or an editor in what you have to offer. If you get one or the other out to your preserve and expose him or her to some good feature material, you are over the hump.[2]

Handling the Media: When writers and photographers visit you, prepare for them in advance. If you plan to take pictures, have a couple of friends on hand to serve as models and have dogs, cover, and birds in top shape. Good photographs of birds flushing and dogs on point are seldom achieved by chance. You may have to resort to "tricks-of-the-trade" to get the necessary action shots. Good birds will only take a given amount of commotion by the dog handler, dogs, hunters, and photographer before flushing. You may have to explain these facts to the writer. The more you do to anticipate a writer, the better story you can expect.

Any outdoor writer on his first visit to a hunting preserve may doubt that he will find sporty shooting, or he will compare your operation to other preserves that he has visited. You must prove the sportiness of your preserve, and the best way to do it is to let him hunt. Get him involved. Let the writer discover your birds are "carbon copy" versions of wild birds, your hunting cover is good (even difficult in spots), your dogs know their work, and he has to hunt hard. The writer who earns his birds will think more of your preserve and write accordingly. Give him a "typical" hunt, with no extra birds or fancy frills. If he is in good physical shape, put him into thickets, weed patches, or swamp edges that will convince him it's a real hunt and not armchair hunting.

Never tell a writer how to write his story, or ask to see the story before it goes to press. But if you cannot tell him how to write, you can at least guide him. Be subtle about this. Stress hunting action and lead him away from the usual interest in penned gamebirds. You are selling hunting and outdoor recreation, and the behind-the-scenes operation is no one's business but yours. If the writer asks when the birds were released, tell him you have no regular schedule; it depends on the need. Be indefinite and unclear about such points, but have clear, crisp answers to questions about how the birds are hunted, the dog work, and interesting hunting anecdotes. Your casual conversation can suggest many things without seeming to be hard sell. Leave the impression that this is tailor-made game cover that produces top-notch sport and action.

After "Guns of Autumn," the anti-hunting TV show of several years ago, many preserve operators became suspicious of any and all TV publicity. However, TV is a powerful media form and the type of TV presentation depends on the TV crew and the preserve operator. Make sure that you have a shooting script of sporty hunting and outdoor recreation to follow before going in the field. Do not allow camera coverage of penned birds or too much emphasis on the kill. Make your hunting dogs, the cover, and hunting the theme of your TV show, and make sure that the TV commentator or reporter participates in the hunt event if he is a complete novice. It's the key to a positive TV program (and be sure that a few birds are missed cleanly).

Keep in regular touch with your publicity contacts, and nurture them tenderly and faithfully. Post them well in advance of your opening dates, and follow this up about a week before the hunting begins. Send in short reports of amusing incidents at the preserve — humor is always useful, if it's in good taste. Same thing with any unusual wildlife happenings.

To remain popular with your publicity outlets, maintain a "sunny" disposition regardless of how you privately react to a story or a TV or radio program. Not every item will be presented to your taste. Don't dwell on minor flaws. The important thing is that your preserve received favorable publicity. Express your personal appreciation to the outdoor writer or program director for their helping hand.

If the article in a newspaper or magazine is a good one, make arrangements for reprints. You can use copies for your newsletter, prospective customers, and clubhouse scrapbook. Start an album to file such stories, along with photographs

A group of happy hunters — the key to repeat business (courtesy Winchester Group, Olin Corp.).

of hunting parties, especially celebrities. Everyone likes to associate with a winner.

If a party of local or sports celebrities had good hunting at your preserve, seek their permission to use the occasion for publicity. If the hunting party grants your permission, let your publicity contacts know about it. It pays to have a good camera and know how to use it. Reporters always need photos.

Some preserve operators use photos of hunting parties for promotion within their membership. They will send a few photos of a hunt to a member as a reminder of a pleasant hunt. More often than not, it will stimulate the club member to enjoy another outing at the preserve. It also helps to post photos on a club bulletin board, but keep the photos current and only post good photos.

The more publicity you offer your contacts, and the better you get to know them, the better the chances are for more publicity. Don't neglect your publicity contacts in the off-season. Phone or drop by their office or home just to say ''hello.''

Bring them a brace of gamebirds ready for the oven. Invite them fishing, if you have a pond or stream. Take them predator calling, crow hunting, or woodchucking. Help them with story material they need for their column or program. It pays to be thoughtful to the ones who help you promote and publicize your preserve.[4]

Videotape: Videotape is a relatively new and powerful form of publicity for your preserve and has a number of applications. Videotape is far less expensive than a movie of your preserve operation. A creditable job of taping sporty hunting on your preserve can be done by amateurs. If the preserve operator doesn't own the equipment, there is a good chance that one of his members does. Prepare a shooting script of the scenes that highlight the sporty hunting on your preserve. Wait for a day with good to excellent light conditions and start taping. With the help of a local professional studio you can edit the videotape and install proper credits for showing on your clubhouse TV, or at sport shows and civic programs. If you should have a good TV program of your preserve, ask the TV producer for a video-tape. Chances are that he'll be happy to let you have it for a small fee.

Public Relations

Public relations is defined as the business of inducing the public to have understanding for and goodwill toward a person, firm, or institution. For a hunting preserve operator, public relations is getting people to like you and what you have to offer. It is the basis of the most powerful promotional effort — word-of-mouth advertising. Lots of advertising and publicity may be desirable, but nothing seems to work quite so well as satisfied customers returning for more hunting, and sending and bringing their friends.

What makes a satisfied customer? Sporty hunting! Hunting preserves must provide hunting, utilizing pen-reared gamebirds, so similar to hunting native birds that the customer cannot tell the difference. No amount of high-class promotion can make up for hunting that is patently artificial and unsporting.

A hunting preserve operator is in the outdoor entertainment business. If he stages a poor show, he will lose his customers. If he produces a good show, his customers will spread the word and his box office will be overwhelmed.

The Customer: All of the promotional suggestions pale into insignificance compared to the importance of the treatment that a hunting preserve operator gives to his customers in his role as their host. As Dickey[1] stated, "The notably successful hunting preserve operators go about their work caring for their sportsmen and families in much the same manner as the legendary inn-keepers of generations ago cared for the guests of their hotels. The hunter-guest is given every consideration and furnished every convenience. . ., not within reason, but well beyond rhyme or reason."

The guest is met with a warm greeting and handshake at the parking area. He is helped with his gear. If he brings his hunting dog, the preserve manager sees that the animal is taken care of promptly. The guest is properly introduced to other sportsmen in the lodge. For the overnight guest, the manager personally makes certain the sleeping quarters and related accommodations are in proper order.

The hunter is treated like a royal visitor. The manager, guides, cooks, field hands — everyone employed by the preserve — are courteous and helpful to the Nth degree. The hunter, as much as possible, is allowed to set the pace. While every phase of the day may be planned, the hunter never gets the impression he is being rushed or on a schedule. No mention is ever made of problems that exist. The hunter doesn't really care; he came, mostly likely, to forget his own problems.

Hunting preserve personnel should be cheerful at all times. Compliment the hunter on his shooting ability when he makes a fair shot. Be helpful to women and youngsters. Don't discipline dogs in front of hunting parties. Wounded game should be quickly and quietly dispatched.

Sounds easy? It isn't over a period of 5–6 months. The preserve operator must maintain a constant vigil over himself and his personnel. As the season rolls on, all preserve personnel, including the operator, must remind themselves every morning that today they are going to meet the finest people on earth — their customers.

A hunting preserve is a commercial enterprise, yet no indication should be given that the operator and his personnel are mercenary. The hunting should be leisurely and pleasant. The guides should constantly give the impression that they are enjoying every minute of the hunt, even if it's "killing" them.

In summary, good public relations with your hunters is treating each one as if he is the best patron you have, and offering sporty hunting as nearly natural in every respect as you can possibly make it. The end result will be a satisfied customer.

Newsletters: Newsletters are an important part of your public relations effort with your hunters. It is second only to the importance of a good brochure in the promotional effort of hunting preserves (Appendix A).

Elliott[3] points out that public relations can be defined as the effort expended communicating with your various publics. Among these publics, and unfortunately forgotten all too often by preserve operators, are the members of his hunting preserve. A preserve operator should communicate with his patrons on a monthly basis. The off-season is even more important than the hunting season. You must send a "hello" to them in a way that indicates your appreciation of their patronage, that you consider them as friends, and that you are looking forward to seeing them soon.

Special events during the off-season (National Hunting and Fishing Day, clay target shoots, dog training activities, picnics, etc.) are essential to maintaining a "lifeline" with your hunters. Whatever the activity, be sure that your patrons are invited.

Hunters are interested in your plantings and how they are progressing, your bird dogs, and the outlook for the coming hunting season. You may want to share some outdoor tips with them — a better way to clean a shotgun, new game recipes, or news about a new litter of pups in your kennels or the activities of other members.

The newsletter should reflect the thought of a letter from 1 friend to another sharing something of common interest. Above all, don't include the newsletter with a monthly billing. In the member's mind, this translates into, "I only hear from him when he wants money."

Wildlife Harvest: The trade magazine of the North American Gamebird Association, *Wildlife Harvest*, is a monthly publication that carries many stories on hunting preserves of a general interest. All one has to do is to check with the Editor: John Mullin, Goose Lake, IA 52750.

Community Service: Community service is a public relations effort that redounds to the benefit of the preserve operator and the hunting preserve concept. Public support is necessary for the very future of hunting preserves, and such support depends on the image that each hunting preserve is projecting within its community.

Hunting preserves are natural areas — mosaics of wild, native vegetation. Plantings, such as pine trees, honeysuckle, sorghum patches, etc., add to the diversity of vegetation and serve to attract all forms of wildlife. Most preserves have a lake or pond, and are excellent examples of good land and water conservation practices. Hence, the landless city dweller is attracted like a magnet to preserves, not only to hunt but to enjoy the natural world. The opportunities for community services are unlimited.

National Hunting and Fishing Day (NHFD) is a natural. On a yearly basis it provides a chance for the preserve operator to have "open house." There is work involved, but there is also a source of revenue from food and refreshments. Or you can let one or more civic organizations furnish such services.

Throughout the year at Nilo we had a stream of requests for tours. In most cases we suggested that the group come out on NHFD, and it saved us time and manpower. By phone and letters we had the cooperation of the Boy Scouts, Ducks Unlimited, National Rifle Association, State Conservation Department, U.S. Fish and Wildlife Service, sporting goods dealers, U.S. Soil Conservation Service, Lions Club, muzzle-loaders and "mountain man" groups, plus archery and rifle clubs. Nilo provided the acreage for such willing groups to participate in NHFD.

The "secrets" to a successful NHFD are to enlist the help of the local newspaper through its outdoor writer, and to keep the youngsters occupied and involved with air rifles, .22 rifles, and shotgun shooting at targets that break and make noise. Other activities that attract and hold the attention of youngsters are archery, canoe races, and bait casting with closed-face spinning equipment. The youngsters bring the adults each year. It also pays to have a gimmick or two, such as a large snapping turtle, giant catfish, or snakes. Most state wildlife agencies have such exhibits for use at state fairs. Other possible events are trick shooting, muzzle-loader shoots, and/or duck or turkey calling contests. Nilo averaged about 1,500 participants a year on NHFD. For more information on how to stage a successful NHFD on your preserve, contact the National Shooting Sports Foundation, 1075 Post Road, Riverside, CT 06878.

Service clubs and sportsmens' organizations are always looking for speakers. One can develop an illustrated talk with 35-mm, colored slides, stressing the preserve's natural habitat and sporty hunting. A 15–20-minute talk is sufficient; leave time in a 30-minute presentation for questions.

Hunter education programs offer excellent public relations opportunities for preserves. Cooperating with such programs provides a chance to cultivate both future customers and their parents. You should consider becoming a certified hunter education instructor. Hunter education programs are beginning to require mandatory live firing, and hunting preserves are ideal for such activity. Details on hunter education programs and requirements to become a certified hunter education instructor are available through your state wildlife agency.

The National Scene

There are more than 15 million hunters in the United States, but less than a million have ever hunted on a preserve. Most hunters don't know what a preserve has to offer, and all too often they have a built-in resistance to preserves because of the "free hunting" tradition. Mullin[6] states that we are still in a new and sensitive experiment in outdoor recreation. We must expend effort (promotion) to achieve widespread understanding and acceptance. Sportsmen must be told what a hunting preserve is and what it can mean to them. Free hunting is a myth, and all hunters know this. They must realize that there has to be an economic incentive for the private landowner to provide wildlife habitat and a place to hunt and to propagate game. Further, the American way is that those who benefit must pay. So, the selling job facing the hunting preserve industry on a national basis is sizeable and will require constant and positive promotion.

Cooperative Promotion

Cooperative promotion can be achieved on the state and national levels. On the state level there are numerous annual outdoor, travel, and sport shows. Seldom does it make sense for an individual preserve operator to take a booth, but it does make sense for a state or national association of hunting preserves. The success of participating in such shows depends on developing an attractive booth and having a good supply of state and national hunting preserve directories on hand for distribution as give-away literature. Equipment rental in the form of projectors, screen, and videotape machines may also be necessary. The manpower for the booth is usually furnished by volunteer hunting preserve operators. The value of such exposure is not only to attract new preserve customers but to inform the public on the hunting preserve concept — private enterprise helping to ensure the future of hunting.

On a national basis, we currently depend on The National Shooting Sports Foundation for news releases to the hunting public, sporting journals, and outdoor writers. We also have good allies in the National Rifle Association (NRA), the Outdoor Writers Association of America (OWAA), and the International Association of Fish and Wildlife Agencies (IAFWA). The hunting preserve industry represented by the North American Gamebird Association (NAGA) is trying to foster and improve contacts with these groups.

Yachik[7] pointed out that there are 3 national issues that will affect the hunting preserve industry: (1) gun control, (2) increased anti-hunting emotions in U.S. society, and (3) potential anti-hunting preserve feelings. He suggested that the hunting preserve industry needs to develop communications objectives and strategies that should ultimately develop into a communications plan for long- and short-term goals.

In recent years, the hunting preserve industry has "suffered" from a lack of good promotional movies on the hunting preserve concept and feature stories in the leading hunting and fishing publications. We have missed the direct support of the Sporting Arms and Ammunition Manufacturers' Institute and the efforts of Charley Dickey and Dr. George Burger. The newness of the preserve concept may have worn off, but the need for positive promotion has not.

One of the best national efforts has been a hunting preserve directory, currently published by the NAGA. Back in the early 1960s the NAGA established a set of minimum standards for hunting preserves for the benefit of the prospective hunter, the preserve industry, and the general public. All respondents in the national hunting preserve directory must attest to observing such minimum standards, and be a member of the NAGA to be listed. It behooves every preserve desiring national promotion to be included in this annual listing.

Summary

The best summary of promotional efforts in the hunting preserve industry was written by John Mullin,[6] a tireless worker in behalf of hunting preserves. He stated, "Continuous business success calls for continuous effort, continuous quality control, continuous improvement of our product, continuous planning of every detail — and above all, continuous selling. As we become more self-conscious and better-organized, we shall become increasingly formidable in obtaining adequate and continuing public support for the hunting preserve's vital role in outdoor recreation.

"Strong, active state and national association effort is urgently needed to inform the public, correct mistaken impressions, promote good will, and further the public's knowledge of hunting preserve operations.

"The public's ignorance of these operations has been the source of most preserve problems. No matter how much you know about gamebirds or hunting, you won't get to first base if you fail to properly inform and favorably impress the public. Without promotion . . . it's like winking at a girl in total darkness. You may know what you are doing, but your prospect doesn't."

John M. Mullin, Editor and Publisher of **Wildlife Harvest.**

References

1. Dickey, C., G. Burger, and H. Hampton. 1961. How to promote shooting preserves. Natl. Shooting Sports Foundation, Inc., 1075 Post Road, Riverside, CT.
2. Elliott, B. 1983. Hunting preserve PR. Wildlife Harvest 14(4):46-48. Goose Lake, IA.
3. _____. 1983. Hunting preserve PR. Wildlife Harvest 14(5):54-55. Goose Lake, IA.
4. Kozicky, E., and J. Madson. 1966. Shooting preserve management — the Nilo system. Winchester Div. (Olin Corp.), E. Alton, IL. 311pp.
5. Miller, H. 1979. How to promote a hunting preserve. The Game Bird Bull. 12(4):1,7,13. Hegins, RD 2, PA.
6. Mullin, J. 1983. Publicity and promotion for hunting clubs. Wildlife Harvest 14(11):8-12. Goose Lake, IA.
7. Yachik, V. 1976. Improving the public image of hunting preserves. Wildlife Harvest 7(5):35-41. Goose Lake, IA.

APPENDIX A

Questions and Answers on Hunting Preserve Promotion

In the 1983–84 tour of successful hunting preserves, there were 13 commercial preserve operators that responded to the following questions:

1. *How important do you consider promotion in the success of your preserve?*

   All 13 agreed that promotion was essential.

2. *What types of promotion have you employed?*
   a. Brochures — 100%
   b. National Hunting Preserve Directory — 85%
   c. Newsletter — 85%
   d. Paid advertising — 69%
   e. Speaking engagements — 62%
   f. Outdoor writers — 54%
   g. Publicity efforts (personalities) — 46%
   h. Special events (NHFD, Father-son Seminars, etc.) — 38%
   i. Promotional movies — 31%
   j. Billboard advertising — 0%

3. *Have you developed a pin or medallion for your hunting preserve?*
   Sixty-nine percent responded "yes."

4. *Do you promote the special packaging for gamebirds or shipping cartons?*
   Thirty-one percent responded "yes."

5. *Do you promote through game recipes?*
   Sixty-two percent responded "yes."

6. *Have you ever had a TV show based on your hunting preserve?*
   Sixty-two percent responded "yes."

Chapter 19

HUNTING SAFETY

Hunting is a safe sport, with an accident rate below playing tennis or swimming,[3] and hunting preserves have an excellent safety record. But, good things just don't happen; they have to be planned.

Safe shooting and hunting on a preserve are a team effort with the operator as coach. Everyone (guides and hunters) must do his/her part, but the basic responsibility rests with the operator.

Nilo has a right to be proud of its hunting accident record — more than a quarter of a century of hunting without an accident. This record reflects more than just luck. In the early years, we were concerned about our first hunting safety efforts. Hunters come to a preserve to relax and enjoy a day in the open with dog and gun, not to listen to safety lectures.

Regimentation can ruin a hunter's day. But, to our pleasant surprise, we found that hunters appreciated being cautioned about safe gun handling. They wanted guidelines on proper hunting etiquette, and hunters liked to hear their companions being told about gun safety. After

all, it is most difficult to shoot oneself with a shotgun unless it is in the foot. Hence, we never sensed any resentment to a short talk on safe gun handling, which we always delivered in a positive manner — ''do's'' instead of ''don'ts.''

All guests are directed to Nilo's gun room, where they can uncase their guns, open or check the actions, and place them in a gun rack (Appendix A). The gun room abounds with hunting safety posters. Then, the guests come upstairs to register, greet friends and, more often than not, drink coffee. We insist that all actions of guns remain open until the hunter is in the field or at the target range. The exception to this rule is a double-barreled shotgun, while on the rack or being transported in a hunting vehicle. But, once the hunter picks up the shotgun, we ask that the action be broken. Shotguns with ''open'' or ''broken'' actions are a matter of safe gun handling and courtesy to other hunters and shooters. One can explain most gun safety as a matter of proper field or sporting etiquette. Everyone likes to practice social graces at or away from home.

Guns and Guests

After licenses have been issued to the guests and the day's hunt is outlined, the hunters are assembled and proper overall gun handling etiquette is discussed.

At this juncture, Nilo personnel will concentrate on 3 safety rules for all shooting and hunting:

1. All gun actions are to be open when a guest picks up his/her shotgun, and are to remain open until it's their time to shoot or hunt. Double-barreled shotguns may be transported to the field in a hunting vehicle with the actions closed, providing the guns have been checked.

2. No exchange of 12- and 20-gauge shotguns. Hunters may want their companions to try the fine pointing qualities of their pet 20-gauge shotguns, and so they exchange shotguns at the clay target range or in the field. Result: a mix-up of 12-gauge and 20-gauge shotshells. In the excitement of shooting, a man may fail to notice that he is putting a 20-gauge shell into a 12-gauge shotgun. Who examines shotshells when the birds are flying? The results can be disastrous!

3. The Nilo manager will offer to help hunting guests with their shotguns — especially with any problems of loading, unloading, or operating the safety.[2]

Hunters often come to a hunting preserve with a borrowed gun, or with no gun at all. If such folks are in the group of hunters, indicate your willingness to help — and admire the good judgment of a hunter who doesn't want to go into the field not knowing his gun. You can give such hunters a demonstration while the rest of the group is getting ready to go afield, and that demonstration is best held outside the clubhouse.

Upland Hunting

Blaze orange hunting coats, and/or caps are no longer an option for upland hunting; they are a downright necessity, not only for reasons of safety but as *a matter of courtesy* to your hunting companions. Nothing is more distracting for a seasoned hunter than not being sure of the location of his companions and/or the guide when a gamebird flushes. Blaze orange outer clothing helps to quickly locate the position of each in-

dividual. Yet, besides Nilo and Richmond Hunting Club, Illinois, few hunting preserves require all hunters and guides to wear blaze orange while hunting.

In the State of Michigan, the mandatory use of blaze orange for small game hunting was required in 1977, and line-of-sight accidents dropped from 111.5 to 55.8 per year after the law was passed.[1] Blaze orange does what it is supposed to do — reduce hunting accidents.

At Nilo every guest wears a blaze orange vest outside his normal clothing. The vests have 2 large pockets for carrying shotshells.

The vests seem to have a psychological effect on hunters. The horseplay of the clubhouse ceases, and the guests seem more receptive to safe gun handling procedures. The bright vests are a constant visual reminder of gun safety.

Prior to upland hunting, the guests are reminded of the proper way to carry a shotgun in the field and about opened and closed actions prior to and following the hunt. Nilo stresses the importance of hunting with the safeties in the "on" position. Safeties should only be slipped into the "off" position when the gamebird is flushed, and immediately placed back in the "on" position as the gun is being brought down from the shoulder. All shotguns can be loaded with the safety in the "on" position.

Nilo encourages a gun handling practice called "fingering the safety" — reminding the hunters to continually check the position of the safety when they are in the field. It is an easy matter to frequently check the safety with one's thumb or forefinger throughout the hunt, and it is an excellent habit to form.

During the hunt, the guide should occasionally glance at the safeties of the shotguns in use, and slip a gun safety into the ''on'' position if it's off when it should not be — a case where action speaks louder than words. The same ''silent'' technique is effective with guests who are lax in how they control the muzzle of their shotguns in the field.

In the 1983–84 tour of hunting preserves, the most frequent gun handling violations noted by the operator were: (1) hunting with the safeties in the ''off'' position and (2) forgetting to control the direction in which the muzzle of the shotgun pointed while hunting (Appendix B).

On chukar and pheasant hunts, the guide lines up the hunters so that 2 men are on each side of him as he works the cover with his dog(s). He watches the line to make sure that no hunter lags behind, or gets in front. A good safety rule is no cross-shooting of flushed gamebirds; hunters on the right of the guide shoot at birds on their side and vice versa on the left side. No gamebirds should be shot on the ground. Left-handed shooters should be on the extreme right of the guide. Shooting at low birds should be avoided, for the safety of the hunting dog.

If rank novices are hunting, it may be wise for the operator to suggest some clay target shooting prior to the hunt and/or accompany the party if possible. The guide will be too busy with his dogs and the general conduct of the hunt to give much personal attention to an individual hunter, and personal attention to novice shooters can be a selling feature of your preserve.

The guide should be prepared to hit the dirt if he happens to be between a flying bird and the shooters. This is not only good field etiquette on his part — it is basic self-preservation!

Quail hunting is the most dangerous type of upland shooting because it is the fastest. It is essential that the shooter know where everyone else is located before the covey is flushed. There is no way of predicting what direction a covey will fly, and it's a case of split-second shooting. The shooter has little time to think; he reacts on conditioned reflexes.

Because of this, quail shooting should be restricted to 2 hunters at a time, or a maximum of 3 if they are really experienced.

If a 4-man party hunts quail, 2 hunters go in on the covey flush and then hunt the singles that they and the guide have ''marked down.'' After the singles are hunted, the other 2 gunners, who remained either with the hunting vehicle or at least 100 yards to the rear with the actions of their guns opened, come up to take their place with the guide.

Gray partridge are new on the hunting preserve scene. Until more hunting experience on preserves is acquired with this species, it may be prudent to follow the same hunting techniques as those prescribed for quail.

Duck Shooting

All mallard shooting should be conducted within blinds that are constructed for shooting safety. The blinds should look like duck blinds, but have high sides except to the front. They should be positioned so that it is impossible for

A shotgun rack being put to good use (courtesy Winchester Group, Olin Corp.).

a hunter in 1 blind to shoot into another blind, or back where other hunters are assembled with the dog handler. It is also advisable to have the blinds on wooden skids so that they can be moved.

A gun rack (Appendix A) is kept in the duck-shooting area for the guns of hunters who are to be assigned blinds, or who have completed their duck hunting. Check on the actions of the guns to make sure that they are open. Again, the most effective reminder to a careless hunter is to open the shotgun without saying a word.

When the hunters are assembled at the duck shoot, they should be told that the gun actions should be open while going to and from the blinds. Guns are loaded only within the blinds and the safety is kept ''on'' until the gun is raised for shooting. When the gun is brought down from the shoulder, the safety is slipped into the ''on'' position.

At Nilo only 2 hunters are permitted in a blind, which gives sufficient space to shoot, load, and unload shotguns. If the hunters are moved from 1 blind to another during a shoot, they are asked to unload their shotguns before leaving the blind. Shooting is never allowed from outside the blind.

In the early years, Nilo had benches in the duck blinds for the comfort of the shooters, but they were removed as a safety precaution. It is dangerous for 1 man to shoot from a sitting position while his partner is standing beside him. Furthermore, some overly enthusiastic hunters will stand on the bench to try to get that last shot at a departing duck.

Hunters should not be allowed to pick up fallen ducks. For safety and efficiency, as well as the pleasure of watching gun dogs at work, use retrievers.

General Comments

Langenau[3] pointed out, in his analysis of hunting accidents in the State of Michigan, that older hunters (45 years or more) need to be warned about fatigue, stumbling, and their reduced ability to handle firearms. Since the vast majority of hunters on preserves are within the older age group, it behooves preserve operators to be aware of this safety problem and to exercise appropriate precautions.

Non-hunters should be kept out of the field. There are always those who want to watch a hunt; if they must do so, let them watch from a car with the windows rolled up. Spectators are not part of the sport of hunting, and they don't add anything to hunters' enjoyment.

There should be an inviolate rule about the use of any alcoholic beverage during the course of a hunt or during the noon luncheon break. At the end of the day, of course, every man is on his own. This rule is appreciated by guests, and it will attract far more customers than it will ever drive away.

It is well to be prepared for emergencies. The telephone numbers of the nearest doctor, ambulance, and hospital should be posted inconspicuously near every phone on the area. A uniform emergency procedure should be developed and understood by all employees in case of serious illness or injury.

Don't overlook the cardiac patient. The hunt can and should be tailored to the physical capabilities of the guest. The good operator will arrange such a hunt without comment or fanfare,

Signs and hunter safety posters discreetly placed help to promote safe gun handling.

and it will be appreciated. No guest should be placed in the embarrassing position of having to admit that a hunt is too strenuous for him. Have a car available should the guest tire in the field. Men often become boys when hunting and forget their physical limitations. It is advisable that the operator and the guides on a hunting preserve take an American Red Cross approved first-aid course and equip every hunting vehicle with an emergency first-aid kit.

Hunting safety is vital to every hunting preserve. It can be so obvious that it can be overlooked, but every possible effort should be made to prevent accidents of all kinds.

Preach hunting safety, *live* hunting safety, and *enforce* hunting safety on your hunting preserve.[2]

References

1. Dabb, J. 1983. Hunting accident deaths and injuries — 1983 report. Michigan Dept. Nat. Resources, Law Enforcement Div., Lansing, MI. 4pp.
2. Kozicky, E., and J. Madson. 1966. Shooting preserve management — the Nilo system. Winchester-Western Press, Winchester Group, Olin Corp., E. Alton, IL. 311pp.
3. Langenau, E., T. Fournier, and J. Dabb. 1985. Analysis of 1977-1983 hunting accidents in Michigan. Michigan Dept. of Nat. Resources, Rose Lake Wildlife Res. Center, 8562 E. Stoll Rd., E. Lansing, MI.

APPENDIX A
Winchester's Shotgun Rack

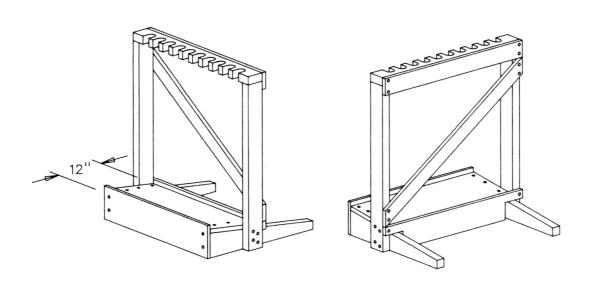

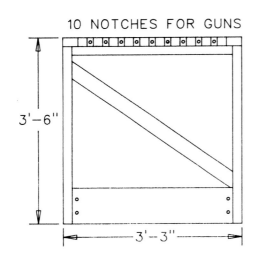

10 NOTCHES FOR GUNS

3'-6"

3'-3"

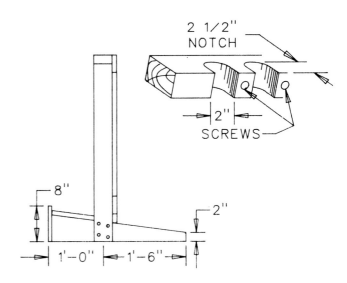

2 1/2" NOTCH

2"

SCREWS

8"

2"

1'-0"   1'-6"

APPENDIX B

Questions and Answers on Hunting Safety

In the 1983–84 tour of successful hunting preserves, there were 12 preserves who responded to queries on hunting safety as follows:

1. *Do you have hunting safety rules for hunting guests?*

All preserves have hunting safety rules. Nine of the preserves post the rules, or they use newsletters or handouts to inform their members.

2. *Does the manager review the hunting safety rules with guests prior to each hunt?*

Six of the preserve operators review hunting safety with their guests prior to each hunt. Other preserves have the guides discuss hunting safety with their party and/or the operator reviews hunting safety on his preserve with each newcomer.

3. *Do your hunting guides check on hunting safety in the field?*

If guides are used for a hunting party, they do check on safety throughout the hunt. Most preserves give the guides instructions to terminate a hunt if the hunting party continues to violate safety rules.

4. *Do you use blaze orange vest or hunting coats?*

Blaze orange hunting coats and/or vests are mandatory on only 2 hunting preserves for upland hunting. Other preserves encourage the use of blaze orange, and 3 preserves considered the use of blaze orange as unnecessary regimentation.

5. *Do you carry liability insurance?*

All hunting preserves contacted carry liability insurance.

6. *What are your most frequent hunting safety violations?*

a. Guests hunting with the safety in the "off" position.

b. Guests failing to control the direction of the shotgun muzzle.

7. *Do you provide clay target shooting; and if so, do you consider clay target shooting valuable to the hunting success of your guests?*

All hunting preserves provide some form of clay target shooting, ranging from a practice trap to automatic trap and/or skeet fields. Besides keeping the guests occupied, preserve operators consider the main benefit of clay target shooting is to serve as a refresher course in shotgun handling for their hunters.

Chapter 20

PROCESSING GAMEBIRDS

The dressing and packaging (processing) of gamebirds is an important item on quality hunting preserves but is often overlooked by new preserve operators. Both the preserve operator and the hunter should be proud of their dressed gamebirds. ''Pres'' Mann, Hunters Creek Club, Michigan, states that shot gamebirds should be treated as trophies, and they are trophies to your hunters.

One of the advantages of patronizing a hunting preserve is the opportunity to take home oven-dressed birds. Game cleaning is a lost art in many modern homes, and hunting preserves must offer this service.

From the moment the bird is shot in the field until it ends as a delightful meal, there are a number of critical steps:

1. Rapidly dissipate body heat from shot birds.

2. Minimize the time between shooting and dressing or picking of the bird. (Some preserves collect shot gamebirds from hunters or from given locations in the field every hour or so.)

3. If the birds are picked, all feathers, including pin feathers, must be removed.

4. Thoroughly remove all blood from the carcass of the bird by soaking it in a chill tank of ice water for at least a few hours and preferably overnight.

5. Use drainage racks after the birds are removed from the chill tank.

6. Package the bird in a shrink-type plastic to minimize the amount of air within the package.

7. Quick-freeze the birds at -10°F and store them at 0–10°F.

8. Follow a time-proven recipe in preparing the birds for the table.

The most common complaints by cooks are that dressed, frozen gamebirds were not picked cleanly or that there is an excessive amount of bloody water when the birds are thawed. Both of these problems can be avoided by attention to details — pick the birds cleanly, and thoroughly soak and wash the carcasses of the birds in ice water after evisceration. Also, allow the birds to remain on the drainage rack long enough to drain properly.

Contracting versus Do-it-yourself

The new hunting preserve operator may be tempted to contract with a poultry house or even a private individual to process his gamebirds. But this has major drawbacks — quality control may be lost, there is little assurance that the contractor will continue to dress your gamebirds both within season and from 1 hunting season to the next. The contractor may escalate his prices from 1 contract to the next. Further, one has the problem of weekends, holidays, and special requests for processing gamebirds. Will the contractor accommodate you and your hunting guests? Of the successful hunting preserves I visited, only two contracted with a poultry plant for dressed birds.

Processing gamebirds is a good source of revenue for a preserve, and it doesn't take long to pay for the necessary equipment. The cost of labor is solved by contracting with responsible individuals on a piecemeal basis. Housewives, high-school students, family members of either the preserve operator or his employees are all good possibilities and have been used successfully on a number of hunting preserves. Most preserves split the charges to the guests for processing gamebirds with their part-time workers.

For dependability, quality control, and peace of mind, hunting preserves should strive to install and operate their own gamebird processing facility.

Skinning versus Picking

There is a growing tendency, especially on southern preserves, to skin gamebirds instead of picking them. Skinning gamebirds does not require as large a financial investment (scalder and picker), and is quicker and more efficient. It helps to solve the problem of the hunter leaving with the birds that he shot. On the other hand, housewives are not accustomed to preparing skinned poultry for meals, and there are fewer suitable cooking recipes. However, proponents of skinning gamebirds offer their hunting guests a number of cooking options that avoid the dryness problem, and some preserve operators have found a market for the skins of gamebirds.

Mullin[1] wrote that everyone agrees that picked gamebirds are more tasty than skinned birds. The skin helps to retain the gamebird's subcutaneous fat, which helps to keep roasted or broiled gamebirds from becoming too dry. Perhaps the most important point is that gamebirds with the skin intact make a more attractive package to your hunter and his family.

The decision whether to skin or pick gamebirds rests with each preserve operator. There is a growing tendency to skin quail on southern hunting preserves, whereas most northern preserves are picking their gamebirds, especially pheasants, ducks, and turkeys. Further, if a preserve operator is considering smoking gamebirds, it is essential to pick the birds.

Processing Gamebirds

Whether you pick or skin, your facility for processing gamebirds must be clean and open to inspection by anyone. Your hunters may be coming to the facility to pick up their gamebirds, and it is important that they be favorably impressed with your processing operation. Along with the clubhouse and the dog kennels, it should be clean and neat.

A clean and pleasant room to process gamebirds.

Dr. L. Schwartz[4] listed the specifications of an acceptable processing plant for gamebirds (Appendix A). He pointed out that even though gamebird processing facilities are not under mandatory public health inspection, rules for processing plants on hunting preserves should nevertheless be rigid. Any new or remodeled gamebird processing facility should be built to U.S. Department of Agriculture (USDA) specifications for building construction, layout, and sanitation. The USDA requires that the killing, scalding, and picking operation must be in a separate room from the room used for evisceration, chilling, draining, packaging, and storing. The building specifications require that the floors must be cleanable, impervious (no wood), and in good repair; the walls must be smooth and cleanable to 6 feet and moisture resistant higher; the ceiling must be moisture resistant, free of rust, or scaling paint; and all equipment must be of non-corrosive cleanable metal.

The USDA regulations also cover water supply, waste disposal, fly and vermin control, and personnel hygiene and apparel. The specifications are rigid and demanding, but they do provide a clean and pleasant place for workers and constitute a source of justifiable pride for management. In the long run, they will save time and money. Contact either the state office of public health or the USDA for the specifications.

Equipment and Supplies

Scalders: There are a number of good scalders on the market (see ''Where to Buy'' in the chapter, ''Short Subjects''). The most important feature is the ability of the equipment to recover to a temperature of 140°F when a number of cold gamebirds are immersed in the holding tank. Don't buy too small a scalder. The best temperature for scalding is the vicinity of 140°F, and the length of scalding time will depend on the type of scalder, the number and species of gamebirds, and the time of year. Some preserve operators add a few drops of detergent to the hot water.

Pickers: Again, there are a number of good mechanical pickers on the market. The larger pickers, such as the Ashley, Pickwick, etc., are more efficient for the larger gamebirds. But, the revival of the Coker machine, with improvements, by the good folks at the Georgia Quail Farm was welcomed by preserve operators who pick quail.[2] Unfortunately, the manufacture of this picker has been discontinued again.

Eviscerating Tables: The best tables are stainless steel, with a large opening in the center to accommodate a garbage can for entrails and for ease in washing down. The table should also be of sufficient height to minimize back strain on your personnel.

Chill Tank: A chill tank should be large enough to easily hold gamebirds from a day's hunt. It must be easy to drain. Stainless steel tanks are the easiest to keep clean and will not rust. An ice machine with sufficient capacity is also an important part of the chilling process. Nothing removes blood from a bird carcass any faster or better than ice-cold water. Shot birds require at least a few hours in a chill tank with ice-cold water, or until rigor mortis is completed. Overnight is even better. To skimp on this phase of bird cleaning is to assure the bird will be encased with bloody water when it thaws in the kitchen of the hunter's home. Further, the quicker the body temperature of the gamebird is brought down to 40°F or lower, the better the quality of the meat.

Drainage Rack: Draining the birds thoroughly after they come out of the chill tank will help avoid the presence of bloody water after the carcass thaws in the plastic bag. One can easily construct a suitable drainage rack for a large number of birds. The front of the rack should be slanted so that the birds on the top row are not draining on the birds on the next row, etc.

Packaging: There are various types of plastic bags for packaging gamebirds, but Cryovac bags have proven to be superb. They maintain the table quality of gamebirds for extended periods of time, if the air is exhausted from the bags just before sealing. All packaged gamebirds should indicate the species of gamebird within the package. It's advisable to have an assortment of bag sizes to accommodate different-size gamebirds. The added advantage of Cryovac bags is that they can be shrunk down on the birds to make an appealing package. If you decide to go first class, add a colorful design of your preserve's emblem on the bag.

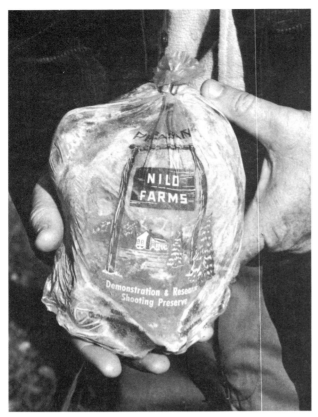

Gamebirds should be well-cleaned and attractively packaged.

The packaged birds should be quick-frozen at -10°F and stored at 0–10°F.

General Comments

A preserve operator should encourage hunters to take their gamebirds when they leave a hunting preserve. To do so, you may have to maintain a "bank" of frozen birds and give them to your hunters in exchange for freshly killed birds. The proper processing of gamebirds takes about 24 hours. If it is necessary to ship game, have a supply of insulated cartons or coolers and a good source of dry ice.

Air express is the best means of shipping. If you can, wait until the weather is cold and ship on Mondays. Mark the cartons "perishable" and check with the shipping agent of the carrier on delivery schedules to specific locations. Then, notify the addressee.

Even with all these precautions and air express, cartons of gamebirds will be lost or will spoil in transit. Also, shipping is time consuming, so avoid it whenever possible. Tell your hunters about shipping problems and urge them to take their quota of gamebirds when they leave. It's a good idea to have an attractive insulated box or cooler for shipping dressed gamebirds, or for the convenience of hunters who wish to carry them home. Shipping boxes or coolers are another good place to advertise your hunting preserve.

As with other services provided by hunting preserves, you should realize a fair profit from dressed birds.

Gamebird Recipes

Have some copies of your favorite gamebird recipes and slip them into the shipping carton with the gamebirds. It's one of those little things that makes life pleasant for both the hunter and the lady in the kitchen.

Every hunting preserve that serves meals should have at least 1 special recipe for gamebirds that titilates the palate of their hunters. As an example, Nilo started serving "Zerkowsky's pheasant potpie" more than 20 years ago and, ever since, their hunters have been contented, happy, and calling for another pheasant potpie luncheon. It is something special, and the recipe has been followed successfully by many a household cook. After all, steak and chicken is available in almost every restaurant, but Zerkowsky's pheasant potpie is not!

Every hunting preserve that serves meals should develop a specialty gamebird meal, one that keeps their hunters coming back for more. An excellent cookbook with gamebird recipes is *Wildlife Harvest Game Bird Cook Book*.[3]

So, when you are packing a box of gamebirds for your hunters, slip a flyer of your favorite gamebird recipes into the box. For example:

"Enclosed are some of _____ Preserve's favorite gamebird recipes for your consideration. They have been highly successful for us, and we hope they will be for you.

"These birds are fully frozen, dressed, and packaged, and should not be thawed until ready for consumption."

Zerkowsky's (Nilo's) Pheasant Potpie

1. Boil 1 pheasant until tender with medium size onion, 2 leaf stalks of celery, salt, and pepper. When phesant is tender, remove from broth, strip meat from bones and dice in large pieces. Strain, and retain 3 cups of broth.

2. Dice fine 1 medium-size onion and some celery. Saute this in 1 tablespoon butter until tender but not brown.

3. Melt 1/2 stick of butter in sauce pan and add 3 heaping tablespoons of flour. Stir until well blended without browning. While hot, add to strained pheasant broth brought to a boil. Stir until thick and smooth.

4. Remove thickened broth from heat and add a little Worcestershire sauce and a few drops of yellow food coloring.

5. Add sauteed onion and celery. Mushrooms may be added if desired.

6. Place diced pheasant in a pan or casserole dish, pour in thickened broth and cover with a rich pie crust. Bake at 450° until pie crust is brown and done. Serves 4.

Nilo
Brighton, IL

Hunters Creek Sauerkraut and Duck

Cut duck in quarters. Lightly salt and pepper pieces. In a baking dish put a layer of sauerkraut, then duck, and sprinkle generously with chopped onion (about 1 onion), and cover with more sauerkraut. Cover baking dish and bake 3 hours in pre-heated oven at 350°.

Hunters Creek Club
Metamora, MI

Hawkeye's Stuffed Quail

12 quail
12 thin slices of bacon
2 sticks margarine
1 lb. pure pork sausage
2 cups flour
3 T. grape jelly
2 cups of red wine

Stuff quail with sausage. Wrap a strip of bacon around quail's breast. Season the flour with salt and pepper. Roll quail in seasoned flour. Melt 2 sticks of margarine in frying pan, place quail in frying pan and brown. Remove quail from pan.

Add seasoned flour to drippings to make enough brown gravy to cover birds. Add wine and grape jelly. Place quail in deep pan or baking dish. Pour gravy over quail. Cover top of pan with foil. Bake in slow oven (about 250°) until tender, about 1 1/2-2 hours.

Hawkeye Hunting Club
Center, TX

Nilo's Roast Chukar

4 chukars
1/4 cup butter
1 recipe brown or wild rice

Clean and dry chukars thoroughly. Stuff with brown or wild rice stuffing. Wrap each chukar separately in aluminum foil. Bake in slow oven (325°) 1 hour. Unwrap birds. Brush with butter. Bake in hot oven (425°) 10–15 minutes, or until brown. Prepare gravy from drippings. Correct seasoning. Serves 8.

Nilo
Brighton, IL

Brown or Wild Rice Stuffing

1 cup brown or wild rice
1 medium onion, chopped
1/2 cup diced celery
1/8 t. pepper
1 can (4 oz.) sliced mushrooms
1/4 cup butter
1 t. salt
1/2 t. seasoned salt
1/2 t. ground marjoram

Cook rice about 5 minutes less than directed on the package. Cook onion, celery, and drained mushrooms (save liquid) in butter until tender. Add to rice. Mix in seasonings. Add mushroom liquid as needed. The mixture should be moist and should hold together very well.

Nilo
Brighton, IL

Smothered Pheasant

Cut 2 pheasants into serving pieces. Shake pieces in seasoned flour. Brown in hot fat on all sides. Remove to large casserole and add 1 medium onion, chopped; 2 stalks of celery, chopped; 1 can cream of mushroom soup; and 1/2 cup dry white wine. Cover and simmer for

177

1 1/2 hours in an oven at 375° or until the meat
is tender.

> Gloria Mullin
> Arrowhead Hunting Club
> Goose Lake, IA

References

1. Mullin, J. 1979. Skinning vs. plucking game birds. Wildlife Harvest 10(4):56. Goose Lake, IA.
2. _____. 1981. New game bird picker. Wildlife Harvest
   12(1):16. Goose Lake, IA.
3. _____. 1984. Wildlife harvest game bird cook book.
   Arrowhead Hunting Club, Goose Lake, IA. 151pp.
4. Schwartz, L. 1978. A processing plant for game birds.
   The Game Bird Bull. 13(3):1,5,16. Rt. 2, Hegins, PA.

APPENDIX A
Processing Plant for Gamebirds

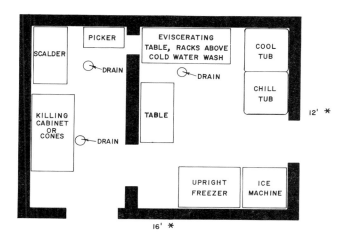

★ DIMENSIONS VARY WITH SIZE AND
TYPE OF EQUIPMENT. THIS IS A
SCHEMATIC LAYOUT ONLY.

ALL DRAINS MUST BE
DEEP-SEAL TRAPPED.

ALL FLOORS MUST SLOPE
TOWARD DRAINS.

PLANT AND PROCESSING SPECIFICATIONS

Separation	Separate rooms are required for killing, scalding, and picking and for eviscerating, chilling, and packing gamebirds.
Water	Potable, as indicated by local health authority.
Floors	Impervious, cleanable, in good repair.
Walls	Smooth, cleanable to 6 ft. above floor – moisture resistant on to ceiling.
Ceiling	Moisture resistant, free of rust, scaling paint.
Openings	Screened or with devices to prevent and control flies and vermin.
Equipment	Rust resistant, non-corrosive, cleanable, non-toxic metal (no wood permitted).

THE PENNSYLVANIA STATE UNIVERSITY
AGRICULTURAL EXTENSION SERVICE

PROCESSING PLANT FOR GAMEBIRDS

DRWN. BY: SLB	ORDER NO.	SHEET 1 OF 1
DSGN. BY: ARG	750-298	
DATE: DEC. 1969		

Chapter 21

GAMEBIRD DISEASES

Stanley A. Vezey, D.V.M.
Poultry Disease Research Center
University of Georgia
953 College Station Road
Athens, GA

L. Dwight Schwartz, D.V.M.
Animal Health Diagnostic Laboratory
Michigan State University
Lansing, MI

Disease prevention, early diagnosis, and treatment are important parts of gamebird husbandry. Wild birds are susceptible to many diseases; however, disease problems are usually intensified when large numbers of birds are concentrated in a relatively small area. Crowding animals that have a large area in their normal habitat results in at least 2 factors that affect the incidence of disease. Social and physical stresses are created, and the density or level of exposure to disease-causing organisms is increased. Both factors are known to increase susceptibility to disease.

The above factors are enough to cause serious problems, but poor management, inadequate nutrition, overcrowding, beak trimming, and vaccinations also are stress factors. Some are necessary, such as beak trimming, but allowing additional stress factors that are avoidable to overlap the necessary ones produces a compound effect that can be disastrous. The preserve operator must eliminate or keep all stress factors at a minimum as the first step in disease prevention.

Most diseases of gamebirds reared in captivity are a direct result of the above factors; but population density, or overcrowding, is the primary predisposing cause of diseases in pen-reared birds. There are few exceptions. For example, quail bronchitis is caused by a highly infectious and contagious virus. There is some evidence to indicate that this disease occurs rather frequently in wild quail. Avian pox is another virus disease that is of frequent occurrence in wild birds as well as those in captivity.

Diseases of pen-reared birds are not usually a serious threat to native birds that may be in the area where pen-reared birds are to be released. In theory, one should consider the release of infected, pen-raised birds as a potential hazard; however, the probability does not warrant the undue amount of concern that has been expressed by some wildlife biologists. Preserve operators should never knowingly release sick birds. Survival of sick birds released (for all practical purposes) is very short. If not harvested immediately, most sick birds that are released will be unlikely to live for more than 24–48 hours.

Prevention of disease should be a preserve operator's primary goal. Treatment is an emergency procedure that is frequently inadequate. Some highly contagious diseases occur in spite of good husbandry and prevention practices; however, most diseases can be prevented. Here are suggested guidelines.

1. Obtain breeding stock, hatching eggs, or young birds from reputable producers that have disease-free flocks.

2. Provide adequate space, water, and feed.

3. Isolation is an absolute must. Free-flying birds should be screened out. Do not allow visitors. Do not visit other premises without showering and changing clothes before attending your birds. Rodents can be carriers of diseases — maintain a rodent control program. Domestic poultry should not be kept on a preserve, nor should employees be allowed to own poultry.

4. Avoid mixing gamebirds from different suppliers.

5. Clean and disinfect waterers daily.

6. Brooding and rearing birds on wire will prevent most internal parasites and many infectious diseases.

7. External parasites are frequently carriers of disease. An adequate control program should be maintained.

8. Clean and disinfect holding pens and equipment after each group of birds is removed.

9. Dogs, cats, and pet birds are potential carriers of disease and should not be allowed near gamebird facilities.

10. Remove dead birds each day and dispose by burning, burying, or use of a disposal pit.

Sanitation

Sanitation is the promotion of good health by the use of proper hygiene to eliminate or reduce the level of disease-causing organisms in a given environment to the point that diseases are reduced to a level of little, if any, economic consequence. Sanitation should be a routine part of all gamebird management programs. Isolation and sanitation are an essential element of gamebird husbandry.

Sanitation principles should be utilized by the people who must visit preserves, on all equipment brought onto a preserve, and before replacing gamebirds in a holding pen. Daily cleaning of waterers and general cleanliness should be practiced to prevent the buildup of disease-causing organisms.

If a contagious disease should occur, complete sanitation and decontamination must be accomplished before repopulating the holding or rearing facilities.

Cleaning

Cleanliness comes first. No disinfectant will do a satisfactory job unless it can reach the surface of the object to be disinfected. Large amounts of organic material can reduce the effectiveness or completely inactivate some commonly used disinfectants.

Thorough cleaning should remove 90–95% of the adhering contaminating material. Hot water is more effective than cold. Detergents or other cleansing agents should be used, and applied with sufficient pressure to remove contaminating debris and to penetrate cracks and crevices. Soap may be used in soft water. Synthetic detergents are usually more effective in hard water. Do not mix different types of detergents, as one may tend to inactivate or decrease the effectiveness of either or both. For example, the effectiveness of quaternary ammonium compounds (usually called "Quats") is reduced by soap and detergents. "Quats" are compatible with trisodium phosphate, washing soda, or lye.

The hunting preserve owner must have good, healthy birds to satisfy his client's needs. If the owner is also the breeder, he is aware of the health status and knows if the birds are suitable for release. Many preserve owners prefer to buy birds from someone who specializes in supplying his industry with good quality "flyers." Reputable breeders do their best to maintain disease-free birds, and most do not object to a random sample of birds being submitted for examination to the nearest diagnostic laboratory. Eight–10, average-quality birds are considered an adequate sample. If in doubt, and assuming the service is available, this is a recommended procedure to assure quality birds.

Cannibalism

Cannibalism is a vice found all too frequently in pen-reared gamebirds. Gamebirds of all breeds and ages are subject to outbreaks of cannibalism, especially ring-necked pheasants.

The 3 broad categories of reasons for cannibalism in gamebirds are management, behavior, and nutrition. However, cannibalism may occur under the most favorable conditions, and not under less favorable conditions.[1]

The control of cannibalism in gamebirds can be best accomplished by the following management techniques:

1. Provide adequate floor or pen space for the birds.

2. Remove dead, sick, or weak birds from the flock immediately.

3. Remove obstacles or equipment that may physically injure birds.

4. Avoid introduction of a few new birds into an established pen population.

5. Restrict human, dog, or predator traffic near bird pens.

6. Provide adequate feeder space and waterers.

7. Avoid sudden changes in the texture of the feed.

8. Provide adequate shelter, ground cover, roost poles, etc.

9. Use proper mechanical devices or management efforts for control of cannibalism — less light, specs, bits, and/or debeaking.

Diagnosis and Treatment of Diseases

Accurate diagnosis of a disease requires experience and training that the average preserve operator does not have. Visible symptoms and postmortem lesions are frequently not sufficient evidence on which to make a positive diagnosis. Laboratory procedures that require considerable equipment are necessary.

The services of poultry diagnostic laboratories are available to the preserve operator. Personnel in these labs are experienced and have the necessary equipment to make an accurate diagnosis.

At the *first* signs of illness, consult the nearest diagnostic laboratory. Do *not* delay action hoping the disease will disappear. It rarely does — and procrastination is an invitation for disaster. The diagnostician is also your best source for information regarding treatment of diseases, what drugs to use, and how to administer them.

Disease prevention by sound husbandry practices cannot be over-emphasized. If disease does occur, make use of available diagnostic facilities for competent advice on how to manage the problem. You cannot afford to do otherwise.

Medication

Drugs and antibiotics should not be indiscriminately used. Some medications are routinely used as a preventative; for example, coccidiostats. Medications can be administered in the feed or drinking water. Very few medications have U.S. Food and Drug Administration clearance for mixing in the feed of gamebirds. This does not necessarily indicate a lack of safety or effectiveness. However, it is not legal for a feed manufacturer to mix a feed containing a non-nutrient additive (medication) that has not been approved. Home mixing is not recommended, because it is difficult to do a satisfactory job with the equipment normally available for on-the-farm use.

Medicated poultry feeds are available. Feeds for domestic turkeys closely approximate feeds for gamebirds and, in many instances, the medication for turkeys within the feeds is an effective treatment for some gamebird diseases.

Water medication is frequently used and is the preferred method of administration for emergency treatment of disease. Generally speaking, the gamebird dosage for water medications is the same as for poultry. Most effective medications are available from suppliers of this type product.

Drugs not labeled with directions for administration to a specific species can be prescribed by your veterinarian. Consult a ''vet'' knowledgeable of gamebird diseases for recommendations.

Common Gamebird Diseases

Quail Bronchitis: This is an acute and highly contagious respiratory infection of young quail, caused by a virus. Difficulty in breathing is the most noticeable and usually an unmistakable sign of the disease. Mortality of chicks under 3 weeks of age may approach 100%. In older birds the symptoms are not usually severe, and mortality is normally less than 20%.

Exactly how quail bronchitis is spread is a mystery. Free-flying birds are suspected as carriers, and the disease is thought by many to be transmitted from the breeder flock to the young chick; however, many breeders report that the best control method is to retain survivors of an outbreak for breeding stock.

Ulcerative Enteritis: A common and serious disease of quail and domestic poultry and a minor disease of other birds, ulcerative enteritis is a bacterial disease caused by one of a group of very common bacteria *(Clostridium)*.

The causative organism is always present in the soil, droppings, litter, and the gut. The level of exposure can be reduced by adequate sanitation. Stress is important in precipitating an active infection (also true of many other diseases) and must be kept to a minimum.

The onset of ulcerative enteritis may be very sudden and death may occur without grossly visible evidence of sickness. In less acute cases, listlessness, loss of appetite, watery white droppings, and a ''humped-up'' position are commonly noted. Unless treatment is started promptly, mortality in young birds may be 100%; 50% mortality is not uncommon.

A postmortem examination will reveal an acute inflammatory enteritis, with ulcers in the intestine and ceca frequently observed. The ulcers may rupture, resulting in an inflammatory infection of the lining of the abdominal cavity. The liver may also be affected, showing light-colored, irregular patches of infected areas.

Some antibiotics are effective for the treatment and prevention of ulcerative enteritis. Brooding and rearing on wire is the most effective means of controlling this disease.

Pullorum and Typhoid: These 2 diseases were once very common in domestic poultry and are at times a problem in gamebirds. They have been (for all practical purposes) eradicated from domestic poultry by a blood-testing program. It is recommended that gamebirds be purchased only from a certified pullorum-typhoid free breeder flock.

Botulism: An acute disease of birds and animals caused by eating materials (feed, dead birds, other animal or vegetable matter) that contain a toxin produced by the bacteria, *Clostri-*

dium botulinum. Normally this bacteria grows in rotting or decaying organic matter. There is good evidence that certain insects may harbor the bacteria and the toxin. There is no treatment. Good sanitation and hygiene are the only effective means of prevention of botulism.

Botulism is also frequently seen in ducks. This is due to rearing methods that usually involve small ponds or other sources of water in which ducks swim. The organism that causes botulism thrives in damp, decaying organic matter, and swimming water for ducks — unless kept clean — may be heavily contaminated with the causative organism. Daily removal of all dead birds, spilled feed, and other organic matter is essential for preventing botulism.

Fowl Pox: Pox is a virus disease that may occasionally infect nearly all species of birds. Turkeys and chickens are probably the most susceptible of all fowl. The occurrence of fowl pox is not unusual in quail, gray partridge, pheasants, doves, pigeons, and other pen-raised wild birds.

The most characteristic sign of the disease is the presence of scaly scabs on unfeathered portions of the body. Occasionally the mouth and throat are involved and the birds are unable to eat. Mosquitoes are considered the primary source of infection, but other blood-sucking insects may also transmit the disease. There is no satisfactory treatment. The vaccines used for domestic poultry are not generally recommended for gamebirds except for turkeys, quail, and pheasants. Mosquito and insect control programs are an aid in preventing fowl pox.

Eastern Equine Encephalitis (EEE): This disease is discussed here primarily because of its public health significance. Many species of birds, domestic and wild, are susceptible to this disease. The virus agent that causes the disease was first isolated from a horse in 1933; hence, the name ''equine'' was applied to the disease. It was probably much more common in birds than in horses. Many mammals including man are susceptible.

EEE is transmitted primarily by mosquitoes and (in actuality) the horse is a dead-end host. Gamebirds most frequently affected are pheasants and turkeys. It has been reported that at least 52 species of wild birds are susceptible.

EEE is sometimes called ''sleeping sickness,'' as a sleepy appearance is the most common clinical sign of the disease. Whenever the disease is suspected, appropriate veterinary and public health officials should be notified.

Blackhead: This is primarily a disease of chickens and turkeys, but nearly all gallinaceous birds, including quail, pheasants, and chukars, are susceptible. There are drugs available that are effective for the prevention and treatment of blackhead. Brooding and rearing on wire is also an aid in the prevention of blackhead.

Avian Influenza (A.I.): A viral disease that reportedly affects many different avian species and waterfowl. The disease is often mild and inapparent (subclinical). There are many variants of the virus, and some of these may cause an acute disease of domestic turkeys and chickens. Serious losses in pen-reared gamebirds have been rare. Migratory ducks are thought to be the primary host of A.I. virus. The disease is nearly always subclinical in ducks. Precautionary measures are isolation and sanitation. Preserve operators should avoid contact with migratory waterfowl. Virulent avian influenza outbreaks usually result in state and USDA quarantine. This could be disastrous to a preserve as it severely restricts movement of all fowl.

Duck Plague (Duck Virus Enteritis - DVE): An acute, contagious viral disease of ducks, geese, and swans. Severe internal hemorrhages and sudden death are noted in acute infections. Mortality may be very high. Milder infections may cause a drop in egg production, but little if any mortality.

The best protection against DVE is to obtain ducks from breeders known to be free of the infection, and keep them in facilities isolated from free-flying waterfowl. A vaccine is available from the Long Island Duck Research Laboratory at Eastport, Long Island, New York. However, their primary purpose is to supply the duck producers on Long Island and the immediate area.

Marble Spleen: Marble spleen disease is a contagious viral disease of pheasants, primarily, and, to a lesser degree, of chukar and guinea fowl. There have been reports of marble spleen in most states where ring-necked pheasants are grown in captivity.

The most characteristic sign of the disease is

sudden death in healthy, well-fleshed, semi-mature and mature pheasants. Sick-appearing birds are not found, as death occurs suddenly. The primary lesions observed are a swollen liver (twice normal size); an enlarged, marbled spleen; and congested, edematous lungs. Death of the bird is the result of pulmonary edema. The name "marble spleen" refers to the splenic swelling and streaking and not to spleen texture. The disease runs its course in 10–14 days; mortality from marble spleen ranges from 5 to 15%. There is no effective medication other than vaccination; however, stress packs with antibiotics may be given. Vaccination for marble spleen should be done routinely on farms known to be infected. Vaccination during outbreaks will shorten the course of the disease and reduce the total mortality.

Mycoplasma gallisepticum (MG): A contagious disease of poultry and gamebirds of all ages characterized by sinusitis and air sacculitis. MG spreads bird-to-bird as well as from hen to chick through the egg. Recovered birds remain carriers for life. Susceptibility to MG varies from species to species. Pheasants and quail are somewhat resistant to the disease, whereas chukar partridges and turkeys are seriously affected.

MG-infected gamebirds develop severe inflammation of the sinuses of the face. The eyes may swell shut, resulting in the bird being unable to find food or water. Sick birds become ruffled, unthrifty, and lose weight. Chronically affected birds ultimately will die without recovering from symptoms. MG is a chronic disease; therefore, affected flocks never fully recover to become sturdy, healthy birds. Control of MG is best accomplished by eradication. In gamebirds that means disposing of affected flocks and purchasing MG-free replacements for next year's breeder flock. Extreme care must be taken to prevent the spread of MG to new stock by employing isolation, separate caretaker, feed source, etc. for the new birds.

MG can be treated but not cured. Several antibiotics are effective against the acute stage of the disease; however, medication should be used only to salvage the infected flock for slaughter purposes. Effective drugs include tylosin, erythromycin, lincomycin, and spectinomycin.

Paratyphoid: Paratyphoid is an acute febrile septicemic disease of poultry and gamebirds chicks. The disease is characterized by diarrhea, pasted vents, stunting, and death. The mortality is decidedly increased in affected flocks. Affected adult birds may not show symptoms; however, infected breeder hens shed the organism in their feces, which contaminate the egg shell, infecting chicks at hatching. Mortality from paratyphoid usually starts in chicks about 7 or 8 days of age. Heavy mortality usually continues to 4 or 5 weeks of age. Because of the stunting there is much unevenness in paratyphoid flocks. Recovered birds remain unthrifty and never regain robustness. Recovered birds remain carriers and shedders of the organism and should not be kept for breeding purposes. Saving recovered birds for breeders carries the problem to the following year.

Paratyphoid can be medicated, but such medication is for the purpose of salvaging the flock for slaughter or hunting. The paratyphoid organism is susceptible to the nitrofuran drugs (NF-180, Furox, NFZ), neomycin, and gentamycin. Paratyphoid control requires an integration of special management, medication, and sanitation.

Diagnostic laboratory personnel and other veterinarians should be consulted for designing treatment and control.

Fowl cholera (FC): FC is an infectious disease affecting most fowl and gamebird species. The disease is caused by a bacterium, and is characterized by acute septicemia, tissue hemorrhage, and high flock mortality. Fowl cholera is more commonly observed in semi-mature and mature poultry. Lesions include hemorrhage and the swelling and congestion of fatty tissue, heart, mucous membranes, liver, spleen, intestines, and reproductive organs. Pinpoint necrotic (white) foci of the liver are common. The disease is confirmed by culturing and identifying the organism. Laboratory diagnosis requires 3–5 days; therefore, flock treatment should be established on the basis of a presumptive laboratory diagnosis.

Fowl cholera is often introduced into the flock by predators. Buildings and ranges normally remain infective to successive flocks unless managed to prevent cholera perpetuation. Buildings should be thoroughly cleaned, sanitized, and rested for 30 days or longer to break the cycle. Ranges should be tilled and left empty for the remainder of the season.

Fowl cholera can be treated. The sulfa drugs are the preferred medications; however, they are quite toxic if misused. Sulfa medication must be used judiciously, and the appropriate drug withdrawal period observed before release, sale, or slaughter of the birds. Vaccines are available, but are seldom totally effective when used as the only source of control.

Internal Parasites

Capillary Worms: Capillary worms are a very common parasite of quail, turkeys, and other gamebirds. These hair-like worms burrow into tissues of the crop; hence, "crop worms" and "threadworms" are common names of this disease. Capillary worms usually build up to a serious level over a period of time (1–3 years) but may become a serious problem within 90 days. Once the ground becomes thoroughly contaminated it is very difficult to prevent the disease and treatment is not always satisfactory.

Brooding and rearing on wire is the most effective means of control. Rotation of floor pens every 60 days, allowing several months between flocks, has been of aid in preventing the disease; but, in the South, winters are not usually severe enough to kill the parasite's eggs.

Coccidiosis: There are several species of this intestinal parasite. All are host-specific. Nearly all gamebirds are affected by 1 or more species of coccidia. Quail reared on the ground in a high-density situation are very susceptible to coccidiosis. Turkeys are also quite susceptible. Brooding and rearing on wire is the best method of prevention. There are several drugs that are effective for the treatment and/or prevention of coccidiosis.

Roundworms: Roundworms are relatively large and grossly visible. A heavy infestation may completely block the intestinal tract. If birds are reared on the floor, frequent medication may be necessary to control roundworms.

Gapeworms: Gapeworms are unusual parasites, confined to the trachea (windpipe) of chickens, turkey, goose, pheasants, peafowl, and quail. These parasites are frequently a serious problem in pen-reared pheasants and cause the condition called the "gapes." Earthworms are the intermediate host for the larvae of gapeworms. Larvae have been reported to remain infective for 4 1/2 years. Reuse of pens without proper sanitation measures is the most common cause of gapeworm infection. Thiabendazole (TBZ) has recently been approved for treatment of pheasants, and it should be administered as a feed additive (0.05%) for 14 days. A withdrawal period of 21 days is required before marketing pheasants for human consumption.

External Parasites

There are many common external parasites of gamebirds. Fortunately, there are several insecticides that are effective in controlling most of these. Recommendations for gamebirds are not usually on the label of these products, but the directions for poultry are applicable to gamebirds.

References

1. Woodard, A. E. 1984. Cannibalism, its cause and control. Game Bird Bull. 17(1):17, 23, 27. Hegins, RD 2, PA.

APPENDIX A

Summary of Results of The Gamebird Drug Use Survey

Drs. Owen D. Keene and L. Dwight Schwartz
Pennsylvania State University
State College, PA

The Gamebird Drug Use Survey was conducted in 1982 as part of a nationwide project on preventing chemical, drug, and pesticide residues in gamebirds. It was a cooperative project between Food Safety Inspection Service (FSIS), Federal Extension Service (FES), Interregional Research Project Number 4 (IR4), and Pennsylvania State University. The survey included identification of the more prevalent diseases in order of importance, common drugs used, and routes of administration used by producers for respective diseases. The survey included only gamebird species of pheasant, quail, and chukars. The summary of the survey data is presented in tables 1 through 6.

Table 1. Ranking of Prevalent Diseases of Pheasants.

Disease	% Incidence	Disease	% Incidence
1. Coccidiosis	54.7	7. Necrotic enteritis	6.6
2. Gapeworm inf.	50.4	8. Fowl cholera	5.8
3. Nematodes	23.4	9. Mycoplasma inf.	4.4
4. Coliform inf.	12.4	10. Staph/Strep inf.	1.5
5. Histomoniasis	12.4	11. Coryza	1.5
6. Paratyphoid inf.	11.7	12. Cestodes	0.7

Table 2. Ranking of Prevalent Diseases of Bobwhite Quail.

Disease	% Incidence	Disease	% Incidence
1. Ulcerative enteritis	60.0	5. Nematodes	10.8
2. Coccidiosis	45.0	6. Paratyphoid inf.	9.2
3. Capillary worms	15.8	7. Staph/Strep inf.	7.5
4. Mycoplasma inf.	10.8	8. Cestodes	0.8

Table 3. Ranking of Prevalent Diseases of Chukar Partridge.

Disease	% Incidence	Disease	% Incidence
1. Coccidiosis	52.4	5. Coliform inf.	11.1
2. Histomoniasis (BH)	31.7	6. Paratyphoid inf.	3.2
3. Nematodes	22.2	7. Fowl cholera	1.6
4. Mycoplasma inf.	11.1		

(BH) Blackhead Disease

Table 4. Prevalent Diseases of Pheasants and Medications Most Frequently Used.

Diseases	Medications	Feed		Water	
		Used*	Eff**	Used*	Eff**
Coccidiosis	Amprolium	39	37	38	34
	S'dimethoxine	5	3	8	7
	Other Sulfas	–	–	5	4
	Furazolidone	3	2	–	–
	Butynorate	2	2	–	–
	Zoalene	1	1	–	–
	Clopidol	1	1	–	–
Gapeworm inf.	Levamisole HC1	8	6	40	37
	Thiabendazole	25	23	7	4
	Buty/Pip/Pheno	1	1	2	2
	Piperazine	1	1	2	2
	S'methazine	–	–	1	1
Nematodes	Levamisole HC1	–	–	13	13
	Piperazine	1	1	12	10
	Thiabendazole	8	6	–	–
	Hygromycin B	3	3	–	–
	Buty/Pip/Pheno	–	–	3	3
Histomoniasis	Dimetridazole	2	2	9	8
	Furazolidone	3	3	–	–
	Carbarsone	2	2	–	–
	Nitarsone	–	–	1	1
	Copper Sulfate	–	–	1	1
Coliform Infections	Neo/Terra	2	1	8	8
	Nitrofurans	5	5	4	4
	Neomycin	2	2	4	4
	Tetracyclines	–	–	3	3
Paratyphoid Inf.	Nitrofurans	10	10	2	2
	Neomycin	1	1	5	4
	Neo/Terra	–	–	4	3
	Terramycin	–	–	1	1
	Bacitracin	–	–	1	1
Necrotic Enteritis	Bacitracin	4	4	1	–
	Neomycin	2	2	3	2
	Streptomycin	–	–	3	2
	Penicillin	–	–	2	1
Fowl cholera	S'dimethoxine	–	–	4	4
	S'quinoxaline	1	1	2	2
Mycoplasma inf.	Tylosin	2	2	2	1
	Erythromycin	–	–	2	1
	Linco/Spect	–	–	2	1
	Boric acid	–	–	1	1
Staph/Strep Inf.	Penicillin	1	1	–	–
	Chlortetracycline	1	1	–	–
Coryza	Erythromycin	–	–	1	1
	Streptomycin	–	–	1	1
Cestodes (Tapeworms)	Hygromycin B	1	1	–	–
	Buty/Pip/Pheno	–	–	1	1

*The number of surveys indicating the medication was *used* in the feed or water.
**The number of surveys indicating the medication was *effective* when used in the feed or water.

Table 5. Prevalent Diseases of Bobwhite Quail and Medications Most Frequently Used.

Diseases	Medications	Feed Used*	Feed Eff**	Water Used*	Water Eff**
Ulcerative Enteritis	Bacitracin	36	33	27	24
	Neomycin	7	6	27	18
	Streptomycin	3	3	12	10
	Tetracyclines	2	2	3	3
	Tylosin	–	–	2	2
	Neo/Terra	–	–	2	2
Coccidiosis	Amprolium	20	16	29	24
	S'quin/S'meth	–	–	17	16
	Furazolidone	3	3	–	–
	Butynorate	1	1	–	–
	Clopidoline	--	–	1	1
Capillary worms	Levamisole HC1	1	1	13	13
	Thiabendazole	2	2	3	3
	Buty/Pip/Pheno	1	1	1	1
	Piperazine	–	–	1	1
Mycoplasma inf.	Tylosin	2	2	10	8
	Erthromycin	–	–	3	1
	Penicillin	–	–	2	1
	Linco/Spect	–	–	1	1
	Tetracyclines	–	–	1	1
	Boric acid	–	–	1	1
Nematodes	Levamisole HC1	1	1	8	8
	Thiabendazole	–	–	3	3
	Buty/Pip/Pheno	1	1	3	1
	Hygromycin B	2	1	–	–
	Piperazine	–	–	1	1
Paratyphoid Inf.	Nitrofurans	4	4	2	2
	Neomycin	1	1	3	3
	Neo/Terra	–	–	3	1
Staph/Strep Inf.	Erythromycin	–	–	4	3
	Penicillin	–	–	2	2
	Tetracyclines	–	–	1	1
Cestodes (Tapeworms)	Buty/Pip/Pheno	1	1	1	1

*The number of surveys indicating the medication was *used* in the feed or water.
**The number of surveys indicating the medication was *effective* when used in the feed or water.

Table 6. Prevalent Diseases of Chukar Partridge and Medications Most Frequently Used.

Diseases	Medications	Feed		Water	
		Used*	Eff**	Used*	Eff**
Coccidiosis	Amprolium	19	15	17	16
	S'quin/S'meth	–	–	9	8
	S'dimethoxine	–	–	7	6
	Other sulfas	–	–	2	2
	Zoalene	1	1	–	–
	Furazolidone	1	1	–	1
Histomoniasis	Dimetridazole	2	2	17	17
	Carbarsone	1	0	1	1
	Nitarsone	1	1	–	–
	Ipronidazole	–	–	1	1
	Copper SO_4	–	–	1	1
Nematodes	Piperazone	1	–	6	6
	Levamisole HC1	–	–	6	5
	Thiabendazole	5	5	1	1
	Buty/Pip/Pheno	1	–	–	–
Mycoplasma inf.	Tylosin	2	1	4	4
	Erythromycin	–	–	3	2
	Linco/Spect	1	1	1	1
Coliform Infections	Neomycin	–	–	3	2
	Nitrofurans	–	–	3	2
	Tetracyclines	1	1	1	1
	Linco/Spect	1	1	1	0
	Neo/Terra	1	1	1	0
Paratyphoid Inf.	Neomycin	–	–	1	1
	Bacitracin	1	1	–	–
Fowl cholera	S'quinoxaline	1	1		

*The number of surveys indicating the medication was *used* in the feed or water.
**The number of surveys indicating the medication was *effective* when used in the feed or water.

Chapter 22

SHORT SUBJECTS

Hunting preserve management is many things, large and small — and the small things must never be overlooked. As the philosopher said, "He that despiseth small things shall fail, little by little."

Since little things are the basics of quality hunting, a number of small but important subjects have been combined in this chapter: Staying Informed, Helpful Organizations, Guns and Ammunition, Clay Target Shooting, Contracts, Liability Insurance, Dead-bird Disposal, and Where to Buy Equipment and Supplies.

Staying Informed

The preserve operator must keep up with developments within the game breeding, gun dog, and hunting preserve industries. The best way is to subscribe to various trade journals or to become a member of associations that have been serving these industries for years. Examples are:

Wildlife Harvest
    John M. Mullin, Editor
    Goose Lake, IA 52750
A monthly magazine devoted to the gamebird breeding and hunting preserve industries — the official publication of the North American Gamebird Association. The magazine carries information on the latest developments in these industries, notices, and summarizations of meetings at regional and national levels, and information on where to buy gamebirds and equipment. Subscription to this trade magazine can be arranged by contacting the Editor or by joining the North American Gamebird Association, P.O. Box 2105, Cayce-West Columbia, SC 29171.

The Game Bird Bulletin
    RD 2
    Hegins, PA 17938
An excellent publication on the gamebird and hunting preserve industries, published on a bi-

monthly basis by the Pennsylvania Game Breeders Association, Inc. The publication contains many timely articles of interest to preserve operators.

The Game Bird Breeders Gazette

Allen Publishing Co.
1328 Allen Park Drive
Salt Lake City, UT 84105

A monthly publication for the game breeding industry, bird fanciers, waterfowl breeders, and aviculturists. The magazine contains leading articles on the above subjects and a large classified-ad section on all phases of gamebird rearing.

American Field

The American Field Publishing Co.
222 West Adams St.
Chicago, IL 60606

This weekly magazine is largely devoted to bird dogs, especially the pointing breeds. It also reports on registered field trials. Departments include game and shooting, natural history, travel, and kennel activities. It contains many ads pertaining to dogs and kennels.

Gun Dog

P.O. Box 343
Mount Morris, IL 61054

One of the leading gun dog magazines in the United States. It is a versatile magazine, and its name reflects the contents. Emphasis is placed on hunting dog owners and their problems, ranging from training to medical problems. The magazine also contains stories on hunting, and information on old and new shotguns.

Retriever Field Trial News

Retriever Field Trial News
435 East Lincoln Ave., Rm. 15
Milwaukee, WI 53207

This publication for retriever enthusiasts is devoted to news of retriever field trials, the sale and breeding of retrievers, and training equipment.

Helpful Organizations

"United we stand; divided we fall" is not only true of our country, but applies equally as well to the game breeding and hunting preserve industries.

Everyone who has an interest in the future of private enterprise in providing hunting opportunities should be a member of the North American Gamebird Association (NAGA), P.O. Box 2105, Cayce-West Columbia, SC 29171. The Association provides essential leadership on a national level.

The NAGA holds an annual meeting, usually in January, in different parts of the country. These meetings — both before and behind the scenes — are packed with the latest information on game rearing, hunting preserve management, and state and national legislation. As a member, you receive monthly issues of *Wildlife Harvest* (discussed under "Staying Informed"). The NAGA also has a number of active committees that address current problems facing the industry.

Another important group includes state associations of game breeders and hunting preserve operators. State associations are necessary to help solve the many problems that breeders and operators face at the state level. Perhaps their most essential function is to maintain a good working relationship with state wildlife agencies.

The purpose of statewide associations is to promote and improve hunting preserves, and to protect the interest of the operators. Such associations are incorporated as non-profit organizations and meet at least once a year. It is essential that hunting preserve operators support such groups, not only by annual membership fees, but by attending the meetings and participating in the activities.

Your state wildlife agency or conservation department can furnish you with the name and address of your state association. If one is not in existence in your state, and there are 5 – 6 hunting preserves and private game farms in operation, it would be well to organize a state association.

In Illinois an association was formed in 1959. This Association has provided excellent leadership in promoting hunting preserves across the state, and in maintaining an excellent relationship with the Department of Conservation. The

Association was also instrumental in having a member of the Department assigned to help game breeders and hunting preserve operators, an assignment that has been the basis of a mutual trust and understanding between the 2 groups for years.

The National Shooting Sports Foundation, 1075 Post Road, Riverside, CT 06878, has provided vital help with the National Hunting Preserve Directory, promoting National Hunting and Fishing Day, national news releases on hunting preserves, and providing information on sporting arms and ammunition and on clay-target shooting facilities.

Guns and Ammunition

It is wise to encourage every patron to own and use his own shotgun. It's a good safety precaution. Safe gun handling is a matter of habit, and the average sportsman is safest when he is handling a gun he knows. With a strange gun, he usually will have problems, such as trying to shoot birds with the safety in the "on" position and/or loading and unloading the shotgun. Further, if the shotgun does not fit him properly, he will never enjoy his full potential as a shooter.

It is advisable for a preserve operator to have 3 or 4 double-barreled and/or semi-automatic shotguns available for hunting guests. Customers may forget their shotguns, or a shotgun may malfunction. A pump shotgun can cause no end of confusion to a man who is not acquainted with this type of gun action — and many men aren't.

It is necessary to stock a limited quantity of ammunition of various gauges and shot sizes. Hunters will forget their ammo or fail to bring enough. However, guns and ammo should be made available to hunter-customers as a service of your preserve and not in a spirit of competition with local sporting goods stores. Cultivate a good relationship with such businesses — the store manager can help by distributing your brochures in his store and recommending your preserve as a good place to hunt.

Clay Target Shooting

Every hunting preserve should have clay target shooting facilities. They are useful for instruction, for practice, and for hunting guests who would like a shooting match between, before, or after a hunt.

Crazy Quail is one of the best clay target games for a hunting preserve. It is inexpensive

Jack Downs, Nilo, helping a hunter with his shotgun shooting (courtesy Winchester Group, Olin Corp.).

for the preserve operator. It is relatively easy to install and a challenge to any shooter (Appendix A). It does require someone to operate the practice trap.

Crazy Quail is a 10-shot game, and each shooter shoots all 10 shot shells to complete a round. The shooter stands in 1 spot, at least 22 yards behind the trap, and may be handicapped additional yardage. However, at Nilo, we never tried to handicap the shooter (it is difficult enough to break all 10 targets at 22 yards). The shooter stands facing the trap and is not permitted to turn around to shoot at a clay target. On the command of ''pull'' by the shooter, a clay target is thrown from the pit by a practice trap. The tension of the trap spring should be set to throw the clay targets at least 50 yards.

To achieve a variety of angles, 8 of the clay targets are thrown at intervals of about 45 degrees to complete a circle of 360 degrees; however, the shooter has no prior knowledge of the angle of any given clay target. The other 2 clay targets are thrown at the discretion of the trap operator. More often than not, he will try to help the shooter by giving him a repeat at an angle where he has broken a clay target. The trap operator is below ground level, and is careful not to establish any given routine on the angles that the targets are thrown within or between a round of 10 ''clays.'' A respectable score is 6 or 7 broken targets. The shooter cannot move his feet once he calls ''pull,'' and a target thrown in his direction (as in No. 8 station at skeet) must be broken before it passes him. A breach of either of these 2 rules constitutes a foul.

Crazy Quail is never the same on any 2 days. Wind direction and velocity change the flight of the targets, and air temperature and changing light make a big difference. As in shooting gamebirds, each target is a different challenge. One cannot learn to ''groove'' targets as in trap or skeet. A 12-gauge shotgun with a modified choke is a good choice for Crazy Quail.

Crazy Quail is ideal for an operator, since you can handle rank novices on straightaway targets behind the sunken trap house and the ''expert'' at the 22-yard line. Also, it is possible to shoot regulation trap on a Crazy Quail field. All the operator has to do is establish 5 stations at 16 yards from the trap house, and place stakes for

A top view of a crazy quail trap pit (courtesy Winchester Group, Olin Corp.).

Busting an incomer at crazy quail. Note location of the trap area, the shelf for 10 shotshells in front of the shooter, and the safety barrier to prevent the shooter from swinging his shotgun to the rear (courtesy Winchester Group, Olin Corp.).

the guidance of the trap operator as to the limit for right- and left-angle targets.

Formal trap and skeet layouts, Riverside Skeet, and Hunter's Clays offer top sport in and out of the preserve season. The decision to install clay target facilities depends on the wishes of your preserve members, and/or the volume of business you might attract throughout the year. Information on trap and skeet layouts, Riverside Skeet, and Hunter's Clays can be obtained from the National Shooting Sports Foundation, 1075 Post Road, Riverside, CT 06878.

Contracts

A contract can be defined as a binding agreement between 2 or more parties and constitutes good business procedure. Further, it helps both game breeder and hunting preserve operator plan for the coming hunting season. Verbal contracts are fine, but things do happen to the parties to such agreements, especially a lapse of memory on specific details.

With either verbal or written contracts, there has to be a degree of mutual trust and understanding. Sometimes the game breeder is not able to produce the number of gamebirds that he planned. At other times, the preserve operator may have ordered more gamebirds than he can use. When such things happen, it behooves either party to notify the other as quickly as possible. By doing so, the other party can make other arrangements, either to sell or purchase necessary gamebirds.

Some of the important points to consider in a written contract are that the birds are or were:

1. Not brailed during the rearing process.
2. Exposed to the weather from the time they were 8 weeks of age (or younger).
3. In good health, normal weight, in full plumage, and without misshapen bills.
4. At least 16 weeks of age and of agreed-upon sex ratio.
5. Subject to your inspection upon delivery, or when you pick them up on specified dates.
6. To cost a specified amount on the agreed-upon delivery dates, with stipulations as to the method and time of payment.

As a rule, the game breeder and preserve operator become good friends — each depends on the other. With the passage of time and good business relationships, the contract can be simplified to the number and price of the birds on a given delivery date and the sex ratio.

Liability Insurance

John Mullin, Editor of *Wildlife Harvest*, has tried for years to obtain national coverage for liability insurance on hunting preserves at a reasonable price, and has this to say: ''We receive numerous phone calls and letters from hunting preserves seeking reasonably priced liability insurance. Such insurance is an important aspect of managing a hunting preserve. None of us are affluent enough to be 'self-insured.' We must depend on 'spreading the risk,' especially considering the lawsuit-happy era we're presently encountering.

"Any kind of insurance is generally very confusing to the purchaser. Everyone in the preserve business realizes that he can't afford to be without the essential basic protection afforded by broad liability coverage. Our biggest problem in dealing with the insurance companies is that every preserve varies a bit in extra activities and sources of ancillary income. These extra-curricular activities are difficult to clearly define and explain to the satisfaction of an insurance company. Some preserves may be forced to eventually purchase some 'standard hunting preserve liability coverage' from 1 company that is a nationwide insurer. Then we might do well to purchase other type 'farm coverage,' or special activity coverage, from our local agent.

"Hunting is a relatively safe sport. Hunting and shooting rank 16th down the list of sports accidents requiring emergency medical care. But we can be easily exposed to the possibility of lawsuits. The insurance industry refers to this as 'exposure.' The public is becoming more prone to litigation, and many lawyers promote such litigation. There is a predilection for courts to rule in favor of plaintiffs. This is why preserves are increasingly 'exposed' to the possibility of lawsuits.

"The best known of the 4 major types of risk is 'legal liability.' In cases other than legal liability, it's relatively easy to establish predictable limits of exposure. If your clubhouse burns down, you can determine its replacement costs. If your intention is to protect your employees, there are 'workmen's compensation' statistics and laws to refer to. But if an outsider were to be injured or killed on your property, your liability exposure is limited only by the imagination of juries and the deliberations of judges.

"There is a wide variety of liability policies on the market, but very few policies are designed specifically for commercial hunting preserves. Maybe you can get a special rider on a general liability insurance. We must work together to obtain more standardized coverage for hunting preserve liability.

"Naturally, you're better off if you can purchase preserve liability within your own state. If possible, purchase your liability insurance through the same company that carries your other insurance. Be sure your insurance company has financial stability.

"There is a great future for the hunting preserve industry. This future must be insured through being underwritten by someone in the business of providing good protection at reasonable prices. Most individuals entrusted by the insurance companies with approving the acceptance of such risks were most generally not sportsmen. They had no idea what a hunting preserve was — nor why they should be encouraged.

"We need someone who understands the situation from both ends. We need someone who can enlighten the underwriters as to just what risks are really involved and what kind of cooperation we could guarantee on the part of the preserve operator with regard to adequate loss-prevention, safety programs, good housekeeping, personal supervision, etc.

"Purchasing sufficient liability insurance at a reasonable price goes through a cycle. When there is competition for our business, it becomes a 'buyer's market.' When a couple of insurance companies cease insuring hunting preserves, it seriously reduces competition for our business and becomes a 'seller's market.' This results in increased cost to hunting preserves.

"The North American Gamebird Association (NAGA) will continually strive to inform you about insurance possibilities. In turn, we would appreciate you informing the association of any good liability insurance you can purchase at a fair price. Then, we'll 'pass the word' in my *Wildlife Harvest* magazine."

It is far better to prevent incidents that lead to lawsuits. Negligence will beat you in court.

Some hunting clubs are requesting their guests to sign "Assumption of Risk and Disclaimer" or a liability release. King[1] points out that the details of a liability release and the customer's understanding of it are crucial because of what the courts call "Informed Consent." An accident victim's lawyer can argue there was no reasonable way the victim could have known of a particular hazard. A detailed release gives hunters notice of more hazards, making successful suits tougher. One should check with his lawyer and insurance company on the legal value of a disclaimer signed by a hunting guest.

One such disclaimer is in this form:

_____ HUNTING PRESERVE ASSUMPTION OF RISK AND DISCLAIMER

The undersigned, being familiar with or having been informed of the risks assumed by those participating in sport hunting, hereby verify their assumption of such risks and for themselves, their survivors or insurers, disclaim and waive any right of action against the landowner or the _____ Hunting Preserve in the event of injury or damage to themselves or their property while participating in sport hunting or other activities on the _____ Hunting Preserve, (insert address).

NAME	ADDRESS
_____	_____
_____	_____
_____	_____

1. For more information see King, F. 1985. Steps to a safe season. Hunting Ranch Business 1(3):2. 5214 Starkridge, Houston, TX 77035.

Dead-bird Disposal

The disposal of dead gamebirds on a hunting preserve can be a problem. Birds in holding pens do die for a variety of reasons. Also, there are a few gamebirds that will not be suitable for dressing for table use, and/or carcasses of dead birds will be found on the preserve that should be picked up and properly disposed of.

There are 3 disposal methods: burial, incinerators, and disposal pits. Burial of carcasses under at least 2 feet of soil is fine, but not practical on a daily basis. Incineration is also excellent, but is costly and involves air quality regulations. As Dr. Tom Smith[1] pointed out, the least expensive yet effective method of disposal is a properly constructed disposal pit. Such a pit can provide a means of disposal for 20 years or more. A pit, 5 feet wide, 5 feet deep, and 7 feet long, can easily decompose 60–70 pounds of carcasses each month without filling up.

Smith states that the pit should be located at least 100 feet from water wells and storage tanks and drain away from these water facilities. The construction site should be in a well-drained location where the water table is deeper than the depth of the pit. The pit bottom should have a subsoil with a low water infiltration rate, which will maintain a moist condition for bacterial ac-

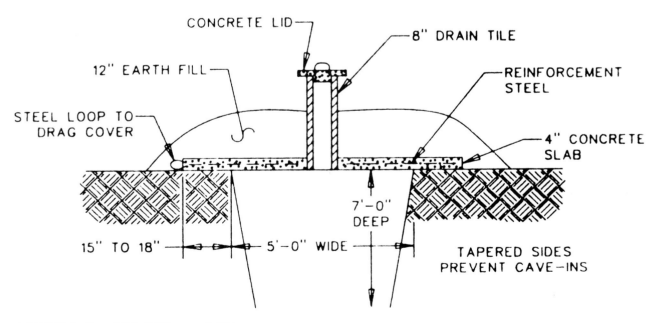

FIGURE 1: Dead-bird Disposal Pit.

tion. However, the pit must not be watertight; there has to be some drainage.

Figure 1 shows the proper dimensions of the pit cover. It is best to make the cover from concrete with a piece of 8-inch drainage tile about 4 feet long serving as a standpipe for the opening. A tight-fitting lid for the standpipe is necessary to prevent children or animals from removing it. The 4-inch thick concrete slab is reinforced with 3/8-inch steel rods on 16-inch centers (each way) or welded steel reinforcement mesh. One can substitute 2 layers of 2-inch lumber for the concrete; however, the wood must be treated with a preservative such as creosote.

The pit can be up to 35 feet long, but is usually limited only by the concrete slab being immovable. If you use a long pit, the openings in the cover should not be more than 6 feet apart. After you dig the pit, you may have to line the walls with old lumber, brick, or concrete blocks to prevent cave-ins and premature filling. After the cover is in position, put a 12-inch layer of soil over the entire slab.

Unless the pit is overfilled, the carcasses will decompose better if you don't use additives. When the pit is filled, you can remove the earth covering and drag the slab over a new pit. Use the earthen fill to cover the exposed pit. A concrete cover can be reused many times.

1. For more information see Smith, T. 1982. Dead bird disposal. Wildlife Harvest 13(1):26-27. Jan. Goose Lake, IA.

Where to Buy Equipment and Supplies

The subject of where to buy gamebirds and gamebird feed has been discussed in various chapters of this book. The best advice is to work with a local feed mill to insure freshness of feed, and it is essential to know your supplier of gamebirds.

Equipment needs require manufacturers and distributors who specialize in supplying hunting preserves. The best way to keep current on suppliers is to check the ads in *Wildlife Harvest*. It is also wise to keep current catalogs from suppliers on hand so necessary items can be ordered when needed.

A partial list of some of the more important suppliers of hunting preserve needs are as follows:

Valentine Equipment Company
7510 S. Madison St.
P. O. Box 53
Hinsdale, IL 60521
Wire for gamebird pens, eviscerating equipment, dog kennel supplies, temperature-controlled scalders, capture nets, traps, etc.

Kuhl Corporation
P. O. Box 26
Flemington, NJ 08822-0026
Fencing for gamebird pens, feeders, waterers, shipping and transfer crates, gamebird processing equipment, packaging materials, and anti-cannibalism devices.

G. Q. F. Manufacturing Co.
P. O. Box 1552
Savannah, GA 31498
Feeders, recovery pens, waterers, pickers, scalders, wire, pliers, literature on bobwhite quail propagation, etc.

Allen and Young Mfg., Inc.
Box 32
Crystal City, TX 78839
Quail and dog feeders and waterers for released birds.

J. A. Cissel Manufacturing Co.
P. O. Box 339
Farmingdale, NJ 07727
Toprite netting, ceco film (anti-spook and disease control), "weathashade" (wind and shade screening), and "fence-it" (specialty netting).

Louis E. Page, Inc.
P. O. Box 2405
Littleton, MA 04160
Wire (galvanized hexagonal and welded before and after weaving), vinyl-coated welded wire, hardware cloth, earth anchors, and plastic wire.

Endurance Net
Box 128
Roebling, NJ 08554
Polyproplene netting — 1/2-, 1-, and 2-inch mesh and shade and wind fabric.

Mangelsdorf Seed Co.
P. O. Box 327
St. Louis, MO 63166
Seeds for hunting preserve food and release-cover patches.

Kester's Wild Game Food Nurseries, Inc.
P. O. Box V
Omro, WI 54963
Seeds for release-cover patches. Specialize in aquatic food plants.

Bob Allen Companies
P. O. Box 477
Des Moines, IA 50302
Specialize in outdoor clothing, shooter supplies, gun cases, and luggage.

Decker Manufacturing Company
P. O. Box 368
Koekuk, IA 52632
Bits and pliers to stop feather picking.

Minuteman
Box 5661
Greensboro, NC 27403
Custom vinyl and plastic signs.

Interstate Graphics
2201-B Range Rd.
Rockford, IL 61111
Signs for hunting preserves.

Southern Emblem Co.
P. O. Box 8
Toast, NC 27049
Custom embroidered emblems, screen-printed shirts and jackets, caps and visors, bumper stickers, decals, and flags.

nappe/babcock
P. O. Box 2028
Richmond, VA 23216
Insulated waterproof bag for transporting frozen gamebirds.

Cryovac Division, W. R. Grace Co.
P. O. Box 464
Duncan, SC 29334
Polyethelene bags for frozen gamebirds.

Woodtream Corporation
Lititz, PA 17543
Traps for predators and live traps for released gamebirds.

Minnesota Trapline Products
Rt. 1, Box 86 B-1
Pennock, MN 56279
Trapping supplies.

Tri-tronics
P. O. Box 17660
Tucson, AZ 85731
Electronic dog-training devices.

National Band & Tag Co.
P. O. Box 430
Newport, KY 41072
Gamebird identification bands and tags.

Trius Products Inc.
Box 25
Cleves, OH 45002
Manufacture clay-target practice traps and traps that can be adapted for Crazy Quail target shooting.

Havahart
115-T Water St.
Ossining, NY 10562
Traps for live-trapping gamebirds and predators.

APPENDIX A

Winchester's Crazy Quail Trap Pit and Revolving Trap Base

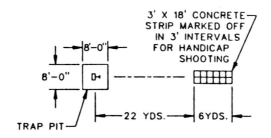

3' X 18' CONCRETE STRIP MARKED OFF IN 3' INTERVALS FOR HANDICAP SHOOTING

8'-0"

8'-0"

TRAP PIT

22 YDS. 6 YDS.

PLOT PLAN OF FIELD

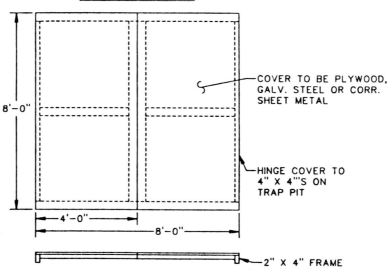

PLAN OF PIT COVER

COVER TO BE PLYWOOD, GALV. STEEL OR CORR. SHEET METAL

8'-0"

HINGE COVER TO 4" X 4'''S ON TRAP PIT

4'-0"

8'-0"

2" X 4" FRAME

TRAP PIT

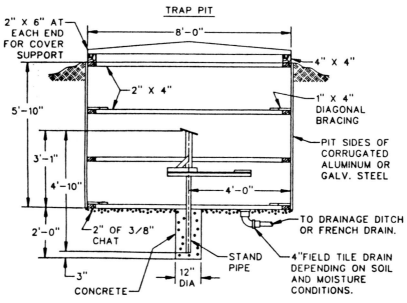

2" X 6" AT EACH END FOR COVER SUPPORT

8'-0"

4" X 4"

2" X 4"

1" X 4" DIAGONAL BRACING

5'-10"

PIT SIDES OF CORRUGATED ALUMINUM OR GALV. STEEL

3'-1"

4'-10"

4'-0"

TO DRAINAGE DITCH OR FRENCH DRAIN.

2'-0"

2" OF 3/8" CHAT

STAND PIPE

4" FIELD TILE DRAIN DEPENDING ON SOIL AND MOISTURE CONDITIONS.

3"

12" DIA

CONCRETE

202

Winchester's Crazy Quail Trap Pit and Revolving Trap Base

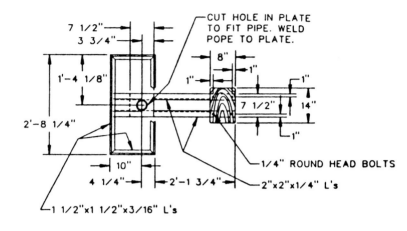

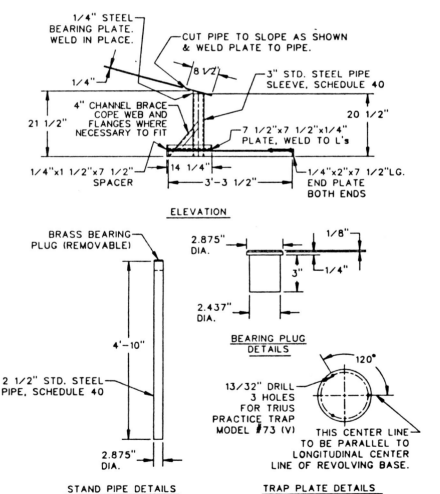

ELEVATION

BRASS BEARING PLUG (REMOVABLE)

2.875" DIA.   1/8"

3"   1/4"

2.437" DIA.

BEARING PLUG DETAILS

4'-10"

2 1/2" STD. STEEL PIPE, SCHEDULE 40

2.875" DIA.

STAND PIPE DETAILS

120°

13/32" DRILL 3 HOLES FOR TRIUS PRACTICE TRAP MODEL #73 (V)

THIS CENTER LINE TO BE PARALLEL TO LONGITUDINAL CENTER LINE OF REVOLVING BASE.

TRAP PLATE DETAILS

BE A SPORTSMAN*

There is something we crave in this world of today;
There is something we need as we struggle along;
There is something God meant we should have as a leaven,
To keep ourselves fit, and contented, and strong.

We must make ourselves friends with the outdoors and nature;
We must breathe the fresh air of woodlands and fields;
We must tread the soft earth of the lowlands and mountains
And spurn cities' dust with an arrogant heel.

There is naught that refreshes, and quiets, and comforts,
There is naught that makes life better under the sun,
There is naught that gives peace to a soul sorely harried
Than tramping abroad with dog and gun.

Let it be but a walk in the frost of the morning;
Let it be but the bell of a hound on the scent;
Let it be but the whirr of small wings in the thicket;
There is solace in this that will keep us content.

What more sweet than the crunch of dry leaves in the autumn;
What more sweet than the work of a dog gaily done;
What more sweet than the sound and bustle of game birds
That makes the blood tingle, and life fairly hum?

So don't let's forget that such pleasures are fleeting;
So don't let's forget that their loss gives us pain;
So don't let's desist in our struggle to keep them
And so be refreshed, yet again, and again.

And yet as we go we must still keep one precept
And try to conserve while the dead feathers fall,
And temper our sport, not be greedy or wasteful,
*But be fair, humane, and a **sportsman,** withal.*

---

*Lawrence B. Smith. American game preserve shooting. 1937. Garden City
Publishing Co., Garden City, NY.

INDEX

Lewis, J., 99-100
Leyland, D., 88
liability insurance,
Long, W., 100
Luttringer, L., 110

M

Madson, C., 9
Madson, J., 1-4, 12, 7-8, 16, 37, 43, 59, 63, 73, 79, 157-158, 165-169
Mann, P., 17-18, 25, 49, 125, 127-128, 150, 173
Mauldin, J., 47
Max McGraw Wildlife Foundation, 11, 97, 99, 101, 114, 119-120, 131, 135, 148
McGraw, M., 12
McLaurin, E., 16
Meng, H., 135
Millbrook Hunt Club, 6
Miller, H., 153-154
Montgomery, R., 135-136, 139
More Game Birds in America, xii
Morris, E., 38
Mosby, H., 100
Mueller, B., 100
Muller, H., 96
Mullin, G., 178
Mullin, J., 12, 47-48, 53, 75, 78, 100-101, 114, 119-121, 130, 144, 146, 160-162, 174-176, 193, 197-198
Musser, T., 9, 18

N

National Rifle Association, 149, 160
National Shoot-to-retrieve Association, 147
National Shooting Sports Foundation, 161, 197
National Wild Turkey Federation, 99
Neil, D., 96
Nickerson, J., 96
Nilo, xiv, 2, 31, 38, 49, 59, 61, 79, 81-82, 89, 91, 97, 116-117, 119, 134, 160, 165-169, 177
Norman, E., 62, 66
North American Gamebird Association, xiv, 10-11, 17, 152, 162, 194

O

Oldenburg, O., 44
Olin, J., x-xv, 11, 59, 96
Olser, P., 6
Ortega y Gasset, J., 57

P

Palmer, G., 12
partridge, chukar
   food and water, 89-90
   gamebird, 40, 87-88
   holding pen, 89, 94
   hunting, 91-92
   pen-reared chukars, 87-88
   quality chukars, 88-89
   release cover, 91
   transportation, 89
   trapping and releasing, 90-91
Patterson, C., 41, 96
Pennsylvania Game Commission, 100
Pershall, T., xiv
pheasant, ring-necked
   catch pens, 47-48
   continental shoots, 53-54
   deep snow, 52
   food and water, 47
   gamebird, 39-40, 43
   holding cover, 50
   holding pens, 22, 45-47, 55
   hunting, 50-52
   rear or buy, 45
   recovery, 51
   releasing, 48-50
   strains, 44-45
Pioneer Valley Gun Association, 18-19
Pratt, A., 46
predators, nuisance animals, and pests
   Bal-chatri raptor trap, 138
   definitons, 133
   laws and regulations, 133
   nuisance animals, 136
   pests, 136
   predators, 134
   starling and sparrow trap, 139
preserve operator
   artificiality, 31
   cleanliness, 31
   diplomacy, 32
   food, 31
   good host, 29-30
   management, 32-33
   part-time help, 33
   regimentation, 31
processing gamebirds
   comments, 176
   contracting, 174
   equipment and supplies, 175
   need, 173
   plant layout, 179
   processing, 174-175
   recipes, 176-178
   skinning versus picking, 174
profitability
   business volume, 144
   dog kennels, 149
   field trials, 147-148
   in-season incentives, 145-146
   metropolitan preserves, 144-145
   off-season activities, 148-149
   personnel, 149

W

Waters, J., 38-39, 61
Weber, J., 62
Weigand, J., 95-96
Wendt, R., 131
Werner, W., 96
Wessel, C., 100
Western Cartridge Company, x
Western-Winchester Game Restoration Plan, xiii
Whalen, B., 77-78
Whalen, L., 12
where to buy equipment and supplies, 200-202
White, R., 110
Wild Wings of Oneka, 26-27, 79, 135, 146
Wildlife Harvest, 12, 20 127, 160, 193, 197, 200
Wildlife Harvest Game Bird Cook Book, 176
Wildlife Management Institute, xi
Winchester Conservation Department, xiii, 2
Winchester, Olin Corp., 170, 202-203
Winchester's Crazy Quail Trap Pit, 202-203
Winchester's Shotgun Rack, 170
Woodstream Corp., 134
Woodward, A., 46, 183

Y, Z

Y.O. Ranch, 103-110
Yachik, V., 161
Zerkowsky, J., 177

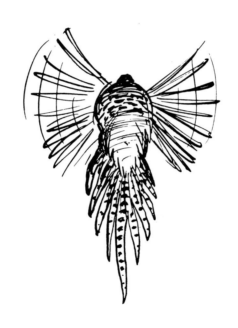